ASPERGER'S SYNDROME

Intervening *ies*

DATE DUE

BRODART   Cat. No. 23-221

ASPERGER'S SYNDROME

Intervening in Schools, Clinics, and Communities

Edited by

Linda J. Baker
Lawrence A. Welkowitz
Keene State College

LEA LAWRENCE ERLBAUM ASSOCIATES, PUBLISHERS
2005   Mahwah, New Jersey   London

Lawrence Erlbaum Associates, Inc., Publishers
10 Industrial Avenue
Mahwah, New Jersey 07430

Cover design by Kathryn Houghtaling Lacey

Library of Congress Cataloging-in-Publication Data

Asperger's syndrome : intervening in schools, clinics, and communities / edited by Linda J. Baker, Lawrence A. Welkowitz.
   p. cm.
Includes bibliographical references and index.
ISBN 0-8058-4570-4 (cloth : alk. Paper)
ISBN 0-8058-4571-2 (pbk. : alk. Paper)
   1. Asperger's syndrome. 2. Asperger's syndrome—Patients—Education. 3. Asperger's syndrome—Social aspects. 4. Learning disabled children—Education. 5. Autistic children—Behavior modification. I. Baker, Linda J. II. Welkowitz, Lawrence A.

RJ506.A9A866 2004
371.92—dc22   2004043264
                                                                        CIP

Books published by Lawrence Erlbaum Associates are printed on acid-free paper, and their bindings are chosen for strength and durability.

Printed in the United States of America
10 9 8 7 6 5 4 3 2 1

Contents

Contributors

Elsa Abele, MS, CCC/SLP
Department of Communicative Disorders, Sargent College, Boston University, Boston, Massachusetts, USA

Tony Attwood, PhD
Petrie Clinic, Brisbane, Australia

Linda J. Baker, PhD
Department of Psychology, Keene State College, Keene, New Hampshire, USA

Teresa Bolick, PhD
Nashua, New Hampshire, and Westford, Massachusetts, USA

Traci A. Gilman, OTR/L
Nashua School District, Nashua, New Hampshire, USA

Susan Gorn, JD
Hatboro, Pennsylvania, USA

Denise Grenier
Lexington, Massachusetts

Isabelle Henault, PhD
Montréal, Quebec, Canada

Robert Hendren, DO
Division of Child and Adolescent Psychiatry, Department of Psychiatry, University of California Davis School of Medicine, Davis, California, USA

The MIND Institute, Sacramento, California, USA

Andrés Martin, MD, MPH
Yale Child Study Center, Yale University, New Haven, Connecticut, USA
Children's Psychiatric Inpatient Service, Yale–New Haven Children's Hospital, New Haven, Connecticut, USA

Joan Safran, PhD
Department of Teacher Education, College of Education, Ohio University, Athens, Ohio, USA

Stephen P. Safran, PhD
Department of Teacher Education, College of Education, Ohio University, Athens, Ohio, USA

Kate Sofronoff, PhD
School of Psychology, University of Queensland, Brisbane, Australia

Larry Welkowitz, PhD
Department of Psychology, Keene State College, Keene, New Hampshire, USA

Acknowledgments

This book came to be because so many people have been willing to share their thoughts with us: our clients, our children, our students, and our colleagues. Andrew Sylvia has followed this project and given us valuable input all along.

Tony Attwood has been an inspiring teacher and a mentor throughout the years we have studied Asperger's Syndrome, and has been forthcoming with his time, his knowledge, and his work. He has never hesitated to share what he knows, and went out of his way to do so when one of the editors (L. Baker) journeyed to Brisbane to see him in action. His generosity, creativity, hard work, and effectiveness are truly remarkable.

The talented contributors to this book have done their jobs well, were fun to work with, and finished their chapters in an unusually timely manner. In addition to contributing her own chapter, Joan Safran read and provided valuable experience, ideas, and feedback on the college chapter.

Our thanks go to the Doug Flutie, Jr. Foundation for Autism for supporting our research and making our peer mentorship program fly.

Michael Matros stepped in when we desperately needed editing assistance.

Suzanne Butcher has been a knowledgeable reader and tireless supporter.

Dan Rath has done crucial work behind the scenes.

Carol Condon has been our dedicated assistant and has made many of our projects possible.

Nikki Crawford ever so patiently read and, when necessary, meticulously reformatted the reference lists at the end of each chapter.

Our mothers, Joan Welkowitz and Dora Baker, have offered their support, unconditional love, and proofreading skills when we most needed them.

Steve Clark has been a shining example of how college faculty members can learn to work supportively with students on the spectrum. His interest and his love have been invaluable.

Dan Rosenn has contributed to both our video and this book by sharing his knowledge and his connections. His insights and kindness put one of us on the road to understanding Asperger's years ago.

The Keene State College community has been curious, encouraging, and supportive as we have pursued our work here. Dean of Sciences Gordon Leversee has been there for us when we've needed help.

Chapter 1

Introduction:
Intervention as Community Building

Linda J. Baker and Lawrence A. Welkowitz
Keene State College

When, we, the editors, began studying Asperger's Syndrome in 1996 there was little information to be found. We were both hungry for more because we had family members and clients struggling with the symptoms of Asperger's Syndrome, and as psychologists, we hoped to be more useful to those we served. We assembled a small study group of faculty, staff, and students and began by reading Asperger's original article (1944/1991), which described children who had many of the characteristics of autism, including sensory and social differences and a variety of neurological problems, but who also appeared more connected to or interested in the world around them. Whereas Kanner's work on children who were more classically autistic was continued in this country, Asperger's work was all but ignored until the last decade.

Thus, our study group moved from reading Asperger's article written in 1944 to studying Attwood's *Asperger Syndrome* (1998) and Frith's *Autism and Asperger Syndrome* (1991), both published in the United Kingdom. We presented case studies of a few individuals we suspected had Asperger's Syndrome, trying to apply what we had learned. At that point, most of our academic colleagues or fellow clinicians had not even heard of the diagnosis, and any time we mentioned our work we were forced to launch into a description and explanation of the syndrome. We were thus inspired to produce a 30-minute descriptive video, *Understanding Asperger's*, filmed and directed by Jesse Gabryle (Welkowitz & Baker, 2000), an enthusiastic student in our college film department. When shown at the

1

annual meeting of the American Psychological Association in 2000, it attracted a large audience that was finally aware of the diagnosis but still searching for information. Since then, not only has the available body of literature grown exponentially, but the number of diagnosed cases has exploded. It was not long before we were inundated with requests from parents, schools, and local psychotherapists for assistance with diagnosis and intervention.

At this point in time there is such proliferation of information and research that those attempting to educate themselves do not know which way to turn. Parents, teachers, clinicians, and those with the diagnosis attempting to figure out what types of intervention make sense find the array of specialists and the diversity of available printed material overwhelming. People with Asperger's Syndrome often face problems at home, in the social world, in the classroom, in the physical world, and sometimes with the law. Ideally, a team of specialists from various disciplines would be available to any diagnosed individual: Special educators, clinicians, occupational therapists, communication specialists, psychopharmacologists, and lawyers would all contribute to the package of interventions assembled for someone needing assistance. Unfortunately, although the expertise is out there, it is rare that any individual has access to the array of services he or she needs. We hope that this collection of chapters will serve as an information team, that readers will benefit from these various specialists, their skills, and their perspectives, and thus be able to determine which services might be helpful to those that need them. Our team of authors has described the state of the art and the recent research in their fields, followed by carefully crafted programs for intervention. From their work might spring new programs and ideas in places where services are lacking. We must also acknowledge that the field is new, that many interventions are the fruit of clinical experience and observation, and that research and program development are still emerging. "Experts" do not always agree and many questions remain unanswered. Although we have attempted to cover a range of issues, many others are not addressed. For instance, we are finding that some young adults with Asperger's Syndrome are vulnerable to encounters with the legal system because they do not understand their social contexts and unknowingly behave in ways that others find threatening.

Any focus on intervention must begin with acknowledgment of the strengths, potential, and significant contributions already made by people with Asperger's Syndrome. Baron-Cohen (2002) suggested that it might be more accurate to think of Asperger's Syndrome as a difference rather than a disability. He proposed that the behavior of people with Asperger's Syndrome, if looked at nonjudgmentally, is neither better nor worse than that seen in neurotypicals and that "being more object focused is clearly a disability only in an environment that expects everyone to be social" (p. 187). He asserted that people with Asperger's Syndrome would no longer be seen as disabled if societal expectations changed, and he suggested that the prevalence of people on the autistic spectrum who work in the sciences, particularly in engineering, exemplifies the talents and potential contributions of people with Asperger's Syndrome. Tony Attwood (personal communication, March 28, 2002) did not hesitate to point out that many well-known artists, musicians, and scientists had profiles indicative of Asperger's Syndrome. At this time, however, as Baron-Cohen (2002) acknowledged, viewing Asperger's Syndrome as a disability is still necessary, primarily because it is the only way to get services for people who are out of step with the dominant social culture.

If we understand that problems faced by people with Asperger's Syndrome are the result of both the limitations of people surrounding them, as well as their own difficulties adapting to the social world, we know that intervention must address both the individual and the environment. Individuals with Asperger's Syndrome will be able to develop and contribute their often extraordinary talents only with the collaboration and support of others. Children with Asperger's Syndrome are particularly vulnerable to the extremes of success and failure. They can grow up to make significant contributions to their communities and societies, or become a constant, and even dangerous drain on limited resources. The rewards of their success are great and the costs of their failures are high. As parents, educators, and clinicians, and as a society, we face the choice of committing time, energy, and resources to providing what it takes to support development in these children or facing the serious consequences of our neglect. Their success is dependent on the quality of all of the interactions they have with people in their lives, whether it is their family members, their teachers, their therapists, their doctors, their bus drivers, their peers, or their one-on-one classroom aides. All of these interactions give them information about whether their efforts will be rewarded or punished, and about whether engagement with others is worth all the hard work. Those of us who are specialists know that the limited amount of time any one of us spends with a child is not enough. It is in the total of everyday interactions that most change happens. To reach their potential, people with Asperger's Syndrome need protection from interactions that punish (e.g., chronic failure, exclusion, teasing, and bullying) and exposure to a wide range of experiences that motivate them to adapt to a social world that is intensely difficult for them to negotiate. The thinking of people with Asperger's and their ways of interacting can be different enough from that of neurotypicals that those in both groups must work to build bridges.

Changes that facilitate the growth and development of people with Asperger's Syndrome benefit not only those with the "disability," but the community at large. For instance, children with Asperger's Syndrome need protection from bullying, but no more than children who bully need to find better ways to interact. We know, for instance, that children who are bullies are at higher risk for criminal behavior later in life (Goleman, 1994); reducing bullying behavior is crucial for bullies and victims alike.

It also benefits all children, not just those with Asperger's Syndrome to learn better friendship skills, and to encounter in their peers more flexible expectations. Children are ostracized for various reasons, yet those who feel different suffer from many of the same pressures. Most children need and want friends, yet many are isolated and lonely. Years of research in the area of friendship by Rubin &

Thomas (2002) and others (Gutstein & Whitney, 2002) have documented the importance of developing friendships. According to these studies, children without friends have ongoing problems with self-esteem, social skills development, and school performance, independent of their intelligence level. It is also crucial that we teach "popular" children to be more respectful of their less conforming peers. As Carrington and Graham (2001) pointed out, for those with Asperger's Syndrome, masquerading their deficits creates inordinate stress. If they could feel better about exposing and explaining their differences, they could function more effectively, and with less agitation, anxiety, and depression. Freedom to do so would benefit many others as well.

Interveners, if well trained, will also know how to build consistent success into the lives of the people they are helping. Tony Attwood (personal communication, March 26, 2002) explained that it is success that motivates children with Asperger's Syndrome to engage with the world, that their daily lives are so fraught with the punishment that comes as a consequence of their social limitations and the ways they are treated by others, that additional punishment only adds to their distress and anxiety. Any new task we ask of the child must meet him or her at his or her level of accomplishment, provide some challenge—but not so much as to be overwhelming—and move the child forward in a way that guarantees success. If you ask a disorganized child who is easily overwhelmed, overstimulated, and distracted to clean his or her messy room and you leave him or her alone for an hour to accomplish this task, the child is likely to fail. If you structure the task, ask the child first to pick the clothes up off the floor and put them in a hamper, throw in a few items yourself, and acknowledge the child's success as he or she progresses, he or she may then take the next suggested step and pick up the books. If you ask a child with no social skills to make eye contact with other children before he or she knows what to say to them or finds the interaction rewarding, what will motivate the child? If he or she succeeds at a short interaction with another child, he or she will want to try again. Success feeds on itself. It is a motivator and a teacher.

As helpers asking children with Asperger's to take on new challenges, we need to keep our priorities in mind. Is it more important that the child learn to control his or her anger, or that he or she complete a math assignment (T. Attwood, personal communication, March 19, 2002)? The child might not yet be able to do both. When deciding on any course of action, the questions must be "What is it most beneficial for this child to learn at this moment?" and "How can I reconstruct the task to guarantee success?"

Because intervention requires effort from the people surrounding those with Asperger's Syndrome, they need support and training. Parents, relatives, and teachers, in particular, who spend the most time relating to individuals with Asperger's Syndrome need and deserve attention. Parents, especially before their children are diagnosed with Asperger's Syndrome, question themselves and their parenting skills (Sofronoff & Farbotko, 2002) Confidence or the lack of it affects parental persistence and mood (Sofronoff & Farbotko, 2002). Intervention on behalf of children with Asperger's Syndrome must include consultation, support, and training for their parents. Publications and Web sites are now available that are responsive to parents' needs, but although the need for teacher training and consultation is often recognized by school systems and training teams, intervention on behalf of parents is often lacking. Because parents can be so well informed—sometimes more knowledgeable than the educators and clinicians they consult—we can overlook the pain and everyday struggles they confront. Parent support groups are becoming more common, and they provide some of what families so desperately need. However, they are not a substitute for the empathy and understanding of intervening professionals.

There are other skills and strategies that all primary helpers must learn, such as ways of avoiding power struggles that can trigger aggressive behavior in people with Asperger's Syndrome (Simpson & Myles, 1998). Gray (Attwood & Gray, 2002) suggested that because children with Asperger's tend to emulate adults, we must make it a habit to look at our own interactions with these children, and repeatedly ask ourselves whether our ways of relating to them are modeling what we would like them to learn about relating to others. Children with Asperger's often behave like pedantic adults. Without help understanding the social culture, they tend to be bossy, want things done their way, be critical and rigid, appear unreasonably sure of themselves, and be insensitive to the thoughts and feelings of others. If we expect a child with Asperger's to follow our orders without questioning us, what are we teaching that child about interacting with others? If we allow his peers to overpower him with insulting words or violent behavior, and we do not intervene, what is he learning about how to treat other people? If we are trying to teach her to think calmly before acting, and we respond to her with impatience, what is she learning from us about managing anger? If we do not listen to the child talk about what interests him or her, what will that child learn about listening to others? We need to stay calm and logical, explain the reasons for our behaviors and demands, learn to communicate effectively with people with Asperger's Syndrome, and make sure that they are treated with the respect we ask them to give others.

The more we learn to be flexible ourselves and the more interactively competent we become, the more effectively we model desirable behavior. Gray (Attwood & Gray, 2002) suggested that when we are working with children with Asperger's Syndrome and confront a challenging behavior, we engage in an introspective process that allows us to evaluate our feelings, thoughts, and assumptions before responding. She proposed that we reflect in the following way: We look at our own emotional response to find out if it is interfering with our judgment; we ask for time to think; we consider that what the child is saying might mean something different to him or her than it means to us; we acknowledge that we might need a translation that includes asking for or providing more information for either party; we acknowledge the child's beliefs and feelings; and we consider an alternative route to the one we would ordinarily choose. In other words, those of us who are more neurotypical need to go through the same cognitive process to understand and communicate with people with Asperger's, that they must learn to communicate with us. The advantages of this approach were apparent recently when one of us was treating a child who was having angry explosions at home and in school. When I suggested the recommended strategy of monitoring his levels of agitation every 15 minutes, scoring these levels with numbers from 1 to 10, and taking preventative action before the numbers got too high, he responded angrily, "No, I hate that!" I took a deep breath, noticed my own discouraged feelings, overrode them, and asked him what he hated about it. He explained that his aide, Mrs. X, had made him assign numbers to his moods in a way that infuriated him, and repeatedly dragged him out of the classroom kicking and punching. We took the time to acknowledge the traumatic nature of those experiences and how often they had occurred. He repeated his refusal to use numbers as monitoring devices. At that point I asked him if he could think of another way to name his mood states. With great gusto, he suggested that we use a "spiciness" scale, and named the agitation levels wimpy, beginner, medium, glass of water, industrial, and nuclear. We wrote them down, he took them home, and he was subsequently able to use his own words to make use of the anger management technique he had previously rejected. When we can curb our own fears and our impatience, be curious about the perspective of the other, legitimize his or her feelings, adopt the flexibility we are trying to teach, and make use of the resources and creativity of the person we are trying to help, we all come out ahead. We challenge ourselves to question our own patterns and assumptions, to adopt the perspective of the other, and to be empathic; in other words, to learn to do what we are asking the individual with Asperger's Syndrome to do. Those helping the child or adult with Asperger's Syndrome, if trained to engage in such a process, are not only better helpers, but become more emotionally intelligent human beings capable of creating better communities.

REFERENCES

Asperger, H. (1991). Autistic psychopathy in childhood. In U. Frith (Ed. & Trans.), *Autism and Asperger's Syndrome* (pp. 37–91). Cambridge, England: Cambridge University Press. (Original work published 1944)

Attwood, T. (1998). *Asperger's Syndrome: A guide for parents and professionals.* London: Jessica Kingsley.

Attwood, T., & Gray, C. (2002, October). *Feelings, friendships, and Asperger's Syndrome: The best of Attwood and Gray.* Conference conducted in Burlington, VT.

Baron-Cohen, S. (2002). Is Asperger Syndrome necessarily viewed as a disability? *Focus on Autism and Other Developmental Disabilities, 17,* 186–191.

Carrington, S., & Graham, L. (2001). Perceptions of school by two teenage boys with Asperger Syndrome and their mothers: A qualitative study. *Autism, 5*(1), 37–48.

Frith, U. (1991). *Autism and Asperger Syndrome.* Cambridge, England: Cambridge University Press.

Goleman, D. (1994). *Emotional intelligence.* New York: Bantam Books.

Gutstein, S., & Whitney, T. (2002). Asperger Syndrome and the development of social competence. *Focus on Autism and Other Developmental Disabilities, 17,* 161–171.

Rubin, K., & Thomas, A. (2002). *The friendship factor: Helping our children navigate their social world—And why it matters for their success.* New York: Viking.

Simpson, R. L., & Myles, B. S. (1998). Aggression among children and youth who have Asperger's Syndrome: A different population requiring different strategies. *Preventing School Failure, 42*(4), 149–153.

Sofronoff, K., & Farbotko, M. (2002). The effectiveness of parent management training to increase self-efficacy in parents of children with Asperger Syndrome. *Autism, 6,* 271–286.

Welkowitz, L. A., & Baker, L. J. (2000). *Understanding Asperger's* [Educational film]. New York: Insight Media.

PART I

Fundamental Issues

Chapter 2

Theory of Mind
and Asperger's Syndrome

Tony Attwood
Petrie Clinic

Psychologists describe children and adults with Asperger's syndrome as having impaired *theory of mind*. The term originates from a study of the chimpanzee by Premack and Woodruff (1978); who described Theory of Mind (ToM) as the ability to attribute independent mental states to self and others to predict and explain behavior. In the 1980s the term was used by developmental psychologists Leslie and Morton, who suggested that young children have an innate mechanism that enables them to think about and distinguish between the real world and thoughts. Frith and Baron-Cohen, colleagues of Leslie and Morton, first started to apply the concept of ToM to children with autism.

Research and clinical experience had established that young children with autism rarely engage in pretend play. Baron-Cohen, Leslie, and Frith (1985) suggested that children with autism lack the crucial mechanism to distinguish things in the real world and things in the mind. They examined whether children with autism would be confused by the concept that a person can know something that someone else does not know. They used a paradigm developed by Wimmer and Perner (1983), in their studies of normal children, which has become known as the Sally-Anne task. A scene is enacted using two dolls (Sally and Anne), a marble, and a miniature box and basket. Sally has the box and Anne has the basket. Sally places the marble in her box, then goes for a walk. While she is out of sight, Anne takes the marble from Sally's box and places it in her basket. The marble is not visible in either the box or the basket. Sally returns from her walk. The child has observed the sequence of events and is asked, "Where will Sally look for the marble first?" Normal children of around 4 years know that Sally still thinks her marble is in the box, and point to the box. However, children with autism, matched on cognitive and linguistic abilities to normal 4-year-old children, have considerable difficulty with this task. (Baron-Cohen et al., 1985).

In the last 20 years there have been hundreds of studies published in research journals that have explored the application of ToM to our understanding of autism and Asperger's Syndrome. The purpose of this chapter is not to provide a comprehensive review of the literature, which has been achieved by Baron-Cohen, Tager-Flusberg, and Cohen (2000), but to provide a brief explanation of the term and then focus on how impaired ToM skills affect the daily life of children and adults with Asperger's Syndrome. Assessment procedures for ToM skills for clinicians and ways in which parents and teachers can design remedial programs are also discussed.

HOW IS ToM IMPAIRED IN ASPERGER'S SYNDROME?

Cognitive psychologists originally used ToM to mean the ability to recognize and understand thoughts, beliefs, desires, and intentions of other people to make sense of their behavior and predict what they are going to do next. It has also been described as mind reading (Baron-Cohen, 1995) and mentalizing and empathy (Gillberg, 2002). There is no consensus regarding the precise definition of the nature of impaired ToM abilities observed in children and adults with Asperger's Syndrome. In psychological terms, the descriptions suggest a cognitive incapacity to impute mental states to others and to the self, which results in a deficit in the ability to explain and predict another person's behavior. The person with Asperger's Syndrome might not recognize or understand the cues that indicate the intentions or feelings of the other person or know how to respond. This has been described as mind blindness (Baron-Cohen, 1995), or more colloquially, a difficulty in putting themselves in another person's shoes.

It has been suggested that impaired ToM also affects self-consciousness and introspection (Frith & Happe, 1999). I was talking to Corey, a teenager with Asperger's Syndrome, about the ability to mind read. He said, "I'm not good at working out what other people are thinking, I'm not sure what I'm thinking now." Thus there might be a pervasive difficulty in thinking about thoughts and feelings, whether they are the thoughts and feelings of another person or oneself.

The Developmental Progression of ToM Abilities

At around 10 to 18 months of age, very young children develop pretend play. They can change the function of an object; for example, a banana can be held and used as if it is a telephone. The mental state of pretense has emerged and the child will know that an adult demonstrating such actions is only pretending.

The next stage in the development of a ToM is an awareness of what another person can see, their visual perspective and knowledge. This ability is usually present in 2-year-old children and becomes the basis of one of the first social games, namely hide-and-seek with an object. At around 3 years of age, children know that another person has to look inside a container to know what is inside. At around 3 to 4 years of age a child knows how someone will perceive the orientation of an object from a different perspective; for example, when another person is sitting opposite to the child, a picture will appear upside down from their perspective.

The third stage in the development of ToM abilities is the understanding of another person's desires and emotions, which helps to explain the behavior and intentions of other people. This ability to understand basic desires can occur around the age of 2 years for some children. We have the term *terrible twos* to describe the conflict between the child's desires and those of his or her parent (Howlin, Baron-Cohen, & Hadwin, 1999). At the same age, children are able to identify the basic facial expressions of happy, sad, angry, and scared. By the age of 4 years they can understand whether another person is likely to express these feelings in everyday situations. For example, if a story is told of a boy who expects a particular toy for his birthday present, but subsequently receives a present he does not want, children at this age can understand that the boy in the story will feel sad or angry.

In theoretical terms, the first level in the development of mental representation or metarepresentation (ToM) is to understand that other people have thoughts: in other words, "I think that you think." The next level in metarepresentation is "I think that you think that she thinks." The final level is "I think that you think that she thinks that he thinks." Children with severe autism might never even acquire the first level, but children with Asperger's Syndrome usually acquire this level later in their childhood, around 4 to 6 years. They continue to be delayed in acquiring Level 2 metarepresentation, which occurs in other children around 6 years; children with Asperger's Syndrome are usually able to pass Level 2 tests by age 10 (Gillberg, 2002). With Asperger's Syndrome, it might not be an eternal absence of ToM skills, but a significant delay in comparison to their development of general intellectual abilities.

Neurological Origins of ToM

The ability to acquire ToM skills is dependent on the efficient functioning of several areas of the brain; so far significant areas have been identified in the frontal and temporal lobes of the brain (Baron-Cohen et al., 1994; Goel, Grafman, Sadato, & Hallett, 1995). In particular, an area of the left portion of the frontal lobe (Brodmann area 8/9) has been identified as functioning when a person is engaged in a task that requires the use of ToM abilities (Fletcher et al., 1995). Do these areas of the brain function as one would expect in individuals with Asperger's Syndrome? Happe et al. (1996) found that individuals with Asperger's syndrome activated a part of the brain 2 cm below and 8 mm in front of the area activated by control participants. Their adult participants could provide correct answers to questions that require ToM skills, but to do this they used an area of the brain adjacent to that used by control participants.

Effects of Impaired ToM Abilities on Daily Life

Research by developmental and cognitive psychologists has provided a description of the concept of ToM in normal children and how it can be impaired in those with an autistic spectrum disorder. How does impaired ToM affect a child or adult's daily life? The answer to this question is provided by clinicians and in the comments and autobiographies of those with Asperger's Syndrome.

Although it might be relatively easy to understand that the person has difficulty knowing what another person might be thinking or feeling, it is much harder to imagine what it must be like on a day-to-day basis. Most people are fortunate in having an intuitive ability to read and respond appropriately to the cues or signals for mind reading. We can read a face and translate the meaning of body language or changes in the prosody of speech. We also recognize the contextual cues that indicate the prevailing or expected thoughts of others. When observing young children with autism or Asperger's Syndrome, I have noticed they often lack awareness of these social signs or cues. Our social rules are, in part, based on the desire not to offend the thoughts and feelings of others, and often the child with Asperger's Syndrome is criticized for breaking these rules. I use the metaphor of a car driver who does not see or cannot read the road signs; he or she might run through a red light, drive too close to another car, fail to observe the speed limit, or drive the wrong way down a one-way street. Similarly, the child with Asperger's Syndrome might hear the teacher clear her throat and think she has a throat infection. Other children will know that this can also mean the teacher is becoming annoyed and they should stop what they are doing or she will become more annoyed. They look at her face to read her mood and see if the warning is directed at them. Much as a motorist who sees an amber traffic light ahead, these children decide to change their behavior. The child with Asperger's Syndrome who does not read the cues and therefore fails to respond as expected to the signal is not being wilfully disobedient; when the teacher says he is annoyed that the child continued what he or she was doing, the child might be perplexed as to the connection between his or her behavior and the teacher's feelings.

The following sections address some of the areas of daily life in children and adults that are affected by impaired ToM skills.

Difficulty Reading the Social and Emotional Messages in the Eyes. How do we know what a person might be thinking or feeling? One way is our ability to read a face, and in particular, the eyes. A series of studies has been conducted to determine if children and adults with Asperger's Syndrome look at the eyes of another person as much as we would expect, and how good they are at deciphering the messages in the eyes. We have known for some time that children and adults with an autistic spectrum disorder appear to engage in less eye contact than anticipated. The first problem for them in mind reading is that they look at a person's face less often. However, when they look at a face, where do they look? Most people tend to focus on the eyes to help determine the other person's thoughts and feelings. Eye-tracking technology can be used to measure visual fixation and recent research has indicated that those with Asperger's Syndrome tend to look less at the eyes and more at the mouth, body, and objects than do control participants (Klin, Jones, Schultz, Volkmar, & Cohen, 2002a, 2002b). These ingenious studies determined where someone was looking as they watched a filmed interaction between actors. In one scene, whereas the control participants fixated on the look of surprise and horror in the actor's wide-open eyes, the participants with high-functioning autism focused on the actor's mouth. The research showed that normal control participants visually fixated on the eye region twice as often as the group of participants with high-functioning autism.

Other research has shown that when a person with Asperger's Syndrome does look at someone's eyes, he or she is less able to read the meaning in the eyes than control participants (Baron-Cohen & Jolliffe, 1997; Baron-Cohen, Wheelwright, Hill, Raste, & Plumb, 2001). A quotation from a person with Asperger's Syndrome suggests this point: "People give each other messages with their eyes, but I do not know what they are saying" (Wing, 1992, p. 131). Thus, those with Asperger's Syndrome have two problems in using information from the eyes to determine what someone is thinking and feeling. First, they tend not to look at the eyes as the dominant source of information regarding social and emotional communication. Second, they are not very good at reading the eyes that they do focus on. For those with Asperger's syndrome, the eyes are not the windows of the soul.

Making a Literal Interpretation.   One of the consequences of impaired ToM skills is a tendency to make a literal interpretation of what someone says. I have noted the literal response to requests such as "Hop on the scales," the emotional reaction to comments such as "Let's toast the bride," and confusion regarding common metaphors such as "It's about time that you pulled your socks up." This also means that the child or adult is bewildered by sarcasm, and prone to teasing by others, as he or she is remarkably gullible. One of the ways that we determine the speaker's intention is to consider the social context, facial expression, and tone of voice. We have known for some time that children and adults with Asperger's syndrome have difficulty recognizing the relevant social cues and reading the thoughts or emotions in another person's face (Baron-Cohen et al., 2001) but we have new evidence that they also have difficulty understanding the significance of the person's tone of voice or prosody (Kleinman, Marciano, & Ault, 2001; Rutherford, Baron-Cohen, & Wheelwright, 2002), which normally would enable the listener to go beyond a literal interpretation. We are able to understand the incongruence between facial expression, tone of voice, and context, and realize when someone is teasing or being sarcastic.

Being Considered Disrespectful and Rude.   The child with Asperger's Syndrome might not respond to an adult's or another child's subtle cues this person is becoming annoyed with egocentric behavior. Those with Asperger's Syndrome appear to break the social rules and do not respond to the warning signs. If the adult or other child does not know that this behavior is due to impaired ToM skills, his or her interpretation of the behavior is to make a moral judgment; the child with Asperger's syndrome can be viewed and described as deliberately rude, selfish, naughty, and wilfully disobedient.

This characteristic can occur in adults. Houston and Frith (2000) published a case history of the infamous Hugh Blair of Borgue. Blair was an 18th-century Scottish *laird* or landowner, whose arranged marriage was annulled on the grounds of his mental incapacity. The authors examined the historical records and identified characteristics of autism or Asperger's Syndrome in his developmental history and profile of abilities. The court papers refer to his difficulties understanding the thoughts and perspectives of others. Blair would visit his neighbors at inappropriate times, "borrow" their clothes, or give gifts that were unwanted. The authors also referred to how some of his servants and local children would mock him, although he appeared to have been unaware of their ridicule.

Honesty and Deception.   I have noted that young children with Asperger's Syndrome are often remarkably honest. Asked by a parent if they have committed an act that they know is not allowed, these children are likely to readily admit that they did it. Other children will recognize that there are some occasions when the adult would not have enough knowledge (i.e., they did not actually see who did it) and they can use deception to avoid the consequences. Such deception usually occurs around 4 years of age (Sodian, Taylor, Harris, & Perner, 1991). Children and adults with Asperger's Syndrome appear to have a greater allegiance to honesty and the truth than to the thoughts and feelings of others.

Another characteristic is not knowing when not to say the truth. They might make an audible and direct comment to someone that is true but likely to cause offense or to isolate them from their peers. For example, they might notice that a woman in the line at the supermarket checkout is obese, and remark, in their usual tone of voice and volume, that the lady is fat and needs to go on a diet. Their opinion is that she should be grateful for the observation and advice; the likelihood that their mother will be embarrassed or the woman angry at such a rude comment is not part of the child's thinking process. Other children would normally inhibit such a response based on their understanding of the other person's thoughts and feelings.

Another such example might occur at school. For instance, while the teacher is distracted, a child might commit a disobedient act. When the teacher recognizes something has happened but does not know who did it, the teacher asks that the culprit confess. The other children often know who it was but they will usually not say, as their allegiance is to the social code of, as the Australians would say, "not dobbing in your mates." However, for children with Asperger's Syndrome, the allegiance is to the truth, not the social group. The teacher asks a question and they quickly provide the answer, and are then confused as to why their peers are annoyed with them, especially if they did not commit the act.

The ability to deceive might occur later in the child with Asperger's Syndrome, as they progress from Level 1 to Level 2 in metarepresentation. This can cause confusion to parents and teachers, as the previously honest (perhaps to a fault) child recognizes the potential value of deception. As a clinician, I am delighted with the progression to Level 2 in metarepresentation, but it is difficult for parents and teachers to accept the immature lying of someone whose intellectual ability is beyond this stage of behavior.

Becoming Aware of Making Social Errors.   Young children with Asperger's Syndrome can be unaware of the thoughts and feelings of others and virtually mind blind. As they mature and acquire basic ToM skills, they can become very conscious of being mind myopic and socially clumsy, which can lead to a social phobia. I have treated many adolescents and young adults with Asperger's Syndrome who have developed agoraphobia or school refusal. In clients who do not have Asperger's Syndrome these psychological conditions are usually due to a fear of what other people might think of them, which requires advanced ToM abilities. From my clinical experience, a client with Asperger's Syndrome is his or her own worst critic and is more likely to develop a social phobia due to self-criticism for making a social mistake.

A Sense of Paranoia.   One of the consequences of impaired ToM skills in the person with Asperger's Syndrome is difficulty distinguishing between deliberate and accidental actions. For example, a child is running down the corridor at school, trips, and accidentally knocks into a child with Asperger's Syndrome. Other children would know by the context, the character of the child who tripped, and his or her apology that although the act might have hurt, it was unintentional. This might not be automatically recognized by the child with Asperger's Syndrome, who retaliates as if the action was a form of deliberate provocation. The ability to accurately determine the intentions of others is impaired, resulting in a sense of paranoia.

I observed a boy with Asperger's Syndrome who was sitting on the classroom floor with the other children in the class, listening to the teacher read a story. The adjacent boy started to tease him by poking his fingers in his back while the teacher was not looking. The boy with Asperger's Syndrome became increasingly annoyed and eventually hit the other boy to make him stop. The teacher was looking at the children at this point, but being unaware of the preceding events, reprimanded the child with Asperger's Syndrome for being aggressive. Other children would have explained that they were provoked, and would recognize that if the teacher knew the circumstances, the consequences would be less severe and more equitable. Yet he remained silent. The teacher continued with her story and a few moments later another child returned to the classroom from going to the toilet. As he carefully moved past the boy with Asperger's Syndrome, he accidentally touched him; the boy with Asperger's Syndrome was not aware that in this situation the action was accidental, so he hit the other boy in the same way as he had the child who had been tormenting him.

If they are in a "negative" mood, they can fail to differentiate between deliberate and accidental acts, or distinguish whether the intention was hostile or benevolent. There can be a difficulty with the causal attribution of negative events. One of the concerns of clinicians is differentiating between the anticipated consequences of an impaired ToM and the paranoia and persecutory delusions associated with schizophrenia. Paranoia can be a clinical characteristic of some children and adults with Asperger's Syndrome. Blackshaw, Kinderman, Hare, and Hatton (2001) examined the potential link between impaired ToM and paranoia in young adults with Asperger's Syndrome. They described how an incident such as being ignored by a friend could be conceptualized in terms of the situation (they did not see you, were in a hurry, etc.), which uses the circumstances as an explanation, or it could be conceptualized in terms of their mental intentions (they do not want to talk to you or they wanted to make you feel embarrassed or ignored). They administered a series of tests and questionnaires to measure the degree of impaired ToM and paranoia. The individuals with Asperger's Syndrome scored lower on tests of ToM and higher on measures of paranoia than controls. However, both groups were equally likely to attribute negative events to themselves as they were positive events, and to use both personal and situational attributions. They also found that the paranoia was due to impaired ToM abilities and was qualitatively different from the characteristics of paranoia observed in people with a diagnosis of schizophrenia. The paranoia is not a defense strategy, as occurs in schizophrenia, but is due to confusion in understanding the subtleties of social interaction and social rules. I would add that the apparent paranoia in Asperger's Syndrome might also be due to very real social experiences, where individuals encounter a greater degree of deliberate and provocative teasing than their peers. Once another child has been antagonistic, any subsequent interaction with that child is confusing; the child with Asperger's Syndrome can make the assumption that the interaction was intentionally hostile, whereas others would be better able to interpret the other child's intentions by the context and social cues. Another example that I have noted is the tendency of the peer group to label the child with Asperger's Syndrome as "psycho." This can lead the young adult with Asperger's Syndrome to wonder if he or she is indeed going insane.

Managing Conflict.   As a child develops, he or she becomes more mature and skilled in the art of persuasion, compromise, and management of conflict. Part of this is the ability to understand the perspective of another person and how to influence that person's thoughts and emotions using constructive strategies. Managing conflict successfully, therefore, requires considerable ToM skills. One would thus expect difficulties in conflict resolution with children and adults with Asperger's Syndrome. Observations and experience of conflict situations suggest that the person with Asperger's Syndrome is relatively immature, lacks a variety of negotiating tools, and tends to be confrontational. They might resort to primitive conflict management strategies, such as emotional blackmail or an inflexible adherence to their own point of view. They might fail to understand that they would be more likely to get what they want by being nice to the other person. When an argument or altercation is over, the person with Asperger's Syndrome might also show less remorse or appreciation of repair mechanisms such as an apology.

Awareness of Hurting Others' Feelings.   Asperger (1944/1991) described "autistic acts of malice" that are perceived by parents and others as unpleasant and hurtful. He considered that "since their emotionality is poorly developed, they cannot sense how much they hurt others, either physically, as in the case of younger siblings, or mentally, as in the case of parents" (p. 77). Perhaps there is some cold comfort in knowing that when they have deliberately hurt someone, physically or emotionally, their lack of empathy might partly explain their actions.

Asperger (1944/1991) also described how the children can inadvertently cause discomfort in others by being unaware not only of the thoughts and feelings of others but of social content. He wrote:

> For personal distance too they have no sense or feeling. Just as they unconcernedly lean on others, even complete strangers, and may run their fingers over them as if they were a piece of furniture, so they impose themselves without shyness on anybody. They may demand a service or simply start a conversation on a theme of their own choosing. All this goes, of course, without any regard for differences in age, social rank or common courtesies. (p. 81)

Impaired ToM abilities can also lead people with Asperger's Syndrome to become notorious for being insensitive to someone's vulnerabilities, or pushing someone's buttons, but they might be unaware of what these vulnerabilities are and why people are consequently annoyed or offended.

Repairing Someone's Feelings.   When we see someone who is distressed, we instinctively know what to do; we have a range of options to repair someone's feelings based on our intuitive ToM abilities. We recognize the cues, depth of emotion, and social context, and select an appropriate repair mechanism such as words and actions that provide comfort, reassurance, or affection. I have observed that many children and adults with Asperger's Syndrome recognize obvious cues of distress such as tears, but due to their impaired ToM or empathy skills, tend to respond with a thoughtful, practical action, such as getting some tissues or leaving the person alone to recover rather than the conventional, quicker, and more effective emotional restorative of words and gestures of affection. It is interesting to note that when the child or adult with Asperger's Syndrome is distressed, the thoughts and feelings of others might not be as powerful an emotional restorative for them as solitude and preferred activities such as their special interest.

Recognizing Signs of Boredom.   People with Asperger's Syndrome might have a remarkable enthusiasm for their special interest. However, they might not recognize that other people do not share the same level of enthusiasm. People with Asperger's Syndrome tend to look less at the other person when they are talking; therefore they might not see or recognize the subtle signs of boredom or be able to judge whether the topic is relevant to the context or priorities of the other person. Equally, those topics or activities that are of interest to others might be perceived as boring by the person with Asperger's Syndrome. For example, at elementary school, children usually have a vicarious interest in the experiences of their peers. They sit still during show and tell and take a genuine interest in the experiences of the child who is standing before the group. Children with Asperger's Syndrome might not be able to empathize with the storyteller or be interested in their experiences. They can become bored and be criticized for not paying attention. The tendency therefore to talk at length without recognizing another person's boredom, or to be inattentive to others' interests, might be due to impaired ToM rather than a lack of respect or a desire to misbehave.

Introspection and Self-Consciousness.   Frith and Happe (1999) suggested that due to differences in the acquisition and nature of ToM abilities in the cognitive development of children with Asperger's Syndrome, they might develop a different form of self-consciousness. They might acquire ToM using their intellectual capacity and experience rather than intuition. This can eventually lead to a heightened degree of self-consciousness as they reflect on their own and others' mental states. Frith and Happe (1999) described this highly reflective and explicit self-consciousness as similar to that of philosophers. I have read some of the essays and autobiographies of adults with Asperger's Syndrome and would agree that there is a quasi-philosophical quality. When the profile of abilities associated with Asperger's Syndrome is combined with advanced intellectual abilities we might achieve new advances in philosophy. It is interesting to note that philosopher Ludwig Wittgenstein had many of the characteristics of an intellectually gifted person with Asperger's Syndrome (Gillberg, 2002).

A lack of introspection also affects psychotherapy with children and adults with Asperger's Syndrome. I have modified cognitive behavior therapy to accommodate the unusual profile of abilities in this particular group of clients. This includes recognition of impaired ToM skills in terms of impaired self-reflection and impaired understanding of the effects of their own words and actions on the thoughts and feelings of others (Attwood, 2003a). Of note to clinicians is my observation that people with Asperger's Syndrome might have difficulty explaining their own and others' mental processes using speech, but can be more eloquent and accurate in explaining subjective feelings using equipment such as an emotional thermometer, and typed communication such as an e-mail.

Clothing and Personal Hygiene.   If one is less aware of the thoughts of others, then conformity to peer pressure is reduced. I have noticed that young people with Asperger's Syndrome might not be aware of current trends in clothes and personal grooming. Their clothes are practical rather than "cool." This can lead to ridicule from their peers. Girls with Asperger's Syndrome might prefer to wear the comfortable and practical clothing of boys, including a short haircut. They can be perceived as being tomboys, and in adolescence such clothing might be misinterpreted by others as an indication of sexual orientation, which could lead to teasing. For teenagers with Asperger's Syndrome there can be a lack of appreciation of the thoughts of other people in response to body odor. Parents can be exasperated about having to remind their child to use a deodorant. Clinical experience has found that one of the reasons for a lack of success in achieving and maintaining employment is poor personal hygiene.

Reciprocal Love and Grief.   With an impaired ToM, there are difficulties with the conceptualization of feelings and desires of others and oneself. Mayes, Cohen, and Klin (1993) examined desire and fantasy from a psychoanalytic perspective in the context of impaired ToM in people with Asperger's Syndrome. Their view is that people with autism and Asperger's Syndrome do not fall in love readily, nor grieve the loss of others to the degree one would expect. Their description is that "generally, their responses to losses are as muted and brief as their displays of affection" (p. 460). In his autobiography, Schneider (1999) explained his confusion regarding love and grief:

> At one point my mother; exasperated at me, said, "You know what the trouble is? You don't know how to love! You need to learn how to love!" I was taken aback totally. I hadn't the faintest notion what she meant. I still don't. (p. 43)

Schneider also described his grief and loss:

> One rather fundamental emotion felt by people is grief when someone close is lost, either through death or permanent departure for a far-off place. Never in my life have I ever felt grief, or even a sense of loss. (p. 51)

I have conducted relationship counseling for couples where one partner has a diagnosis of Asperger's Syndrome. A question that I ask each partner is his or her description of love. The following are the thoughts of several partners who do not share their husband's diagnosis of Asperger's Syndrome:

Love is: Tolerance, non-judgmental [sic], supportive.

Love is: A complex of beliefs that tap into our childhood languages and experiences; it is inspired when you meet someone that has a quality that maybe you admire, or do not have (admiration and respect)—or that they (someone you admire) reflects back to your ideal self—which is what you want to be or see yourself as.

Love is: Passion, acceptance, affection, reassurance, mutual enjoyment.

Love is: What I feel for myself when I am with another person.

The following are some of the descriptions given by their husbands with Asperger's Syndrome:

Love is: Helping and doing things for your lover.

Love is: An attempt to connect to the other person's feelings and emotions.

Love is: Companionship, someone to depend on to help you in the right direction.
Love is: I have no idea what is involved.

Love is: Tolerance, loyal, allows "space."

People with Asperger's Syndrome might express their love in more practical terms; or, to change a quotation from *Star Trek* (as Spock is examining an extraterrestrial), "It's life, Jim, but not as we know it." In Asperger's Syndrome, it is love, but not as we know it.

The child with Asperger's Syndrome might find confusing or misinterpret expressions of love from his or her parents. For example, the mother of an actively anxious 8-year-old boy with Asperger's Syndrome would lie next to him in his bed as he fell asleep. This was an expression of her love for him, to ensure that, as he fell asleep, he would be next to someone who loves him. When I asked the child why his mother lay next to him, his reply was, "She's tired and she said that my bed is the most comfortable bed."

I have noticed that children and adults with Asperger's Syndrome can be remarkably stoic in grief situations. Their perspective is to be practical rather than emotional; death is inevitable and the person no longer exists. The grieving process can be brief and less intense than one would expect. However, I have noted that although the child might have a limited grief reaction to the death of a close relative, there can be intense grief over the death of a pet.

Understanding of Embarrassment and Faux Pas.   At around 6 to 8 months of age, the basic emotions of fear, anger, sadness, happiness, surprise, and disgust can be observed in an infant, but self-conscious emotions such as embarrassment usually occur around the second year. Between the ages of 3 and 5 years, a child develops advanced self-conscious emotional expressions such as pride, shame, and guilt, which involve self-reflection and evaluation. We know that the feeling of embarrassment matures through three stages. The second stage occurs at about 5 years of age, and is primarily a response to negative reactions from others; however, at around 8 years of age, it can be a response to an assumed evaluation of oneself (Lewis, 1995). Hillier and Allinson (2002) examined the understanding of embarrassment in children with high-functioning autism and found a link between ToM skills and the understanding of embarrassment. However, they found that their participants with high-functioning autism showed a reasonable understanding of this rather complex emotion. When they examined the autistic participants' responses in detail they found that there were some interesting characteristics. They tended to rate some situations as embarrassing whereas controls did not, and they had some difficulty justifying why someone would be embarrassed. At an intellectual level, they had an understanding of the concept of embarrassment, but they were less able to use the concept in novel situations. In practical terms, I have noted that some children with Asperger's Syndrome can appear to have little embarrassment or stage fright when making a presentation or acting in front of others. Observation of social situations that would be expected to include the body language of embarrassment suggests that people with Asperger's Syndrome make fewer gestures of embarrassment (e.g., a hand over the mouth, or a red face) than their peers (Attwood, Frith, & Hermelin, 1988).

Baron-Cohen, O'Riordan, Stone, Jones, and Plaisted (1999) developed a faux pas detection test using a series of stories, and examined whether children with Asperger's Syndrome recognized a faux pas. They found that, in comparison to control children, children with Asperger's Syndrome were less skilled at detecting faux pas and tended to commit faux pas in their everyday behavior. I have noted that people with Asperger's Syndrome tend to make comments based on their perspective, preferring to tell the truth rather than modify their comments to take into account the other person's feelings.

Coping With Criticism.   Children at around 8 years of age can inhibit their comments or criticism on the basis of their prediction of the emotional reaction of the other person; for example, they keep their thoughts to themselves so as not to embarrass or annoy their friend. However, due to their immature ToM skills, people with Asperger's Syndrome can be very keen to point out another person's mistakes. Their comments can be interpreted as deliberately critical and hostile, but they might have intended simply to enlighten the other person and are oblivious to their feelings. For example, I have observed teenagers with Asperger's Syndrome at high school criticize their teacher in front of the whole class. The mistake can be trivial, such as an incorrect spelling of a word, but the desire to correct the mistake takes precedence over the feelings of the teacher.

Speed and Quality of Social Processing.   We are usually very quick in using our ToM abilities when engaged in social reasoning tasks. Research has shown that although some children and adults with Asperger's Syndrome can demonstrate quite advanced ToM skills, they can take longer with their cognitive processing than one would expect, and require more prompts. Their answers to questions that rely on ToM abilities can be less spontaneous and intuitive than those of control participants and more literal, idiosyncratic, and irrelevant (Bauminger & Kasari, 1999; Kaland et al., 2002).

One of the consequences of using conscious calculation rather than intuition is the effect on the timing of responses. In a conversation or social interaction, people with Asperger's Syndrome can be slow in processing aspects that require ToM skills. This delayed reaction time can cause the other person to perceive them as somewhat formal or pedantic, or to even consider that they are intellectually retarded. They are simply following the social rules and are less able to be spontaneous and flexible. Observation suggests that the time delay leads to a lack of synchrony to which both parties try to adjust. Other children often torment children with Asperger's Syndrome, calling them stupid, which adds insult to injury and can lead to low self-esteem or anger.

Exhaustion.   We know that the acquisition of ToM skills can be delayed in those with Asperger's Syndrome but that they can eventually achieve advanced ToM abilities. However, we also need to recognize the degree of mental effort required by people with Asperger's Syndrome to process social information. They appear to use cognitive mechanisms to compensate for impaired ToM skills, which lead to mental exhaustion. I have also noted that ToM abilities in children and adults with Asperger's Syndrome can be influenced by the degree of stress. When relaxed, they can more easily process mental states, but when stressed, as with any skill, their performance declines. This can have an effect on the formal testing of ToM abilities and could explain some of the differences between formal knowledge in an artificial testing situation and real life.

Advanced Ability in Other Cognitive Skills.   Although people with Asperger's Syndrome might have difficulty with ToM abilities, in contrast, they can be remarkably skilled in other cognitive abilities. It appears that if the social brain is less well developed, other mental abilities flourish. While other children are socializing and practicing their ToM abilities, those with Asperger's Syndrome are developing and practicing other mental skills. They can be remarkably able in understanding machines, leading to precocious abilities with construction toys, electronics, mechanics, and science. Other cognitive abilities might flourish, such as musical, mathematical, and language abilities. Some of these skills can become the foundations of a successful career.

THE ASSESSMENT OF ToM ABILITIES

We recognize that impaired ToM abilities have a significant impact on the daily lives of those with Asperger's Syndrome, but as clinicians, parents, and teachers, we hope to encourage and facilitate the development of ToM skills. The first stage is to assess the child or adult's current level of functioning with regard to ToM.

Infants to 3 Years

At around 9 to 12 months of age, infants engage in joint attention. They will be interested in where an adult is looking. Infants will also point to an object, not simply because they want it, but to declare to the other person that they might both find the object interesting, a form of gestural communication described as *proto-declarative pointing*. Infants also check to see that the adult is looking at the interesting object or event. Thus the infants are becoming aware of what someone knows and likes. However the ability to direct someone's attention might be delayed in a very young child with an autistic spectrum disorder such as Asperger's Syndrome (Baron-Cohen, 1989).

Other indicators of the precursors of ToM abilities are imaginative or make-believe play, where a doll or figure represents a person with thoughts and experiences, and the use of mental state terms in speech with the correct use of words such as *believe, think, know, feel*, and so on. Children with an autistic spectrum disorder are known to be delayed in their imaginative play and to be less likely to use mental state terms in their speech.

4 to 5 Years

The Sally–Anne Task. We now have several tests to measure the development of ToM skills in young children between the ages of 4 and 5 years. The most frequently used test is known as the Sally–Anne false belief task (Wimmer & Perner, 1983). Two dolls are used, one named Sally, the other, Anne. There are three toy items; a box, a basket, and a marble. The child listens as a story is told. Sally places her marble in the box and closes the lid. While she is away (the doll is removed from the scene), Anne removes the marble and places it in the basket, covered by a piece of cloth. Questions are asked of the child during the story that confirm that the child knows where the marble was and is now. The crucial question is, when Sally returns, "Where will Sally look for the marble first?" Normal 4-year-olds point to where Sally thinks she left the marble, rather than where it was subsequently placed.

Smarties Task. The Smarties task involves a content change that is unexpected (Hogrefe, Wimmer, & Perner, 1986). The child is shown a container of sweets popular among their peers (the original task used a tube of Smarties, which are sugar-coated chocolate beans similar to M&Ms). The child is asked "What is in the closed container?" with the expected reply being "Smarties." The container is opened to reveal not Smarties, but another, unexpected object, such as a pencil. The next part of the assessment is to explain to the child that their friend (or mother) is going to come into the room and will be shown the same container. The key question is "What will he or she say is in the tube?" Again, normal 4- to 5-year-olds will understand the difference between what they know and what another person knows.

One of the advantages of having two different tests that assess the same ability is that they can be used in research designs where two parallel tests are required, for example, in the evaluation of ToM training programs.

6 to 12 Years

The Strange Stories Test.   Happe (1994a) developed the Strange Stories test that examines more advanced ToM abilities. Each story describes an event that results in a person saying something that is not strictly true. The child is asked to explain why the person in the story made such a comment. There are two examples for each of the 12 story types: Lie, White Lie, Joke, Pretend, Misunderstanding, Persuasion, Appearance/Reality, Figure of Speech, Irony, Forgetting, Double Bluff, and Contrary Emotions. The Strange Stories test facilitates an examination of the understanding of a character's mental states. An example is the story about a White Lie in Happe (1994b):

> Helen waited all year for Christmas because she knew at Christmas she could ask her parents for a rabbit. Helen wanted a rabbit more than anything in the world. At last Christmas day arrived, and Helen ran to unwrap the big box her parents had given her. She felt sure it would contain a little rabbit in a cage. But when she opened it, with all the family standing round, she found her present was just a boring old set of encyclopaedias, which Helen did not want at all! Still, When Helen's parents asked her how she liked her present, she said, "It's lovely, thank you. It is just what I wanted."
>
> Is it true what Helen said?
>
> Why did she say that to her parents? (p. 78)

The concept of a white lie, said so as not to hurt someone's feelings, is an example of advanced ToM abilities, and an ability expected in the development of friendship and interpersonal skills at around the age of 7 years (Attwood, 2003b). I use some of the Strange Stories test in my diagnostic assessment of children and adults with Asperger's Syndrome. Stories such as this one can produce some interesting responses from children with Asperger's Syndrome. The reply to the question at the end of the story from children with Asperger's Syndrome can be "I don't know," but such children can also reply with plausible responses without an appreciation of why the child might tell a white lie. An example is, "She can read about rabbits in the encyclopaedia, that's why she said it was just what she wanted," or "You wouldn't wrap a rabbit in a cage, it couldn't breathe, perhaps the rabbit is outside and this is just another present." I have also noted that some children with Asperger's Syndrome can provide the anticipated answer, such as "Not to hurt their feelings," which is evidence of advanced ToM abilities, but can take several seconds to cognitively determine why she said that, whereas normal children provide an almost instantaneous answer. They might also restrict their answer to their own immature and egocentric perspective and reply that she said that so that her parents would not smack her.

The TOM Test.   The TOM test was developed in Holland and is designed for children between 5 and 12 years of age (Muris et al., 1999). The test consists of vignettes, stories, and drawings, and the child answers a series of questions. There are three subscales:

1. Precursors of ToM, such as the recognition of the emotions from facial expressions and posture, and the understanding of pretense.
2. First-order ToM such as false belief.
3. More advanced aspects of ToM, which enables an assessment of second-order belief and humor.

The test has a total of 78 questions with a score of failed (0) or passed (1) that can be divided between the three subscales. For example, in one of the test items the child looks at a picture of a street scene that includes a house fire and two people calling for help from an upstairs window. A traffic jam is causing the delay of the arrival of the fire rescue vehicle and numerous bystanders display several contrasting facial expressions. The questions require the child to identify who is expressing a particular feeling and why.

The test is sensitive to the developmental progression in ToM abilities and can be used by academics, clinicians, and teachers. In particular, the test can provide invaluable information on an individual child's abilities that can assist with the design of remedial programs to improve the child's maturity with regard to ToM abilities. The TOM test can also be readministered to determine whether the remedial programs have been successful.

Detecting Faux Pas.   This test is designed for children from 7 to 11 years old and assesses the ability to recognize a faux pas (Baron-Cohen et al., 1999). Ten faux pas stories are recorded on an audiocassette and the child answers a series of questions such as whether someone said something they should not have said. An example of one of the 10 stories is as follows:

Sally has short blonde hair. She was at her Aunt Carol's house. The doorbell rang. It was Mary, a neighbor. Mary said "Hello," then looked at Sally and said, "Oh, I don't think I've met this little boy. What's your name?" Aunt Carol said "Would you like a cup of tea?"

In this story, did someone say something that they should not have said?

What did they say that they should not have said?

Adolescence

Stories From Everyday Life.   The Stories From Everyday Life (Kaland et al., 2002) was designed and developed in Denmark, and is a new test battery extending the original Strange Stories test developed by Happe, but based on vignettes or stories about everyday situations for adolescents. The test comprises 26 short stories or

13 pairs of different types of stories. The last part of the stories contains two questions assessing the ability to infer a mental state from the story context, such as a lie, white lie, figure of speech, misunderstanding, double bluff, irony, contrary emotions, forgetting, jealousy, intentions, empathy, and social blunders. There is a series of control questions to ensure the listener understands the gist of the story. The scoring includes 2 points for fully correct answers and 1 point for partly correct answers. The authors of the test found that, in comparison to control participants, the participants with Asperger's Syndrome had significantly more problems attributing mental state inferences, had significantly longer reaction time, and needed significantly more prompt questions.

Social Attribution Task.   The Social Attribution Task was originally developed by Heider and Simmel (1994). They made a cartoon animation film with a cast of characters that are geometric shapes that move in synchrony, against one another, or as a result of the action of the other shapes. The film lasts only 50 seconds but has six sequential segments presented one at a time. After each segment, the observer is asked, "What happened there?" to provide a narrative to the silent film. The observer is also asked questions such as "What kind of a person is the big triangle or the small circle?" The authors of the task found that college students used anthropomorphic words to describe the actions (*chasing, entrapping,* and *playing*), and feelings (*frightened, elated,* or *frustrated*) of the characters.

The Social Attribution Task has recently been used to determine if adolescents with high-functioning autism and Asperger's Syndrome can attribute social meaning to ambiguous visual stimuli (Klin, 2000). There are six index scores that can be obtained from an analysis of the observer's narrative:

- *Animation Index:* Provides a measure of the capacity to attribute social meaning to ambiguous visual stimuli.
- *Theory of Mind Index:* The frequency of mental state terms and emotions.
- *Salience Index:* The number of social elements.
- *Pertinence Index:* The degree of relevance.
- *Person Index:* The ability to create personality attributions or anthropomorphize.
- *Problem-Solving Index:* The ability to answer explicit questions about the cartoon.

When the Social Attribution Task was used with adolescents with Asperger's Syndrome significant differences were found between such participants and their controls. Their narratives were shorter with less elaborate social plots. Many of their comments were not pertinent to the video and they identified only one quarter of the social elements identified by the control participants. They used fewer ToM terms and less social sophistication. They also produced fewer and more simplistic personality attributions. The narratives of the control participants, who easily attributed social meaning to the ambiguous scene, included descriptions of bravery or elation, complex personalities, and social attributions that provided a coherent social story. In contrast, one of the narratives from a participant with an autistic spectrum disorder was an accurate description of the facts:

> The big triangle went into the rectangle. There were a small triangle and a circle. The big triangle went out. The shapes bounce off each other. The small circle went inside the rectangle. The big triangle was in the box with the circle. The small triangle and the circle went around each other a few times. They were kind of oscillating around each other, maybe because of a magnetic field. After that, they go off the screen. The big triangle turned like a star—like a Star of David—and broke the rectangle. (Klin, 2000, p. 840)

Adults

The original studies of ToM abilities were conducted with young children but the last few years have seen the development and evaluation of several tests that measure ToM abilities in adults.

Reading the Mind in the Eyes Test.   The original Reading the Mind in the Eyes Test was described in a research paper by Baron-Cohen and Jolliffe (1997) and revised several years later (Baron-Cohen et al., 2001). The test uses 40 photographs of the eye region taken from magazine photographs. All pictures are in black and white, with the same region of the face in each photograph. The task is to choose which of four words describes the thoughts or feelings of the person in the photograph. The thoughts or emotions conveyed in the photographs include sympathy, desire, fantasy, skepticism, interest, suspicion, and other complex thoughts. I have often used this test in the diagnostic assessment of adults. Some adults with Asperger's Syndrome have had considerable difficulty reading the mind in the eyes, and some have achieved reasonable test scores but have taken some time to analyze in detail each face, often lamenting the lack of further information from other facial features, such as the mouth. In contrast, those adults who do not have signs of Asperger's Syndrome can complete the task and achieve a high score with relative ease.

The Awkward Moments Test.   The Awkward Moments test uses short excerpts from television commercials and programs and questions regarding a central character's feelings (Heavey, Phillips, Baron-Cohen, & Rutter, 2000). The test was designed to be sensitive to the more subtle aspects of ToM abilities of adults in naturalistic settings. Most of the scenes involve a character experiencing a socially awkward moment. The test requires more than recognition of facial expression, examining the ability to understand false belief as well as the social significance of the actors' actions, in particular, what other characters in the film clip think about the main character's behavior. Eight film clips are used, and the test score is based on the quality of the answer and the number of prompts required to obtain a correct answer. The authors of the test compared adults with high-functioning autism and Asperger's Syndrome with control participants, and found that the participants with an autistic spectrum disorder were less able to explain the characters' intentions and motives.

Mental State Voices Task.   In this test a recording has been made of an actor reading aloud, "The quick brown fox jumped over the lazy dog" with different verbal intonations (Kleinman et al., 2001). The 12 intonations represent the basic emotions (happy, sad, angry, afraid, surprised, and disgusted) and more complex emotions (arrogant, guilty, calm, anxious, bored, and interested). Two actors (male and female) were used, resulting in 24 stimulus sentences.

Reading the Mind in the Voice Test.   In this test the person listens to a brief sample of dialogue on audiotape and then chooses between two adjectives to describe the mental state of the speaker (Rutherford et al., 2002). Each speech segment is a sentence or a phrase and the test comprises 40 segments.

REMEDIAL PROGRAMS

After the child or adult has been assessed on a test of ToM abilities, a range of remedial programs can be applied to facilitate the maturity of ToM abilities.

Social Stories

Social stories were the first activities specifically designed to improve ToM abilities. Carol Gray originally developed social stories in 1991, not from the academic application of a theoretical model of social cognition, but from working directly and collaboratively with children with an autistic spectrum disorder (Gray, 1998). It is an imaginative technique that, among other attributes, explains the perspective, thoughts, and feelings of the person with Asperger's Syndrome and others in a story. They have become part of the social curriculum for children with Asperger's Syndrome throughout the world.

A social story provides information on the where, when, who, what, and why of social situations. Social stories aim to inform more than direct, and provide user-friendly information and tuition on what each person in a given interaction or situation might be thinking or feeling. They use a written medium to identify which details or cues to attend to and what they mean. They explain the code to decipher what is relevant to the situation, and the thread or theme that links specific events. Social stories also correct false assumptions. The stories are written in a style that is consistent with the child's chronological age, reading abilities, and level of cognitive development, sometimes using drawings, photographs, and illustrations There are four types of sentence—descriptive, perspective, directive, and control—and a ratio that designates the proportion of each type of sentence to be used in each social story. The *descriptive* sentences describe where a situation occurs, who is involved, what they are doing, and why. They set the scene for the story, and describe the relevant cues to the situation, such as the social context and verbal and nonverbal communication. The *perspective* sentences provide valuable information regarding ToM abilities. They describe each character's knowledge, thoughts, beliefs, and feelings that are relevant to the situation. One of the essential characteristics of preparing and writing a social story is the acquisition of information on the perspective of all participants, especially the child with Asperger's Syndrome. *Directive* sentences are statements that explain what to do (i.e., the script) in terms of speech, thoughts, and actions. The social story can be customized to include the special interests or writing style of the child with Asperger's Syndrome using *control* sentences (Gagnon, 2001; Gray, 1998). A social story dictionary can improve knowledge and vocabulary with regard to mental state terms, with pictorial explanations of vocabulary such as *know, guess, expect,* and *opinion.* The first social story, and at least half of all subsequent ones, describes a particular social success of the child with Asperger's Syndrome. These stories are a means of recording achievements as well as providing information on situations that require ToM abilities.

Gray's original work on social stories has now been examined in several research studies and found to be remarkably effective in improving both understanding and social and emotional behavior in people with autism and Asperger's Syndrome. (Hagiwara & Myles, 1999; Lorimer, 2002; Norris & Dattilo, 1999; Rogers & Myles, 2001; Rowe, 1999; Scattone, Wilczynski, Edwards, & Rabian, 2002; Smith, 2001; Swaggart et al., 1995; Thiemann & Goldstein, 2001). However, although social stories are a remedial strategy that would be expected to improve ToM abilities, to date there have been no published studies that have examined whether and how social stories improve such abilities using the standard ToM tests. However, I recognize that teachers, parents, and practitioners need remedial strategies such as social stories now, and cannot wait until the research studies determine whether they improve maturity in ToM abilities.

ToM Training

Several studies have investigated whether ToM abilities can be improved using treatment programs designed specifically to improve social cognition. The programs have used social skills training using a group format (Ozonoff & Miller, 1995), simple computer programs (Swettenham, 1996), and teaching (Hadwin, Baron-Cohen, Howlin, & Hill, 1996). Pre- and posttreatment assessment using the standard measures of ToM abilities has confirmed that the programs facilitate the ability to pass ToM tasks. However, these studies have not found a generalization effect to tasks not included in the training program.

Subsequent studies used an interesting approach to teach ToM abilities by using a picture in the head strategy (McGregor, Whiten, & Blackburn, 1998; Swettenham,

Baron-Cohen, Gomez, & Walsh, 1996). The training procedure included placing a photograph into a slot in a doll's head to explain the concept that another person can see or know something different to that seen or known by one's self. This procedure was conducted with very young children, with some degree of success in encouraging the ability to pass a Sally–Anne false belief task.

Comic Strip Conversations

Comic strip conversations (CSCs) use simple drawings such as stick figures, thought and speech bubbles, and text in different colors to illustrate the sequence of actions, emotions, and thoughts in a specific social situation. This practical technique was developed by Carol Gray based on her extensive experience working with children with an autistic spectrum disorder (Gray, 1994). Children are familiar with thought bubbles from reading comics and cartoons. We know that children as young as 3 to 4 years old understand that thought bubbles represent what someone is thinking (Wellman, Hollander, & Schult, 1996).

With CSC, a single cartoon or comic strip is a conversation between the child and adult, with the drawings used to determine what someone is thinking, is feeling, said or did, or could do. Color can be used to identify the emotional tone or motivation, and a color chart can be used to associate a specific color or depth of color with a specific emotion. For example, the child might decide to use a red crayon to indicate that the words spoken by the other child were perceived as being said in an angry tone of voice. This provides an opportunity to learn the child's perception of the event and to correct any misinterpretations. One of the advantages of this approach is that the child and adult have a conversation, but are not looking at each other; their joint focus is on the evolving drawing in front of them. The general approach is one of joint discovery, of the thoughts and feelings being portrayed, rather than an attempt to determine who is at fault. CSCs provide a clear, visual explanation of what someone is thinking and feeling. They can be used to explain misinterpretation of intentions (of both parties); explain figures of speech such as sarcasm; and illustrate alternative outcomes by changing actions, speech, and thoughts. It is interesting that when we express our new understanding, we say, "Yes, I see what you mean," rather than "I hear what you mean."

I make regular use of CSC in my clinical practice. Children with Asperger's Syndrome often communicate their thoughts and feelings more eloquently using drawings rather than speech. Although children with Asperger's Syndrome have difficulty knowing what someone else might be thinking or feeling, clinical experience suggests they have even greater difficulty defining the degree of expression of a particular emotion. Their perception can be very black and white. I add another component to CSC: the use of a numerical scale to measure the degree of expression; for example, how sad someone is feeling, using a scale from 1 to 10. This strategy is particularly useful for children who have a limited vocabulary for the subtle and precise description of emotional intensity.

A recent research study has examined whether thought bubbles can be used to acquire ToM abilities (Wellman et al., 2002). The study described the use of thought bubbles as a prosthetic device that led to an increased ability to pass false belief tests and other ToM tests in children with autism with a mental age of 4 years and older. In addition, the use of thought bubbles led to greater generalization of ToM abilities than had occurred with previous educational strategies.

Programs for Teachers and Parents

Teachers and parents now have a practical guide to teach mind-reading skills (Howlin et al., 1999). The guide provides resource materials, assessment and teaching procedures, and an outline of the principles underlying theory and practice. The understanding of mental states is divided into three separate components:

- Understanding informational states.
- Understanding emotion.
- Understanding pretense.

The section on informational states provides a range of activities to teach visual perspective taking, the principle that seeing leads to knowing, and how to predict actions on the basis of another person's knowledge.

The section on teaching emotions examines several levels of emotional understanding, namely recognizing facial expression from photographs and schematic drawings through to identifying both situation-based emotions, and desire- and belief-based emotions.

The material requires the child to have a language age of at least 5 years and a knowledge of the concept that other people have desires and thoughts. In some activities the child is required to make a forced choice as to whether the person will feel happy or sad according to the situation. One example uses a drawing of a car situated between closed railway crossing barriers with a train approaching. The text describes the scene:

> Jamie is in the car. The barrier comes down. The train is coming. How will Jamie feel when the train is coming?

The child has a prompt of happy/sad/angry/afraid. Although the answer appears to be obvious, I have observed that, if the child with Asperger's Syndrome has a special interest in trains, he or she might consider the situation solely from his or her perspective, and would be happy to come so close to a train. If this was the child's response, one can discuss that although Jamie would be happy, his father, who is driving the car, probably feels afraid. This can help explain how two people would perceive the same situation in very different ways.

The resource material uses simple drawings with clear cues and no irrelevant detail. The child is also provided with a logical and progressive structure with sufficient time to think about his or her response. With practice, as provided by the wide range of examples, the child becomes more fluent and able to interpret mental states. The authors of the guide have conducted a quantitative analysis of the program and found that improvements in ToM abilities were maintained long after intervention ceased.

Computer Programs

A remarkable new DVD has been published that is an electronic encyclopedia of emotions, entitled *Mind Reading: The Interactive Guide to Emotions* (2002). Baron-Cohen and his colleagues at the University of Cambridge discovered that there are 412 human emotions (excluding synonyms). They examined the age at which children understand the meaning of each emotion, and developed a taxonomy that assigned all the distinct emotions into one of 24 different groups. A multimedia company then developed software that is suitable for children and adults to learn about emotions based on the work of the Cambridge team.

On the DVD, six actors portray each of the 412 emotions using video recordings of facial expression, body language, and speech. The DVD also includes audiorecordings and stories that illustrate the circumstances and contexts for each emotion. There is an emotions library, a learning center, and a games zone. A controlled treatment trial is currently being conducted to determine the effectiveness of the program in teaching an understanding of emotions and any improvements in ToM abilities.

I recommend the program as particularly suitable for children and adults with Asperger's Syndrome. Such individuals can have considerable difficulty learning cognitive skills in the live social theater of the classroom, where they have to divide their attention between the activities in front of them and the social, emotional, and linguistic communication of the teacher and the other children. With a computer, the feedback is instantaneous; they do not have to wait for a response from the teacher and they can repeat a scene to identify and analyze the relevant cues many times without annoying or boring others. They are also not going to receive public criticism for mistakes and are more likely to relax when engaged in a solitary activity. The program is designed to minimize any irrelevant detail, highlight the relevant cues, and enable the students to progress at their own pace. It might be somewhat ironic that those with Asperger's Syndrome might be better able to learn about people by using a computer than observing real-life situations.

Cognitive Behavior Therapy

Cognitive behavior therapy (CBT) has been designed and refined over several decades and proven to be effective in changing the way a person thinks about and responds to feelings such as anxiety, sadness, and anger (Graham, 1998; Kendall, 2000). CBT focuses on aspects of cognitive deficiency in terms of the maturity, complexity, and efficacy of thinking, and cognitive distortion in terms of dysfunctional thinking and incorrect assumptions. Thus, it has direct applicability to clients with Asperger's Syndrome who are known to have deficits and distortions in thinking.

The therapy has several components, the first being an assessment of the nature and degree of mood disorder using self-report scales and a clinical interview. The next stage is affective education, with discussion and exercises on the connection between cognition, affect, and behavior, and the way in which individuals conceptualize emotions and construe various situations. Subsequent stages are cognitive restructuring, stress management, self-reflection, and a schedule of activities to practice new cognitive skills. Cognitive restructuring corrects distorted conceptualizations and dysfunctional beliefs. The person is encouraged to establish and examine the evidence for or against his or her thoughts and build a new perception of specific events. Stress management and cue-controlled relaxation programs are used to promote responses incompatible with anxiety or anger. Self-reflection activities help the person recognize his or her internal state, monitor and reflect on his or her thoughts, and construct a new self-image. A graded schedule of activities is also developed to allow the person to practice new abilities, which are monitored by the psychologist.

The following sections provide an examination of two of the components of CBT, affective education and cognitive restructuring.

Affective Education.   The main goal is to learn why we have emotions, their use and misuse, and the identification of different levels of expression. A basic principle is to explore one emotion at a time as a theme for a project. The choice of which emotion to start with is decided by the psychologist but a useful starting point is happiness or pleasure. A scrapbook can be created that illustrates the emotion, including pictures of situations that have a personal association with the feeling (e.g., a photograph of a rare lizard for a person with a special interest in reptiles). The scrapbook illustrates and lists pleasurable things in the person's life, and can also include the sensations associated with the feeling, such as favorite aromas, tastes, and textures. The scrapbook can be used as a diary to include memorabilia, compliments, and records of achievement such as certificates.

When a particular emotion and the levels of expression are understood, the next stage of affective education is to use the same procedures for a contrasting emotion. After exploring happiness, the next topic explored would be sadness. Feeling relaxed would be explored before a project on feeling anxious.

Cognitive Restructuring.   The next component of CBT is cognitive restructuring. This includes knowing which thoughts or emotions are an antidote to a feeling; for example, which strategies or activities associated with feeling happy could be used to counteract feeling sad.

When exploring positive emotions such as happiness and affection, clinical experience suggests that some clients with Asperger's Syndrome have difficulty coping with and responding to moderate levels of expression of these feelings in other people. When family members express physical signs of delight or affection, clients can report feeling uncomfortable and not knowing how to respond. They might need guidance in the appropriate response and in how to inform others of their discomfort. In particular, affection from others might not be as effective a means of emotional repair or recovery as one would expect. If people are generally confused about why other people express affection physically, and unsure how to show affection themselves, they can develop a fear of what they do not understand.

Some individuals with Asperger's Syndrome can have considerable difficulty translating their feelings into conversational words. There can be greater eloquence, insight, and accuracy using other forms of expression. The psychologist can use prose in the form of a conversation by typing questions and answers on a computer screen, or techniques such as CSCs, as previously described. When designing activities to consolidate the new knowledge on emotions, one can use a diary, e-mail, art, or music as means of emotional expression, possibly providing a greater degree of insight for both client and therapist.

Cognitive restructuring enables people with Asperger's Syndrome to correct distorted conceptualizations and dysfunctional beliefs. The process involves challenging their current thinking with logical evidence and ensuring the rationalization and cognitive control of their emotions. The first stage is to establish the evidence for a particular belief. People with Asperger's Syndrome can make false assumptions of their circumstances and the intentions of others. They have a tendency to make a literal interpretation, and a casual comment could be taken out of context or to the extreme.

We are all vulnerable to distorted conceptualizations but people with Asperger's Syndrome are less able to put things in perspective, seek clarification, or consider alternative explanations or responses. The psychologist encourages these people to be more flexible in their thinking, and to seek clarification using questions or comments such as "Are you joking?" or "I'm confused about what you just said." Such comments can also be used when misinterpreting someone's intentions such as, "Did you do that deliberately?" and to rescue the situation after they have made an inappropriate response with a comment such as "I'm sorry I offended you," or "Oh dear, what should I have done?"

Cognitive restructuring also includes a process known as *attribution retraining*. People might exclusively blame others and not consider their own contribution, or they can excessively blame themselves for events. One aspect of Asperger's Syndrome is a tendency to adopt an attitude of arrogance or omnipotence where the perceived focus of control is external; specific others are held responsible and become the target for retribution or punishment. Individuals with Asperger's Syndrome have considerable difficulty accepting that they themselves have contributed to the event. However, the opposite can occur when they have extremely low self-esteem and feel personally responsible, which results in feelings of anxiety and guilt. There can also be a strong sense of what is right and wrong, and conspicuous reaction if others violate the social laws (Church, Alisanski, & Amanullah, 2000). These people might be notorious as "policemen," dispensing justice but not realizing what is within their authority. Attribution retraining involves establishing the reality of the situation, establishing the various participants' contribution to an incident, and determining how clients can change their perception and persona.

The psychologist will incorporate and review conventional behavioral strategies such as rewards and consequences, but there are modifications when considering clients with Asperger's Syndrome. Some rewards might be less effective, particularly expressions of delight and approval. Due to impaired ToM abilities, creating a pleasurable response in others might not be as much of a priority or motivational factor. Appealing to their intellectual vanity rather than altruistic desire to please the therapist can be far more effective, such as the comment that their response was an illustration of their intelligence, wisdom, or maturity.

One of the goals of CBT that is particularly important for those with Asperger's Syndrome is to increase their awareness of the impact of their behavior on others. They tend to be egocentric, to be less aware of other people's inner thoughts and feelings, and to need to move from a consideration of self to others. They need to learn the value of aspects of repair such as an apology and restitution. The program is as much one of tuition in ToM and affective education as a psychological therapy. It also incorporates strategies to repair the feelings of others to improve their social cohesion with family and friends.

This chapter has explained our understanding of the psychological term *theory of mind*, and how a relative impairment in the ability to mind read affects the daily life of children and adults with Asperger's Syndrome. The chapter has also included explanations of some of the remedial programs to teach ToM abilities. However, the last words should be from someone with Asperger's Syndrome: Liane Holliday-Willey (2002, personal communication) wrote, "You wouldn't need a Theory of Mind if everyone spoke their mind."

REFERENCES

Asperger, H. (1991). Autistic psychopathy in childhood. In U, Frith (Ed.), (1991). *Autism and Asperger Syndrome* (pp. 37–91). Cambridge, England: Cambridge University Press. (Original work published 1944)

Attwood, T. (2003a). Cognitive behaviour therapy. In L. Holliday-Willey (Ed.), *Asperger Syndrome in adolescence* (pp. 38–68). London: Jessica Kingsley.

Attwood, T. (2003b). Frameworks for behavioural interventions. *Child and Adolescent Psychiatric Clinics, 12,* 65–86.

Attwood, T., Frith, U., & Hermelin, B. (1988). The understanding and use of interpersonal gestures by autistic Down's Syndrome children. *Journal of Autism and Developmental Disorders, 18,* 214–257.

Baron-Cohen, S. (1989). The autistic child's theory of mind: A case of specific developmental delay. *Journal of Child Psychology and Psychiatry, 30,* 285–297.

Baron-Cohen, S. (1995). *Mind blindness: An essay on autism and theory of mind.* Cambridge, MA: MIT Press.

Baron-Cohen, S., & Jolliffe, T. (1997). Another advanced test of theory of mind: Evidence from very high functioning adults with autism or Asperger's Syndrome. *Journal of Child Psychology and Psychiatry, 38,* 813–822.

Baron-Cohen, S., Leslie, A., & Frith, U. (1985). Does the autistic child have a "theory of mind"? *Cognition, 21,* 37–46.

Baron-Cohen, S., O'Riordan, M., Stone, V., Jones, R., & Plaisted, K. (1999). Recognition of faux pas by normally developing children and children with Asperger Syndrome or high-functioning autism. *Journal of Autism and Developmental Disorders, 29,* 407–418.

Baron-Cohen, S., Ring, H., Moriarty, J., Schmidt, C., Costa, & Ell, P. (1994). Recognition of mental state words: A functional neuroimaging study of normal adults, and a clinical study of children with autism. *British Journal of Psychiatry, 165,* 640–649.

Baron-Cohen, S., Tager-Flusberg, H., & Cohen, D. (2000). *Understanding other minds II: Perspectives from autism and cognitive neuroscience.* Oxford, England: Oxford University Press.

Baron-Cohen, S., Wheelwright, S., Hill, J., Raste, Y., & Plumb, I. (2001). The "reading the mind in the eyes" test revised version: A study with normal adults with Asperger Syndrome or high-functioning autism. *Journal of Child Psychology and Psychiatry, 42,* 241–251.

Bauminger, N., & Kasari, C. (1999). Brief report: Theory of mind in high-functioning children with autism. *Journal of Autism and Developmental Disorders, 29,* 81–86.

Blackshaw, A. J., Kinderman, P., Hare, D. J., & Hatton, C. (2001). Theory of mind, causal attribution and paranoia in Asperger Syndrome. *Autism, 5,* 147–163.

Church, C., Alisanski, S., & Amanullah, S. (2000). The social, behavioural and academic experiences of children with Asperger Syndrome. *Focus on Autism and Other Developmental Disabilities, 15,* 12–20.

Fletcher, P. C., Happe, F., Frith, U., Baker, S. C., Dolan, R. J., Frackowiak, R. S. J., et al. (1995). Other minds in the brain: A functional imaging study of "theory of mind" in story comprehension. *Cognition, 57,* 109–128.

Frith, U., & Happe, F. (1999). Self-consciousness and autism: What is it like to be autistic? *Mind and Language, 14,* 1–22.

Gagnon, E. (2001). *Power cards: Using special interests to motivate children and youth with Asperger Syndrome and autism.* Shawnee Mission, KS: Autism Asperger Publishing.

Gillberg, C. (2002). *A guide to Asperger Syndrome.* Cambridge, England: Cambridge University Press.

Goel, V., Grafman J., Sadato, N., & Hallett, M. (1995). Modelling other minds. *Neuroreport, 6,* 1741–1746.

Graham, P. (1998). *Cognitive behaviour therapy for children and families.* Cambridge, England: Cambridge University Press.

Gray, C. (1994). *Comic strip conversations.* Arlington, TX: Future Horizons.

Gray, C. (1998). Social stories and comic strip conversations with students with Asperger Syndrome and high-functioning autism. In E. Schopler, G. Mesibov, & L. J. Kunce (Eds.), *Asperger's Syndrome or high-functioning autism* (pp. 167–198). New York: Plenum.

Hadwin, J., Baron-Cohen, S., Howlin, P., & Hill, K. (1996). Can we teach children with autism to understand emotions, belief, or pretence? *Development and Psychopathology, 8,* 345–365.

Hagiwara, T., & Myles, B. S. (1999). A multimedia social story intervention: Teaching skills to children with autism. *Focus on Autism and Other Developmental Disabilities, 14*, 82–95.

Happe, F. (1994a). An advanced test of theory of mind: Understanding of story characters' thoughts and feelings by able autistic, mentally handicapped, and normal children and adults. *Journal of Autism and Developmental Disorders, 24*, 129–154.

Happe, F. (1994b). *Autism*. Cambridge, MA: Harvard University Press.

Happe, F., Ehlers, S., Fletcher, P., Frith, U., Johansson, M., Gillberg, C., et al. (1996). "Theory of Mind" in the brain: Evidence from a PET scan study of Asperger Syndrome. *Neuroreport, 8*, 197–201.

Heavey, L., Phillips, W., Baron-Cohen, S., & Rutter, M. (2000). The Awkward Moments Test: A naturalistic measure of social understanding in autism. *Journal of Autism and Developmental Disorders, 30*, 225–236.

Heider, F., & Simmel, M. (1994). An experimental study of apparent behaviour. *The Autism Journal of Psychology, 57*, 243–259.

Hillier, A., & Allinson, L. (2002). Beyond expectations: Autism, understanding embarrassment, and the relationship with theory of mind. *Autism, 6*, 299–314.

Hogrefe, G.-J., Wimmer, H., & Perner, J. (1986). Ignorance versus false belief: A developmental lag in attribution of epistemic states. *Child Development, 57*, 576–582.

Houston, R., & Frith, U. (2000). *Autism in history: The case of Hugh Blair of Borgue*. Oxford, England: Blackwell.

Howlin, P., Baron-Cohen, S., & Hadwin, J. (1999). *Teaching children with autism to mind-read: A practical guide*. Chichester, England: Wiley.

Kaland, N., Moller-Nielsen, A., Callesen, K., Mortensen, E. L., Gottlieb, D., & Smith, L. (2002). A new "advanced" test of theory of mind: Evidence from children and adolescents with Asperger Syndrome. *Journal of Child Psychology and Psychiatry, 43*, 517–528.

Kendall, P. C. (2000). *Child and adolescent cognitive behavioral therapy procedures*. New York: Guilford.

Kleinman, J., Marciano, P. L., & Ault, R. L. (2001). Advanced theory of mind in high-functioning adults with autism. *Journal of Autism and Developmental Disorders, 31*, 29–36.

Klin, A. (2000). Attributing social meaning to ambiguous visual stimuli in higher-functioning autism and Asperger Syndrome: The social attribution task. *Journal of Child Psychology and Psychiatry, 41*, 831–846.

Klin, A., Jones, W., Schultz, R., Volkmar, F., & Cohen, D. (2002a). Defining and quantifying the social phenotype in autism. *American Journal of Psychiatry, 159*, 895–908.

Klin, A., Jones, W., Schultz, R., Volkmar, F., & Cohen, D. (2002b). Visual fixation patterns during viewing of naturalistic social situations as predictors of social competence in individuals with autism. *Archives of General Psychiatry, 59*, 809–816.

Lewis, M. (1995). Embarrassment: The emotion of self-exposure and evaluation. In J. P. Tangney & K. W. Fischer (Eds.), *Self-conscious emotions: The psychology of shame, guilt, embarrassment and pride* (pp. 198–218). New York: Guilford.

Lorimer, P. A. (2002). The use of social stories as a preventative behavioral intervention in a home setting with a child with autism. *Journal of Positive Behavior Interventions, 4*, 53–60.

Mayes, L., Cohen, D., & Klin, A. (1995). Desire and fantasy: A psychoanalytic perspective on theory of mind and autism. In S. Baron-Cohen, T. Tager-Flusberg, & D. Cohen (Eds.), *Understanding other minds: Perspectives from autism* (pp. 450–465). Oxford, England: Oxford Medical Publications.

McGregor, E., Whiten, A., & Blackburn, P. (1998). Teaching theory of mind by highlighting intentions and illustrating thoughts: A comparison of their effectiveness with three-year-olds and autistic subjects. *British Journal of Developmental Psychology, 16,* 281–300.

Mind reading: The interactive guide to emotions [Computer software]. (2002). Human emotions. Retrieved Feb. 3, 2003 from http://www.human-emotions.com

Muris, P., Steerneman, P., Meesters, C., Merckelbach, H., Horselenberg, R., van den Hogen, T., et al. (1999). The TOM test: A new instrument for assessing theory of mind in normal children and children with pervasive developmental disorders. *Journal of Autism and Developmental Disorders, 29,* 67–80.

Norris, C., & Dattilo, J. (1999). Evaluating effects of a social story intervention on a young girl with autism. *Focus on Autism and Other Developmental Disabilities, 14,* 180–186.

Ozonoff, S., & Miller, J. N. (1995). Teaching theory of mind: A new approach to social skills training for individuals with autism. *Journal of Autism and Developmental Disorders, 25,* 415–433.

Premack, D., & Woodruff, G. (1978). Does the chimpanzee have a theory of mind? *The Behavioural and Brain Sciences, 4,* 515–526.

Rogers, M. F., & Myles, B. S. (2001). Using social stories and comic strip conversations to interpret social situations for an adolescent with Asperger's syndrome. *Intervention in School and Clinic, 38,* 310–313.

Rowe, C. (1999). Do social stories benefit children with autism in mainstream primary school? *British Journal of Special Education, 26,* 12–14.

Rutherford, M. D., Baron-Cohen, S., & Wheelwright, S. (2002). Reading the mind in the voice: A study with normal adults and adults with Asperger Syndrome and high-functioning autism. *Journal of Autism and Developmental Disorders, 32,* 189–194.

Scattone, D., Wilczynski, S. M., Edwards, R. P., & Rabian, B. (2002). Decreasing disruptive behaviours of children with autism using social stories. *Journal of Autism and Developmental Disorders, 32,* 535–543.

Schneider, E. (1999). *Discovering my autism.* London: Jessica Kingsley.

Smith, C. (2001). Using social stories with children with autistic spectrum disorders: An evaluation. *Good Autism Practice, 2,* 16–23.

Sodian, B., Taylor, C., Harris, P. L., & Perner, J. (1991). Early deception and the child's theory of mind: False trails and genuine markers. *Child Development, 62,* 468–463.

Swaggart, B. L., Gagnon, E., Bock, S. J., Earles, T. L., Quinn, C., Myles, B. S., et al. (1995). Using social stories to teach social and behavioral skills to children with autism. *Focus on Autistic Behavior, 10,* 1–16.

Swettenham, J. (1996). Can children with autism be taught to understand false belief using computers? *Journal of Child Psychology and Psychiatry, 37,* 157–165.

Swettenham, J., Baron-Cohen, S., Gomez, J. C., & Walsh, S. (1996). What's inside a person's head? Conceiving of the mind as a camera helps children with autism develop an alternative theory of mind. *Cognitive Neuropsychiatry, 1,* 73–88

Thiemann, K. S., & Goldstein, H. (2001). Social stories, written text cues and video feedback: Effects on social communication of children with autism. *Journal of Applied Behavior Analysis, 34,* 425–446.

Wellman, H., Hollander, M., & Schult, C. (1996). Young children's understanding of thought bubbles and of thoughts. *Child Development, 67,* 768–788.

Wellman, H. M., Baron-Cohen, S., Caswell, R., Gomez, J. C., Swettenham, J., Toye, E., et al. (2002). Thought-bubbles help children with autism acquire an alternative theory of mind. *Autism, 6,* 343–363.

Wimmer, H., & Perner, J. (1983). Beliefs about beliefs: Representation and the constraining function of wrong beliefs in young children's understanding of deception. *Cognition, 13,* 103–128.

Wing, L. (1992). Manifestations of social problems in high-functioning autistic people. In E. Schopler & G. B. Mesibov (Eds.), *High-functioning individuals with autism* (pp. 129–142). New York: Plenum.

Chapter 3

Diagnosis

Stephen P. Safran
Ohio University

Over the past two decades, diagnosis of Asperger's Syndrome has been a topic of continuing professional debate. Although Asperger's Syndrome is universally viewed as a neurologically based pervasive developmental disorder (PDD) associated with deficits in social interactions and narrow or obsessional interests (Meyer & Minshew, 2002; Volkmar & Klin, 2000), experts disagree over its diagnostic validity. Is Asperger's Syndrome a distinct condition, qualitatively different than autistic disorder? Or is it equivalent to high-functioning autism, existing at the mild end of the autistic spectrum (Szatmari, 1992, 1998, 2000)? The meaning and the scope of the concept of *diagnosis* also generate differing views. For many professionals, diagnosis is simply analogous to classification. However for others, the true value of diagnosis lies within the broader concept of assessment as an "analytic information gathering process directed at understanding the nature of the problem, its possible causes, treatment options and outcomes" (Mash & Terdal, 1997, p. 12).

From this wider assessment perspective, accurate diagnosis is critical to individuals with Asperger's Syndrome, their families, and service providers for several reasons. First, early intervention programs can improve social, pragmatic, and cognitive skills necessary for improved life adjustment and also help parents develop effective behavior management skills. If recognition is delayed, the severity of peer rejection, depression, suicide, and other long-term negative effects might increase (Howlin & Asgharian, 1999). Next, accurate diagnosis can provide insight into developmental changes over time (Volkmar & Klin, 2000). For example, families and professionals can be more aware of problems related to bullying and teasing during middle childhood and early adolescence (Church, Alisanski, & Amanullah, 2000). Finally, Asperger's Syndrome is a unique condition often accompanied by unusual behaviors and narrow, idiosyncratic interests. Diagnosis therefore opens a window toward better understanding. If Asperger's Syndrome is undetected, many behaviors can be misconstrued as intentional or rude, placing blame on a person for acting in a socially unacceptable manner (S. P. Safran, 2001). Diagnosis is truly the first step in supporting persons with this sometimes invisible and perplexing disability.

AN OVERVIEW OF DIAGNOSIS

In 1944 the Austrian psychiatrist Hans Asperger reported a new condition among children he termed *autistic psychopathy*. Whereas Kanner's original work from the same period on autism was widely disseminated, it was not until 1981 that Wing introduced Asperger's Syndrome to the English-speaking world. Over the ensuing two decades, there were numerous attempts to delineate diagnostic criteria with varying degrees of consistency and success (i.e., American Psychiatric Association [APA], 1994, 2000; Gillberg, 1989; Szatmari, Bremner, & Nagy, 1989; Wing, 1981; World Health Organization [WHO], 1993). Until the release of the *International Classification of Diseases (ICD–10;* WHO, 1992) and the *Diagnostic and Statistical Manual of Mental Disorders* (4th ed. [DSM–IV]; APA, 1994; see Table 3.1), no formal classification system acknowledged Asperger's Syndrome as a distinct disorder. Howlin (2000) posited that part of the current diagnostic confusion is due to the half-century delay between Asperger's initial work and the professional adoption of Asperger's Syndrome. This is only one of many reasons why there remains substantial uncertainty about what constitutes an accurate and reliable diagnosis (Freeman, Cronin, & Candela, 2002; Szatmari, 1998, 2000).

PDD, also referred to as autistic spectrum disorders, the autistic continuum, or disorders of empathy (Gillberg, 1996), are a set of related conditions under the *DSM–IV–TR* (APA, 2000) that present three types of developmental delays: skills in reciprocal social interaction, communication, and stereotypic behavior. Specific syndromes included within the PDD umbrella are Autistic Disorder, Rett's Disorder, Childhood Disintegrative Disorder, Asperger's Syndrome, and Pervasive Developmental Disorder–Not Otherwise Specified (APA, 1994, 2000; Szatmari, 1998). Although Asperger's Syndrome is considered the mildest form, its combination of symptoms can be confusing to parents and professionals. According to the *DSM–IV–TR*, Asperger's Syndrome is specifically composed of two primary clusters. The first, qualitative impairment in social interactions, consists of delays in using and understanding nonverbal behavior, problems establishing peer relationships, and deficits in social reciprocity. The second, restricted areas of interest and stereotypic behaviors and activities, includes preoccupation with one narrow special-interest area or parts or objects, rigidity (sticking with one set, sometimes dysfunctional routine), or repetitive, stereotyped movements (J. S.

TABLE 3.1

DSM–IV–TR Diagnostic Criteria for Asperger's Disorder

A. Qualitative impairment in social interaction, as manifested by at least two of the following:
1. Marked impairments in the use of multiple nonverbal behaviors such as eye-to-eye gaze, facial expression, body postures, and gestures to regulate social interaction.
2. Failure to develop peer relationships appropriate to developmental level.
3. A lack of spontaneous seeking to share enjoyment, interests, or achievements with other people (e.g., by a lack of showing, bringing, or pointing out objects of interest to other people).
4. Lack of social or emotional reciprocity.
B. Restricted repetitive and stereotyped patterns of behavior, interests, and activities, as manifested by at least one of the following:
1. Encompassing preoccupation with one or more stereotyped and restricted patterns of interest that is abnormal either in intensity or focus.
2. Apparently inflexible adherence to specific, nonfunctional routines or rituals.
3. Stereotyped and repetitive motor mannerisms (e.g., hand or finger flapping or twisting, or complex whole-body movements).
4. Persistent preoccupation with parts of objects.
C. The disturbance causes clinically significant impairment in social, occupational, or other important areas of functioning.
D. There is no clinically significant general delay in language (e.g., single words used by age 2 years, communicative phrases used by age 3 years).
E. There is no clinically significant delay in cognitive development or in the development of age-appropriate self-help skills, adaptive behavior (other than social interaction), and curiosity about the environment in childhood.
F. Criteria are not met for another specific Pervasive Developmental Disorder or Schizophrenia.

Safran & S. P. Safran, 2001; S. P. Safran, 2001). According to these criteria, there is also no significant delay in language development, cognition, or self-help skills, and an individual might not be diagnosed with another type of PDD, most often autistic disorder (APA, 1994, 2000).

Although the most recent *DSM–IV–TR* (APA, 2000) does not change the diagnostic criteria of Asperger's Syndrome, additional clarifying information has been added. Associated features, including motor clumsiness, variability in cognitive functioning, overactivity and inattention, plus secondary emotional problems (i.e., depression) are described in greater detail. Further, despite normal language development (described as the use of single words by age 2, communicative phrases by age 3), pragmatics or the social use of language might be impaired. Persons with Asperger's Syndrome might also have egocentric relationships with others and have narrow interests that facilitate the accumulation of large amounts of often nonfunctional information that lead to topical obsessions (i.e., *Star Wars*, Transformers, railroad timetables). Atypical conversational skills can include verbosity, limited self-monitoring, lack of response to social cues, difficulty regulating voice volume, and failure to comply with basic social conventions. According to most authorities, there remains a significant diagnostic overlap with autistic disorder, suggesting that after controlling for intellectual functioning, differences are primarily due to symptom severity (Gillberg, 1998; Meyer & Minshew, 2002; Szatmari, 1998, 2000).

Over the last decade, researchers have analyzed many components of the Asperger's Syndrome criteria to address issues of diagnostic validity (Ghaziuddin, Tsai, & Ghaziuddin, 1992; Gillberg, 1998; Howlin, 2000; Szatmari, 1998). Despite careful consideration of such factors as age of onset of language, cognitive delays, autistic social impairment, abnormal communication, all-absorbing interests, pedantic speech, clumsiness, age of onset and exclusion of autism, there remain many questions. For example, Howlin (2000) concluded that it was far more problematic to diagnose Asperger's Syndrome than autistic disorder for several reasons. First, the *DSM–IV–TR* (APA, 2000) assumes a "hierarchical stance," so if criteria for autistic disorder are met, then by exclusion, an individual may not be diagnosed with Asperger's Syndrome. However, if this exclusion clause were carefully followed, the number of persons diagnosed with Asperger's Syndrome would decline dramatically. In seeming contradiction to the *DSM–IV–TR*, Howlin (2000) noted that some researchers assume that if intelligence and language development are in the typical range then their sample population can be diagnosed as Asperger's Syndrome, thereby ignoring the exclusion of autistic disorder. Second, the current *ICD–10* (WHO, 1992) and *DSM–IV–TR* criteria, although acknowledging overlap, are unclear about what differentiates Asperger's Syndrome from autistic disorder. This is particularly true when assessing delays in early language development, a cornerstone of differential diagnosis. Third, research attempts at distinguishing Asperger's Syndrome and autism have added to the diagnostic confusion because of inconsistent standards for identifying participants in research studies. This increases difficulties related to the external validity and generalization of results (Szatmari, 1992). Fourth, the overlap between Asperger's Syndrome and related conditions such as schizoid personality, nonverbal learning disability, semantic pragmatic disorder, and other types of PDD has created many diagnostic questions (Volkmar & Klin, 2000).

Despite less than perfect classification criteria and the ongoing debate over differential diagnosis, the need to understand the nature of Asperger's Syndrome, potential causes, treatment options, and long-term outcomes remain critical international priorities. The enormity of the challenge lies in the incidence rates. The most reliable current prevalence estimates of Asperger's Syndrome range from between .26% and .71% of the general population based on Swedish data (Ehlers & Gillberg, 1993; Kadesjoe, Gillberg, & Hagberg, 1999). If, as is currently believed, Asperger's Syndrome is equally represented across all ethnic and national groups, incidence rates within national boundaries can be estimated. In the United States, for example, with a population of approximately 280 million persons, this equates to between 728,000 and 1,988,000 persons with Asperger's Syndrome, the vast majority of whom remain undetected. These numbers dramatize the need to evaluate current early identification and screening practices so the long journey toward more comprehensive and effective services can begin.

COMPONENTS OF THE DIAGNOSTIC PROCESS

The diagnosis of Asperger's Syndrome is a complex process that should include trained and experienced interdisciplinary team members ideally composed of psychologists, speech language pathologists, psychiatrists, pediatricians, social workers, educators, and other professionals, as well as family members (Howlin, 1998). There are many types of data that can be collected during a comprehensive assessment and accurate identification depends on reliable and valid data obtained from multiple and independent sources. First, information on developmental history should include pregnancy and early development (particularly social, communication, and motor skills), medical background, psychiatric or health disorders of family members, and psychosocial factors. Although standardized tests are a necessary element, information from observations in structured and unstructured environments, interviews, behavioral assessment, and other sources should also be obtained (Freeman et al., 2002). An individual profile of strengths and weaknesses can then be developed after careful consideration of chronological age and developmental level. Although types of assessment vary across individuals, the following are the general components of the diagnostic process (see Howlin, 1998):

1. *Assessment of cognitive ability*—A wide range of intelligence tests (i.e., Wechsler scales) can be used, preferably using an instrument that provides separate verbal and nonverbal (performance) scores.
2. *Assessment of language development*—This should be done for both receptive and expressive language, but validity and reliability of standardized instruments are often suspect.
3. *Assessment of behavior*—A determination must be made whether a behavior is appropriate for an individual's chronological and mental age, or level of language development.
4. *Assessment of special problem areas*—These include behaviors often related to Asperger's Syndrome, including social skills, play, and communication.
5. *Assessment of medical conditions*—There might be a variety of medical conditions including Fragile X and other genetic anomalies that must be distinguished from Asperger's Syndrome.

Mindful of these components, the current status of early identification and screening for Asperger's Syndrome is examined next.

DIAGNOSIS AND EARLY IDENTIFICATION

Although it occurs infrequently, early identification of Asperger's Syndrome is a crucial first step for youngsters and their families. For children whose disability is more evident at an earlier age, such as with low-functioning autism, early diagnosis is a simpler process. However, when impairments are more subtle and symptoms appear at later ages, the process of identification can be more problematic, causing delays and visits to multiple service providers for families looking for answers (Howlin, 2000; Howlin & Asgharian, 1999). In the case of Asperger's Syndrome, with language development and intellectual functioning usually in the normal range, many symptoms are masked (S. P. Safran, 2001), making professionals and parents more likely to downplay early difficulties (Howlin & Asgharian, 1999). Any delays in early identification can cause families undue hardship and hold up critical services.

Addressing important questions related to early identification in the United Kingdom, Howlin and Asgharian (1999) compared the experiences of families of children with autistic disorder and Asperger's Syndrome. They investigated the age at which parents first became concerned with their child's difficulties and compared the age of diagnosis for youngsters diagnosed with Asperger's Syndrome versus autistic disorder. Of 2,488 surveys distributed, 1,295 (55.1%) were fully completed. As anticipated, parents first voiced concern at an earlier age if their child was diagnosed with autistic disorder (18 months) compared to Asperger's Syndrome (2.53 years). In addition, the average age of confirming a diagnosis was substantially higher for the Asperger's Syndrome group (11.13 vs. 5.49 years), with a high percentage of those with Asperger's Syndrome unidentified until after their 20th birthday (9.8%). Parents of the Asperger's Syndrome group were also less satisfied with the diagnostic process, to some degree due to the delay in diagnosis ($r = .38$). There was also significant variability with the number of cases of Asperger's Syndrome and autistic disorder identified in different age groups. By 5 years of age, virtually all children with autism were identified. In contrast, it was not until age 10 that the percentage of all children diagnosed with Asperger's Syndrome exceeded the percentage identified with autism. Overall, there were four times as many families reporting that their child had autistic disorder, suggesting substantial underidentification of Asperger's Syndrome in the United Kingdom, where services are arguably more available than in other parts of the developed world. In sum, Howlin and Asgharian's (1999) findings strongly reflect that "parents of children with less severe cognitive and linguistic impairments are likely to face more delays and difficulties in obtaining a diagnosis. Such delays have practical, psychiatric, and even genetic implications" (p. 838).

SCREENING

Screening is the initial step in the diagnostic process and is designed as a quick, inexpensive method to identify individuals at risk for Asperger's Syndrome from a large population group. Typically individuals who know a child or adult complete a behavior checklist or rating scale that concentrates on a specific condition (Asperger's Syndrome) or a more general group of related disorders (PDD). These instruments should not be used in isolation to determine a diagnosis, but should be part of a more comprehensive evaluation. Although screening for Asperger's Syndrome was previously dependent on checklists designed for autism or other PDD such as the Childhood Autism Rating Scale (Schopler, Reichler, DeVellis, & Daily, 1980), more recently scales focusing specifically on Asperger's Syndrome have been developed (S. P. Safran, 2001). It should also be noted that none of these have been designed to differentiate Asperger's Syndrome from high-functioning autism. The following are brief overviews of English-language screening instruments for Asperger's Syndrome that have either been published or are under development.

Australian Scale for Asperger's Syndrome (ASAS; Attwood, 1998)

This 24-item scale is divided into five categories that describe Asperger's Syndrome: social and emotional abilities, communication skills, cognitive skills, specific interests, and movement skills. Each item provides an example to help users respond to queries, but several are couched in Australian and British culture and idioms and might not be as suitable for North Americans. Although the scale has a high degree of face validity, there are no reliability, validity, or factor analysis structure provided (S. P. Safran, 2001). Although the ASAS was developed to make decisions about children needing a more complete assessment, according to Howlin (2000), scoring is unclear.

Autism Spectrum Disorders Screening Questionnaire (ASDSQ; Ehlers, Gillberg, & Wing, 1999)

This 27-item clinical instrument, developed and standardized in Sweden, is based on a sample of 110 6- to 17-year-old children, and a "validation" group of 34 youngsters clinically identified with Asperger's Syndrome. Teachers and parents rate each behavior (i.e., "lives somewhat in a world of his/her own with restricted idiosyncratic interests") using a 3-point scale. Data obtained from teachers indicated a 2-month test–retest reliability of .94, plus an 84% success rate for diagnosing Asperger's Syndrome by parents and a 65% success rate for teachers. These results are considered acceptable by psychiatric standards (S. P. Safran, 2001). The ASDSQ has also been used as the screening measure for a study to obtain prevalence rates of Asperger's Syndrome (Ehlers & Gillberg, 1993) and has undergone professional review as a research and assessment tool. However, the sample size for standardization is small and it is designed for use primarily with clinical populations, limiting its use with school and other more mainstream groups (Howlin, 2000).

Asperger Syndrome Diagnostic Scale (ASDS; Myles, Bock, & Simpson, 2001)

This 50-item scale standardized in the United States is divided into five subscales of 7 to 13 items each (language, social, maladaptive, cognitive, and sensorimotor). Parents, teachers or other persons who know the child rate whether they have "observed" or "not observed" a specific behavior. Based on these scores, children then receive an Asperger Syndrome Quotient and are evaluated on their likelihood of being diagnosed as having Asperger's Syndrome on a scale of very unlikely to very likely. A group of 115 students with Asperger's Syndrome (ages 5–18 years from 21 states) were used as the normative sample. Interrater reliability is reported as .93 and an internal consistency reliability of .83 was obtained for the 50 items. The technical manual also reports that the scale correctly classifies students with Asperger's Syndrome with 85% accuracy (J. S. Safran & S. P. Safran, 2001). Although the ASDS appears to be reliable to refer youngsters for more extensive evaluation, it has yet to be used as a research tool.

Gilliam Asperger's Disorder Scale (GADS; Gilliam, 2001)

This screening device is based on a sample of 371 individuals with Asperger's Syndrome from 46 American states plus Canada, Mexico, the United Kingdom, and Australia. Four areas—social interaction, restricted patterns, cognitive patterns, and pragmatic skills—are assessed using 32 questions pertaining to specific characteristics (i.e., "The person uses exceptionally precise or pedantic speech") that are rated on a scale ranging from 0 (*never observed*) to 3 (*frequently observed*). An optional fifth section on early development, measured by eight yes–no questions, is also included. Based on total scale score, individuals are either identified as unlikely, borderline, or likely to have Asperger's Syndrome. The sample was identified by information supplied by school personnel who knew youngsters with an Asperger's Syndrome diagnosis, or by parents who responded to Internet requests. Total scale internal consistency reliability was reported as .87, interrater reliability as .89, and test–retest reliability as .93. The manual also claims an 83% accuracy rate for correct diagnosis of Asperger's Syndrome. Although this scale appears to be of technical adequacy, with a larger Asperger's Syndrome normative group than other instruments, the sources of the 371 diagnoses of Asperger's Syndrome is questionable given the large number of third-party referrals (school professionals, parents, and clinicians). According to a review of professional databases, the GADS has yet to be used in a research study.

Childhood Asperger Syndrome Test (CAST; Scott, Baron-Cohen, Bolton, & Brayne, 2002)

In the absence of a suitable screening instrument for mainstream students in the United Kingdom, this 37-item instrument is under development for screening Asperger's Syndrome and related PDD conditions. The pilot study involved 13 children with Asperger's Syndrome and 37 typical youngsters and established an initial cut-off score plus individual item validation data. A second study included 199 families who completed this scale (17.9% return rate on a postal survey). Using the pilot cut-off score, 6.5% of the sample were deemed at risk for Asperger's Syndrome, well above current prevalence estimates. The instrument correctly identified 87.5% of the group with Asperger's Syndrome or autistic spectrum disorders, but with a 36.4% rate of false positives. The authors concluded that the instrument remains a work in progress.

Autism-Spectrum Quotient (ASQ; Baron-Cohen, Wheelwright, Skinner, Martin, & Clubley, 2001)

This unique 50-item, five-area (social skill, attention switching, attention to detail, communication, and imagination) U.K. instrument is designed to distinguish adults with Asperger's Syndrome or high-functioning from several groups. In the initial study, comparison groups included a typical control population, Cambridge University undergraduates and Mathematics Olympiad winners. Eighty percent of the 58 individuals with Asperger's Syndrome were correctly identified, compared with 2% of the control group. Internal consistency reliability was reported as .63 to .77 for each of the five areas. The instrument, developed with the assumption that autistic characteristics exist on a broad continuum, indicates several cognitive similarities among scientists, mathematicians, and those with Asperger's Syndrome. The ASQ might be helpful to identify higher functioning individuals in need of additional assessment (Howlin, 2000). However, the ASQ appears to be more useful for research purposes and for "identifying the extent of autistic traits shown by an adult of normal intelligence" (Baron-Cohen et al., 2001, p. 15).

DIAGNOSTIC INTERVIEWS

Whereas screening devices are designed to be a quick and inexpensive means to identify individuals at risk, there are more in-depth methods that can be used for diagnosis. One such strategy, the diagnostic interview, contains questions that are asked in a standard order by a trained clinician, who then rates the presence or absence and severity of symptoms. These interviews have several potential advantages including enhanced objectivity by the interviewer and interviewee, improved clarity of definitions and questions due to standardization, and simplified diagnosis (Handen, 1997).

The Autism Diagnostic Interview–Revised (*ADI–R*; Lord et al., 1997; Lord, Rutter, & Le Couteur, 1994) is a semistructured interview containing developmental and behavioral aspects of autism, with a child's primary caregiver serving as informant. The interview consists of five sections: (a) opening questions, (b) communication, (c) social development and play, (d) repetitive and restricted behaviors, and (e) general behavior problems. After the 2- to 3-hour interview process, behaviors are coded on a severity scale ranging from 0 to 3. Based on these scores, a mathematical algorithm determines the severity of autistic symptomatology (Lord et al., 1997). Commenting on the relevance of the ADI–R for diagnosing Asperger's Syndrome, Klin, Sparrow, Marans, Carter, and Volkmar (2000) believed that the administration time is well worth it because of the in-depth information received. In addition, use of severity ratings increases sensitivity to milder forms of PDD. The *ADI–R*, often termed the gold standard for diagnosis because of the extensive training and experience required for administration, however, does not require delayed language development as a criteria for autistic disorder identification. Therefore the instrument is not designed to facilitate a differential diagnosis between Asperger's Syndrome and autistic disorder (Klin et al., 2000; Meyer & Minshew, 2002).

Citing the absence of a diagnostic interview for Asperger's Syndrome, Gillberg, Gillberg, Rastam, and Wentz (2001) began development of the Asperger Syndrome (and high-functioning autism) Diagnostic Interview (ASDI). The interview is based on clinical experiences with several hundred individuals with milder PDD, including Asperger's Syndrome, and incorporates Asperger's original case histories rather than *ICD–10* (WHO, 1992) or *DSM–IV–TR* (APA, 2000) criteria. The scale contains 20 items divided into six clusters: social, interests, routines, verbal and speech, nonverbal, and motor (see Gillberg et al., 2001, for a copy of the interview). Based on interviews, each item is rated on a 2-point scale ranging from 0 (*does not apply*) to 1 (*applies to some degree or very much*). Their validation study uncovered an interrater reliability of .91 and a test–retest reliability of .92 based on completion by neuropsychiatrists. All 13 individuals with Asperger's Syndrome or atypical autism met five of six criteria for Asperger's Syndrome per cluster scores. The authors concluded that despite a small sample, they were satisfied with reliability data and instrument validity. However, Gillberg et al. (2001) emphasized that differential diagnosis of Asperger's Syndrome and autistic disorder was not a function of the ASDI. Further, given the current diagnostic confusion, the authors suggested that to minimize the stigma associated with the term *autism*, it might be preferable to use *Asperger Syndrome* for all cases where an average range IQ of 70 or above is achieved. The authors recommended that ASDI results could be used for preliminary results, but not as the final word for diagnosis. The interview can serve as a guide for further assessment.

DIAGNOSTIC PROFILES OF ASPERGER'S SYNDROME

A primary assumption of diagnostic systems is that persons receiving the same classification share common characteristics. With some degree of homogeneity within classification groups, there might be similar developmental trends or standardized test results (e.g., a similar pattern of intelligence test subtest scores) that assist diagnostic efforts. In this section, I selectively analyze research to determine the extent to which cognitive, academic, and social and behavioral data can assist the diagnostic process. The focus is on recent or important investigations employing standardized assessment instruments with larger samples of individuals with Asperger's Syndrome.

Cognitive Profiles

Although there have been numerous studies examining intelligence test scores of individuals with autistic spectrum disorders, there are fewer specifically on Asperger's Syndrome (Barnhill, Hagiwara, Myles, & Simpson, 2000). In one earlier frequently cited Swedish study, Gillberg (1989) examined numerous areas of assessment information in children ages 5 to 18 with Asperger's Syndrome ($n = 23$) and autism ($n = 23$), including several intelligence tests. He found a wide range of Full Scale IQ scores among those with Asperger's Syndrome, including 9% with mild mental retardation (< 70), 35% near average (70–84), 39% average (85–115), and 17% above average (> 115). Despite initial attempts to match participants with Asperger's Syndrome and autism using IQ scores, the Asperger's Syndrome group still achieved higher scores. With consideration of all assessment results, although individuals with Asperger's Syndrome all demonstrated some language difficulties, usually in abstract comprehension and decoding of social information, children with autism showed more severe language problems prior to the age of 5. Gillberg described Asperger's Syndrome as a mild variation of autism, supporting the notion of an autistic spectrum.

In another Swedish study, Ehlers et al. (1997) evaluated whether Wechsler IQ scores could help differentially diagnose Asperger's Syndrome from autism. The sample contained 40 children in each group (ages 6.0–15.4) with either a Full Scale, Performance, or Verbal IQ score of at least 70 (above the mental retardation range). Results showed an average Full Scale IQ of 102, Verbal IQ of 108.4, and Performance IQ of 95.6 for the Asperger's Syndrome group. Further, the highest subscale scores were on the Information, Similarities, Comprehension, and Vocabulary subtests, with lower levels on the Performance subtests of Object Assembly and Coding. Overall, the Asperger's Syndrome sample reflected higher verbal ability but relative weakness in perceptual processing. The autistic group, in contrast, demonstrated stronger visual and spatial skills. Based on subtest scores, a discriminant function analysis was also conducted to attempt to classify youngsters into one of three groups: Asperger's Syndrome, autistic, and a third attention deficit group. Findings produced an overall correct diagnosis rate of 63%. The authors concluded that Wechsler scores did not support the creation of specific cognitive profiles for Asperger's Syndrome or autistic disorder.

Barnhill, Hagiwara, Myles, and Simpson (2000) examined Wechsler IQ results of 37 participants diagnosed with Asperger's Syndrome by a physician, psychologist, or psychiatrist. Overall average scores were calculated for Verbal IQ (99.32; range = 55–146), Performance (96.72; range = 59–137), and Full Scale (98.2; range = 66–144). Although the Verbal scores were slightly higher than Performance scores, the difference was not statistically significant. Further, the distribution of Verbal and Performance scores was similar to a normal curve distribution. All mean subtest scores also fell in the average range except Coding. Relative strengths on the Block Design, Information, Similarities, and Vocabulary subtests were discovered, reflecting a strong range of knowledge and information (Myles, Barnhill, Hagiwara, Griswold, and Simpson, 2001). Barnhill, Hagiwara, Myles, and Simpson (2000) concluded that their results varied from previous studies and suggested that cognitive profiles might not help diagnose Asperger's Syndrome.

Overall, selected research into cognitive assessment and Asperger's Syndrome indicates that test scores will be of minimal assistance in diagnosing Asperger's Syndrome. Although there is some support for differences in Verbal and Performance scores (Ehlers et al., 1997), this is far from a consistent finding (Barnhill, Hagiwara, Myles, & Simpson, 2000). In addition, individuals with Asperger's Syndrome span the IQ continuum, and counter to popular belief, can also include persons within the mild range of mental retardation.

Academic Profiles

There has been only a trickle of research focusing on the academic characteristics of children with Asperger's Syndrome. According to Griswold, Barnhill, Myles, Hagiwara, and Simpson (2002), students with Asperger's Syndrome have relatively strong skills when fact-based material is required. However, many encounter difficulty if conceptualization is needed, particularly in comprehension, critical thinking and problem-solving abilities.

Griswold et al. (2002) examined standardized test score patterns from the Wechsler Individualized Achievement Test (WIAT; Psychological Corporation, 1992) and the Test of Problem Solving–Elementary Revised (TOPS-R; Bowers, Huisingh, Barrett, & Orman, 1994) and the Adolescent (TOPS-A; Bowers, Huisingh, Barrett, Orman, & LoGiudice, 1991) edition. The WIAT consists of eight subtests including an array of basic academic and school-related competencies. In contrast, the TOPS-R and TOPS-A were developed to assess problem solving and language-based critical thinking requiring student verbal responses. The elementary version provides illustrated scenarios accompanied by examiner verbal stories, whereas the adolescent edition combines identical written and verbal information for students. WIAT results reflected a wide variation of student achievement, ranging from low to very high. Compared with typical peers, no differences were found in Reading, Mathematics, and Language composite scores, but significant differences were found for the Basic Reading, Oral Expression, and Language composites. The TOPS–R and TOPS–A also resulted in a wide range of scores, but the average performance of students with Asperger's Syndrome was almost 2 *SD* below average. Griswold et al. concluded that the classification of Asperger's Syndrome was of little value in determining individual learning strengths and deficits. In addition, findings from the TOPS–A and TOPS–R suggest that poor language skills should be evaluated through multiple sources, varying the input and output channels. Further, low math skills indicated a strong need for hands-on instruction and visual instructional materials. Overall, although some students were very verbal, many had difficulty understanding others and finding practical solutions to home, school, and community problems (Myles, Barnhill, et al., 2001). Griswold et al. (2002) recommended that other measures of learning were needed to plan appropriate instruction.

Myles et al. (2002) examined the scores of 16 students with Asperger's Syndrome aged 6 years, 6 months to 16 years, 9 months on the Classroom Reading Inventory (*CRI*; Silvaroli & Wheelock, 2001). This instrument provides a Global, Independent (defined as comfortable reading), instructional (95% word recognition with 75% comprehension) and frustration (< 95% word recognition and < 75% comprehension) reading levels, as well as measures of listening capacity and silent reading. Results showed children with Asperger's Syndrome were at grade level in three of five *CRI* levels; instructional, frustration, and listening capacity. In contrast, silent reading and independent reading were significantly below grade level. Myles et al. concluded that students with Asperger's Syndrome experience difficulty with silent reading and tend to do better when reading aloud. There were also differences on literal and factual versus inferential comprehension material, suggesting once again the frequent deficit involving comprehension skills.

The limited data available on the academic learning of students with Asperger's Syndrome indicates a wide range of achievement levels across all areas, with particular difficulties in conceptualization skills and sustaining attention (Griswold et al., 2002; Hooper & Bundy, 1998; Myles et al., 2002). Similar to cognitive assessment, school learning must be evaluated on an individual basis, with standardized test scores offering few clues to assist diagnostic efforts. Clearly, using techniques such as curriculum-based assessment, examining classroom work samples, and other types of authentic assessment that directly relate to academic instruction can enhance the assessment process.

Social and Behavioral Profiles

Until recently, understanding of social and behavioral dimensions of Asperger's Syndrome was limited primarily to case studies (Barnhill, Hagiwara, Myles, Simpson, Brick, et al., 2000). Researchers are now just beginning to employ larger samples to address many unanswered questions. For example, are there social development pathways for young children with Asperger's Syndrome Do children seek out friends during the early years? The diagnostic process is further complicated by the increasing evidence that psychiatric conditions frequently coexist with Asperger's Syndrome. Ghaziuddin (2002) stated that seldom are in-depth evaluations conducted solely for social or communication deficits, but for a combination of factors that might include physical aggression, hyperactivity, bizarre behavior, or depression. One behavioral concern that arises is whether individuals with Asperger's Syndrome are more likely to engage in violent actions. According to Ghaziuddin, violence is more likely to be related to an individual's special interest or obsession (i.e., pipe bombs, trains, law enforcement) or to a comorbid psychiatric condition. Diagnosis of Asperger's Syndrome must include consideration of potential coexisting disorders.

Are there social and behavior patterns at varying developmental stages that can assist diagnostic efforts? Church et al. (2000) conducted a qualitative retrospective chart review of 40 children with Asperger's Syndrome enrolled at a university child development center between 1986 and 1998. Records on the complete set of 40 preschoolers, who later matriculated to elementary school, middle school, and high school were included. (Because many children had yet to reach middle and high school, only data from the preschool and elementary levels are summarized here.) In preschool, children were generally found to get along well with adults but were already experiencing difficulty with peer interactions. Most children with Asperger's Syndrome appeared comfortable on the "periphery" of activity, but several were very forward in their interaction style. When socialization did occur, it usually consisted of parallel play, with only 12% of the records reporting interactive play, usually with siblings. Misperception of social cues, along with such behaviors as being inappropriately silly (75%), loud (62%), aggressive (50%), and completely withdrawn (15%) were also frequent. In addition, a need for routine and ritual (e.g., using the same juice cup or requiring a specific morning or evening routine at home) was reported. Transitions between activities were described as problematic and a variety of stereotypic behaviors were present. Further, a large number of children were beginning to show their strengths in rote skills through their ability to memorize the content of videotapes. Children were also fascinated with collecting toys but rarely used them in creative ways. Eighty-eight percent experienced either normal or accelerated language development, but 90% were believed to have pragmatic problems, including difficulties with voice volume, gestures, and holding conversations.

By the age of 6 or 7, records indicated that all children experienced social skill problems (Church et al., 2000). Parents described their children as having "superficial" relationships with peers, and when social contacts were made, they centered on special interests such as the solar system with little "small talk." Interestingly, children also fell into two distinct social patterns—either quiet or more "in your face"—with some children having difficulty keeping their hands to themselves. The variety of social skill deficits often resulted in social ostracism and negative interactions. By the middle of elementary school, stereotypic behavior had often been replaced by such actions as humming or pacing. Children with Asperger's Syndrome also became very rule oriented, demonstrating great rigidity during board games and tattling on peers who were considered transgressors. The need for sameness and obsessions with special interests also were paramount for many, but special interests were sometimes channeled into productive peer and academic directions. A child, for example, might become the "computer expert" and be sought after by peers. A high percentage of the children were also viewed as hyperverbal, but could maintain adult fascination by their knowledge of their special area. Unfortunately, the lack of awareness of listener interest often led to long, pedantic monologues. The results of the Church et al. (2000) study must be interpreted with caution because of the use of retrospective records. These sources might contain subjective comments and the researchers did not report a systematic method to review content in the study's methodology.

Citing the absence of empirical studies on social and behavioral functioning of individuals with Asperger's Syndrome, Barnhill, Hagiwara, Myles, Simpson, Brick, et al. (2000) analyzed 20 sets of teacher, parent and student responses on the Behavior Assessment System for Children (Reynolds & Kamphaus, 1992). These scales are designed to measure perceptions of student behavior at home and school, and results can help design treatment plans. Generally, findings demonstrated that parents rated behavioral symptoms as more serious than teachers. Reflecting this trend, parents also judged students' behavioral symptoms and externalizing problems as "clinically significant," whereas teachers viewed them as "at risk." (Both groups viewed internalizing problems as at risk.) Why did parents voice greater concerns than teachers did? The authors speculated a greater degree of structure at school could improve a child's behavior. Alternatively, teachers might better understand developmental norms, thereby not viewing behaviors as problematic as parents do. In addition, children as a group rated themselves as no different than their typical peers, indicating that limited self-awareness could be influencing self-perceptions. Despite a small representation of adolescents in the sample, there was also a growing concern for depression. In sum, although youngsters with Asperger's Syndrome might be viewed "as socially and verbally difficult and immature" (Barnhill, Hagiwara, Myles, Simpson, Brick, et al., 2000, p. 163), there was no evidence of physical harm or threats to others.

Research into the social and emotional characteristics of Asperger's Syndrome has offered several preliminary insights. First, patterns of behavior and social interactions are manifested in different ways at the preschool and elementary levels, including stereotypic behavior, misperception of social cues, limitations in self-awareness, and the need for routine (Church et al., 2000). Parents also generally rate behavior of children with Asperger's Syndrome more severely than do teachers and believe that behavioral symptoms and externalizing problems are clinically significant (Barnhill, Hagiwara, Myles, Simpson, Brick, et al., 2000). Although this information can assist diagnostic efforts, individual variability among children with Asperger's Syndrome was also noted (Church et al., 2000), raising a cautionary flag to link specific behavioral patterns to diagnosis. Clearly more research with larger samples at different developmental levels is called for.

CONCLUDING THOUGHTS

Since the early work of Asperger and Kanner in the 1940s, there has been a substantial increase in the number of individuals identified with autistic spectrum disorders. Although this was originally considered a low-incidence disability, Wing and Potter (2002) recently concluded that recognition of the entire autistic spectrum and changes in diagnostic criteria are largely responsible for these dramatic changes. We are still clearly in the early stages of identifying individuals with Asperger's Syndrome and the demand for clinical diagnostic services will only continue to accelerate. For these reasons, issues in diagnosis will take on even greater importance in the coming decades.

The debate over differential diagnosis of Asperger's Syndrome, autistic disorder, and related conditions remains unresolved despite extensive international research efforts. This lack of consensus only adds to concerns about reliable classification, and the effects of labeling and stigma across the entire autistic spectrum. These issues are not new in the United States, where diagnosis and classification practices play a major role in legislative compliance for service eligibility and insurance reimbursement for treatment. In special education, for example, where identification of a specific disability is the gateway to assistance, some labels are considered preferable to others. The term *learning disability* (compared with mental retardation and emotional disturbance), where definitional ambiguity remains a fact of life after 40 years, quickly became the most common special educational category, largely due to social acceptability. Similarly, Asperger's Syndrome might become preferred over autism simply because families might consider it less stigmatizing. Along these lines, Gillberg et al. (2001) proposed a practical solution to this current diagnostic dilemma, suggesting that Asperger's Syndrome be used for all cases where an average range IQ of 70 or above is achieved. This reality is already reflected in the latest screening instruments and structured interviews specifically developed for Asperger's Syndrome (i.e., Gillberg et al., 2001; Gilliam, 2001; Myles et al., 2001; Scott et al., 2002), as none are designed to differentially diagnose Asperger's Syndrome and autistic disorder. Limited resources would better be directed toward training professionals and developing a gold standard for diagnosing Asperger's Syndrome (see Gillberg et al., 2001).

In closing, we have witnessed tremendous advances in the diagnosis of Asperger's Syndrome. Researchers, professionals, families, and persons with Asperger's Syndrome will continue to make valuable contributions in our efforts to identify all individuals with Asperger's Syndrome in need of support. Improvements in early identification, screening, and other practices are now only in their early stages and the Asperger's Syndrome community can expect future advances. As many continue to look for answers as to why their loved ones are different, have constant problems with social interactions, and narrowly focus on special interests, reliable diagnosis remains the critical first step.

REFERENCES

American Psychiatric Association. (1994). *Diagnostic and statistical manual of mental disorders* (4th ed.). Washington, DC: Author.

American Psychiatric Association. (2000). *Diagnostic and statistical manual of mental disorders text revision* (4th ed.). Washington, DC: Author.

Attwood, T. (1998). *Asperger's Syndrome: A guide for parents and professionals.* London: Jessica Kingsley.

Barnhill, G., Hagiwara, T., Myles, B. S., & Simpson, R. L. (2000). Asperger Syndrome: A study of the cognitive profiles of 37 children and adolescents. *Focus on Autism and Other Developmental Disabilities, 15,* 146–153.

Barnhill, G. P., Hagiwara, T., Myles, B. S., Simpson, R. L., Brick, M. L., & Griswold, D. E. (2000). Parent, teacher, and self-report of problem and adaptive behaviors in children and adolescents with Asperger Syndrome. *Diagnostique, 25,* 147–167.

Baron-Cohen, S., Wheelwright, S., Skinner, R., Martin, J., & Clubley, E. (2001). The autism-spectrum quotient (AQ): Evidence from Asperger Syndrome/high-functioning autism, males and females, scientists and mathematicians. *Journal of Autism and Developmental Disorders, 31,* 5–17.

Bowers, L., Huisingh, R., Barrett, M., & Orman, J. (1994) *Test of problem-solving–Elementary revised.* East Moline, IL: LinguiSystems.

Bowers, L., Huisingh, R., Barrett, M., Orman, J., & LoGiudice, C. (1991) *Test of problem-solving–Adolescent.* East Moline, IL: LinguiSystems.

Church, C., Alisanski, S., & Amanullah, S. (2000). The social, behavioral, and academic experiences of children with Asperger Syndrome. *Focus on Autism and Other Developmental Disabilities, 15,* 12–20.

Ehlers, S., & Gillberg, C. (1993). The epidemiology of Asperger Syndrome: A total population study. *Journal of Child Psychology and Psychiatry, 34,* 1327–1350.

Ehlers, S., Gillberg, C., & Wing, L. (1999). A screening questionnaire for Asperger Syndrome and other high-functioning autism spectrum disorders of school age children. *Journal of Autism and Development Disorders, 29,* 129–141.

Ehlers, S., Nyden, A., Gillberg, C., Sandberg, A. D., Dahlgren, E. H., & Oden, A. (1997). Asperger Syndrome, autism and attention disorders: A comparative study of the cognitive profiles of 120 children. *Journal of Child Psychology and Psychiatry, 38,* 207–217.

Freeman, B. J., Cronin, P., & Candela, P. (2002). Asperger Syndrome or autistic disorder? The diagnostic dilemma. *Focus on Autism and Other Developmental Disabilities, 17,* 145–151.

Ghaziuddin, M. (2002). Asperger Syndrome: Associated psychiatric and medical conditions. *Focus on Autism and Other Developmental Disabilities, 17,* 138–144.

Ghaziuddin, M., Tsai, L. Y., & Ghaziuddin, N. (1992). Brief report: A comparison of the diagnostic criteria for Asperger Syndrome. *Journal of Autism and Developmental Disorders, 22,* 643–649.

Gillberg, C. (1989). Asperger Syndrome in 23 Swedish children. *Developmental Medicine and Child Neurology, 31,* 520–531.

Gillberg, C. (1996). The long-term outcome of childhood empathy disorders. *European Child & Adolescent Psychiatry, 5,* 52–56.

Gillberg, C. (1998). Asperger Syndrome and high-functioning autism. *British Journal of Psychiatry, 172,* 200–209.

Gillberg, C., Gillberg, C., Rastam, M., & Wentz, E. (2001). The Asperger Syndrome (and high-functioning autism) diagnostic interview (ASDI): A preliminary study of a new structured clinical interview. *Autism, 5,* 57–66.

Gilliam, J. E. (2001). *Gilliam Asperger's Disorder scale.* Austin, TX: Pro-Ed.

Griswold, D. E., Barnhill, G. P., Myles, B. S., Hagiwara, T., & Simpson, R. L. (2002). Asperger Syndrome and academic achievement. *Focus on Autism and Other Developmental Disabilities, 17,* 94–102.

Handen, B. L. (1997). Mental retardation. In E. J. Mash & L. G. Terdal (Eds.), *Assessment of childhood disorders* (3rd ed., pp. 369–407). New York: Guilford.

Hooper, S. R., & Bundy, M. R. (1998). Learning characteristics of individuals with Asperger Syndrome. In E. Schopler, G. B. Mesibov, & L. J. Kunce (Eds.), *Asperger Syndrome or high functioning autism* (pp. 317–342). New York: Plenum.

Howlin, P. (1998). *Children with autism and Asperger Syndrome: A guide for practitioners and carers.* Chichester, UK: Wiley.

Howlin, P. (2000). Assessment instruments for Asperger Syndrome. *Child Psychiatry and Psychology Review, 5,* 120–129.

Howlin, P., & Asgharian, A. (1999). The diagnosis of autism and Asperger Syndrome: Findings from a survey of 770 families. *Developmental Medicine and Child Neurology, 41,* 834–839.

Kadesjoe, B., Gillberg, C., & Hagberg, B. (1999). Autism and Asperger Syndrome in seven-year-old children: A total population study. *Journal of Autism and Developmental Disorders, 29,* 327–332.

Klin, A., Sparrow, S. S., Marans, W. D., Carter, A., & Volkmar, F. R. (2000). Assessment issues in children and adolescents with Asperger Syndrome. In A. Klin, F. R. Volkmar, & S. S. Sparrow (Eds.), *Asperger Syndrome* (pp. 309–339). New York: Guilford.

Lord, C., Pickles, A., McLennan, J., Rutter, M., Bregman, J., Folstein, S., et al. (1997). Diagnosing autism: Analyses of data from the Autism Diagnostic Interview. *Journal of Autism and Developmental Disorders, 27,* 501–517.

Lord, C., Rutter, M., & Le Couteur, A. (1994). Autism Diagnostic Interview–Revised: A revised version of a diagnostic interview for caregivers of individuals with possible pervasive developmental disorders. *Journal of Autism and Developmental Disorders, 24,* 659–685.

Mash, E. J., & Terdal, L. G. (1997). Assessment of child and family disturbance: A behavioral-systems approach. In E. J. Mash & L. G. Terdal (Eds.), *Assessment of childhood disorders* (3rd ed., pp. 3–68). New York: Guilford.

Meyer, J. A., & Minshew, N. J. (2002). An update on neurocognitive profiles in Asperger Syndrome and high-functioning autism. *Focus on Autism and Other Developmental Disabilities, 17,* 152–160.

Myles, B. S., Barnhill, G. P., Hagiwara, T., Griswold, D. E., & Simpson, R. L. (2001). A synthesis of studies on the intellectual, academic, social/emotional and sensory characteristics of children and youth with Asperger Syndrome. *Education and Training in Mental Retardation and Developmental Disabilities, 36,* 304–311.

Myles, B. S., Bock, S. J., & Simpson, R. L. (2001). *Asperger Syndrome diagnostic scale.* Austin, TX: Pro-Ed.

Myles, B. S., Hilgenfeld, T. D., Barnhill, G. P., Griswold, D. E., Hagiwara, T., & Simpson, R. L. (2002). Analysis of reading skills in individuals with Asperger Syndrome. *Focus on Autism and Other Developmental Disabilities, 17,* 44–47.

Psychological Corporation. (1992). *Wechsler individual achievement test.* San Antonio: Author.

Reynolds, C. R., & Kamphaus, R. W. (1992). *Behavior assessment system for children.* Circle Pines, MN: American Guidance Service.

Safran, J. S., & Safran, S. P. (2001). School-based consultation for Asperger Syndrome. *Journal of Educational and Psychological Consultation, 12,* 385–395.

Safran, S. P. (2001). Asperger Syndrome: The emerging challenge to special education. *Exceptional Children, 67,* 151–160.

Schopler, E., Reichler, R. J., DeVellis, R. F., & Daily, K. (1980). Towards an objective classification of childhood autism: Childhood Autism Rating Scale. *Journal of Autism and Developmental Disorders, 10,* 91–101.

Scott, F. J., Baron-Cohen, S., Bolton, P., & Brayne, C. (2002). The CAST (Childhood Asperger Syndrome Test): Preliminary development of a UK screen for mainstream primary-school-age children. *Autism, 6,* 9–31.

Silvaroli, N. J., & Wheelock, W. H. (2001). *Classroom reading inventory* (9th ed.). New York: McGraw-Hill College.

Szatmari, P. (1992). The validity of autistic spectrum disorders: A literature review. *Journal of Autism and Developmental Disorders, 22,* 583–600.

Szatmari, P. (1998). Differential diagnosis of Asperger Disorder. In E. Schopler, G. B. Mesibov, & L. J. Kunce (Eds.), *Asperger Syndrome or high-functioning autism?* (pp. 61–76). New York: Plenum.

Szatmari, P. (2000). Perspectives on the classification of Asperger Syndrome. In A. Klin, F. R. Volkmar, & S. S. Sparrow (Eds.), *Asperger Syndrome* (pp. 403–417). New York: Guilford.

Szatmari, P., Bremner, R., & Nagy, J. N. (1989). Asperger's Syndrome: A review of clinical features. *Canadian Journal of Psychiatry, 34,* 554–560.

Volkmar, F. R., & Klin, A. (2000). Diagnostic issues in Asperger Syndrome. In A. Klin, F. R. Volkmar, & S. S. Sparrow (Eds.), *Asperger Syndrome* (pp. 25–71). New York: Guilford.

Wing, L. (1981). Asperger's Syndrome: A clinical account. *Psychological Medicine, 11,* 115–129.

Wing, L., & Potter, P. (2002). The epidemiology of autistic spectrum disorders: Is the prevalence rising? *Mental Retardation and Developmental Disabilities Research Review, 8,* 151–161.

World Health Organization. (1992). *International classification of diseases, ICD–10* (10th revision). Geneva, Switzerland: Author.

Chapter 4

Pharmacotherapy

Robert Hendren
University of California

Andrés Martin
Yale University

Autism spectrum disorders (ASDs) are characterized by a spectrum of abnormal behaviors that include marked impairment in reciprocal social interaction, communication difficulties; and restricted, repetitive, and stereotyped patterns of interests and activities (American Psychiatric Association, 1994). ASDs can also be associated with hyperactivity, impulsivity, anxiety, cognitive disorganization, affective instability, aggression, and distractibility, symptoms that overlap with other disorders such as obsessive–compulsive disorder (OCD) and other anxiety disorders, affective disorders, attention deficit hyperactivity disorder (ADHD), and sometimes even having similarities to psychotic disorders. Treatment of ASD requires psychological and social approaches including special education, speech and language therapy, occupational therapy, and behavioral therapies, the symptoms in individuals with ASD might improve with additional psychotropic medication treatment.

Although psychotropic medications might not reduce the core symptoms of ASDs, it has become increasingly common for patients to be on one or more psychotropic medications for the associated symptoms. It is estimated that as many as half of the individuals with a diagnosis of ASD are treated with one or more psychotropic medications (Martin, Scahill, Klin, & Volkmar, 1999). Children and adolescents with ASD often respond preferentially to different psychopharmacologic agents, but it is difficult to predict in advance which agent is likely to produce the best response in a particular patient. Few studies exist to guide this selection (Scahill & Koenig, 1999).

Although this book is focused on Asperger's Syndrome, few of the published medication studies distinguish the response of youth with autistic disorder from those with Asperger's Syndrome. Where authors describe distinctions, we note them in this chapter. Controversy exists regarding whether high-functioning autism is distinct from Asperger's Syndrome or exists along a continuum (Gillberg, 1998; Klin, Volkmar, Sparrow, Cicchetti, & Rourke, 1995; Miller & Ozonoff, 2000; Ozonoff & Griffith, 2000; Volkmar 2001), but it is probably more useful to think of ASD subtypes in terms of potentially overlapping developmental trajectories (Szatmari et al., 2000; Szatmari et al., 2002) when considering psychotropic medications.

In current clinical practice, the medications believed to provide the greatest benefit in reducing core and associated symptomatology are selective serotonin reuptake inhibitors (SSRIs) and atypical neuroleptics (Buitelaar & Willemsen-Swinkels, 2000; Posey & McDougle, 2000; Scahill & Koenig, 1999; Volkmar, 2001). Within these two classes of medications, however, only the atypical neuroleptic risperidone has proven efficacious in a controlled clinical trial in children with autism (Research Units on Pediatric Psychopharmacology Autism Network, 2002). Current pharmacotherapy for children with ASD often includes long-term treatment with a single agent or a combination of agents, but there are few data on the long-term safety and efficacy of such interventions. This chapter reviews the evidence for the efficacy of the psychotropic agents used in the treatment of ASD, including SSRIs, neuroleptics, mood stabilizers, stimulants, alpha adrenergic agonists, and several other less commonly used agents. It concludes with a discussion of practice guidelines for choosing which medications to try first and how to use combinations of agents.

SSRIs

Although little is known about the pathogenesis of autism, abnormalities in the serotonin (5-hydroxytryptamine or 5-HT) system have been identified in at least a subgroup of about one third of individuals with pervasive developmental disorder (PDD) and in their first-degree relatives (G. Anderson et al., 1987). Hemispheric asymmetries of serotonin synthesis in the frontal cortex, thalamus, and cerebellum are found in autistic boys but not in their siblings (Buchsbaum et al., 2001). Serotonin levels can also vary by age and developmental level (Croonenberghs et al., 2000). Lower whole-brain serotonin values are shown in children with autism younger than 5 years of age, whereas higher values are observed in older children with autism (Chugani et al., 1999).

In addition, there is increasing evidence that serotonin system homeostasis is critical to the genesis, differentiation, and maturation of neuronal cells and networks in brain regions controlling sensory inputs, stimulus processing, and motor output related to autism (see Lesch, 2001, for a review). Based on this literature, using psychotropic medications that help regulate the serotonin system in children with autistic disorder seems a potentially valuable treatment strategy. Clinical reports also indicate administration of SSRIs might improve anxiety, compulsive symptoms, repetitive movements, and social features in patients with autism (Cook, Rowlett, & Jaselskis, 1992; Gordon, State, Nelson, & Hamburger, 1993; McDougle et al., 1996). Although uncontrolled studies suggest that SSRIs are effective in reducing symptoms such as impulsivity, hyperactivity, anxiety, repetitive behaviors, and social withdrawal in children with ASD, to date there are no controlled clinical trials of these agents.

Clomipramine, a serotonin and norepinepherine reuptake inhibitor with a range of other pharmacodynamic effects, has shown efficacy for certain symptoms of autism (anger, hyperactivity, and repetitive behavior) in children, adolescents, and young adults (Gordon et al., 1993; Luiselli, Blew, Keane, Thibadeau, & Holzman, 2000), but it has also been associated with seizures and cardiac side effects. Significant adverse effects were also observed in a large, prospective, open-label study of clomipramine with 35 adults with different subtypes of ASD (Brodkin, McDougle, Naylor, Cohen, & Price, 1997). Furthermore, there is some evidence that clomipramine is less well tolerated and less effective in younger children than in adolescents and adults (Brasic, Barnett, Sheitman, & Tsaltas, 1997; Sanchez et al., 1996).

Because of their apparent efficacy and better side-effect profiles compared with clomipramine and other antidepressants, SSRIs have increasingly become the preferred medication for many mood and anxiety disorders. To date, only one double-blind, placebo-controlled study of an SSRI in patients with autistic disorders has been published. McDougle et al. (1997) demonstrated the effectiveness of fluvoxamine in 30 adults with autism. Eight of the 15 patients in the fluvoxamine group (compared to none in the placebo group) were categorized as much improved or very much improved on the Clinical Global Impressions Scale (CGI). Fluvoxamine significantly reduced repetitive behavior, maladaptive behavior, and aggression with minimal adverse effects. In addition, fluvoxamine increased the communicative use of language.

McDougle and colleagues implemented an unpublished fluvoxamine double-blind, placebo-controlled trial in children and adolescents, which was less encouraging (Posey & McDougle, 2000). Only 1 of the 18 fluvoxamine-treated children (25–250 mg per day) demonstrated a significant clinical improvement with the drug and adverse effects were seen in 14, including insomnia, hyperactivity, agitation, aggression, anxiety, and anorexia. This potential behavior-activating side effect was also observed in an open-label study of low-dose fluvoxamine (Martin, Koenig, Anderson, & Sachill, 2003), as well as a cause of fluoxetine discontinuation in one case (Damore, Stine, & Brody, 1998) and in two different open-label trials (Cook et al., 1992; DeLong, Teague, & McSwain, 1998).

Small case studies and open-label studies report beneficial effects from fluvoxamine (Fukuda, Sugie, Ito, & Sugie, 2001; Kauffmann, Vance, Pumariega, & Miller, 2001; Martin et al., 2003; Yokoyama, Hirose, Haginoya, Munkata, & Iinuma, 2002) and fluoxetine (Alcami Pertejo, Peral Guera, & Gilaberta, 2000;

DeLong et al., 1998; Fatemi, Realmuto, Kahn, & Thuras, 1998; Peral, Alcami, & Gilaberte, 1999). Treatment with these SSRIs resulted in improvement in symptoms of anxiety, aggression, stereotypical behaviors, repetitive behaviors, and prelinguistic and social behaviors in children with ASD. It was generally well tolerated, although a small number of children experienced mild activation requiring discontinuation. One study of 6 adult participants with ASD in a crossover trial of fluoxetine found 3 of the 6 responded positively on rating scale measures of symptom change. The researchers also found that those who responded positively had distinctive positron emission tomography measures of metabolism similar to those found in depression (Buchsbaum et al., 2001).

No double-blind, placebo-controlled trial using SSRI treatment in children with ASD has been published to date. Sertraline appears to be one of the most frequently reported SSRIs to be used in the ASD population, and open-label studies have been encouraging (Posey, Litwiller, Koburn, & McDougle, 1999). In a 28-day trial of sertraline (at doses of 25–150 mg daily) in 9 adults with mental retardation (5 with autism), significant decreases in aggression and self-injury occurred in 8 (Hellings, Kelley, Gabrielli, Kilgore, & Shah, 1996). In addition, a large, prospective, 12-week, open-label study of 42 adults with ASD found sertraline effective in improving aggression and repetitive behavior, but not social relatedness (M dosage = 122 mg per day; McDougle et al., 1998). Three of the 42 patients dropped out of the study due to intolerable agitation or anxiety.

In pediatric populations, there is an increasing number of retrospective case series and open-label studies. One case series of 9 children with autism (age 6–12 years) treated with sertraline (25–50 mg daily) reported that 8 demonstrated significant improvement in anxiety, irritability, and "transition-induced behavior deterioration" or "need for sameness" (Steingard, Zimnitzky, DeMaso, Bauman, & Bucci, 1997, p. 9). Three of the responders demonstrated a return of symptoms after 3 to 7 months. Two children experienced agitation when the dose was raised to 75 mg daily. Citalopram also demonstrated efficacy and safety in a population of 17 participants with ASDs who were in treatment for at least 2 months at an average upwardly titrated dose of 20 mg. Ten children (59%) were judged much improved or very much improved regarding target behaviors, although the core symptoms of social interactions or communication did not show clinically significant improvement (Couturier & Nicolson, 2002). Two participants had increased agitation, one had insomnia, and another might have developed tics. In another citalopam study, 11 of 15 adolescents with Asperger's Syndrome, autism, or PDD Not Otherwise Specified (NOS) demonstrated improvement in anxiety and mood symptoms with side effects reported in 5 patients (Namerow, Thomas, Bostic, Prince, & Monuteaux, 2003).

A large case series of 129 children (2–8 years of age) with well-diagnosed ASD treated with fluoxetine for 5 to 76 months reported that 22 (17%) had an excellent response, 67 (52%) had a good response, and 40 (31%) had a fair to poor response (DeLong, Ritch, & Burch, 2002). Family history of major affective disorder, unusual intellectual achievement (organizing large amounts of emotionally neutral material), and hyperlexia correlated robustly with fluoxetine response.

Norepinephrine reuptake inhibitors also have demonstrated efficacy in open-label trials and retrospective studies with children with ASD. Venlafaxine demonstrated improvement in repetitive behaviors and restricted interests, inattention, and social defects in 6 of 10 completers and was well tolerated (Hollander, Kaplan, Cartwright, & Reichman, 2000). Nine of 26 children with ASD treated with mirtazapine, a medication with both serotonergic and noradrenergic properties, showed modest improvement in aggression, irritability, anxiety, and depression with few adverse effects (Posey, Guenin, Kohn, Swiezy, & McDougle, 2001).

These open-label trials are encouraging and support the need for a double-blind, placebo-controlled trial to evaluate the unique benefits of using an SSRI medication for particular symptoms associated with ASD in a population of well-characterized children.

NEUROLEPTICS

Hyperdopaminergic activity is thought to be associated with increased motor activity and stereotypic movements, and there is evidence that dopamine is also dysregulated in ASD. The dopamine metabolite homovanillic acid is found in high concentration in the cerebral spinal fluid of severely affected children with autism (Gillberg & Svennerholm, 1987). Significant group and age effects were reported in 156 children with autism for dopamine and its derivatives (Martineau, Barthelemy, Jouve, Muh, & Lelord, 1992). Further evidence that the dopaminergic system might be dysregulated in ASD comes from several double-blind, placebo-controlled studies that indicate beneficial effects of haloperidol among children with ASD (Campbell et al., 1978; Cohen et al., 1980; Naruse et al., 1982; Remington, Sloman, Konstantareas, Parker, & Gow, 2001).

Treatment with neuroleptic medication has also demonstrated benefit in the treatment of symptoms associated with ASD and is often used when SSRIs are not effective, are only partially effective, or have intolerable side effects. Neuroleptic medications are beneficial for treatment of marked anxiety, aggression, social withdrawal, stereotypies, and sleep disturbance in ASD. Only haloperidol, a potent postsynaptic dopamine-receptor blocker, has been shown in more than one controlled study to be superior to placebo in the treatment of serious behavioral problems associated with ASD (L. Anderson et al., 1989; L. Anderson et al., 1984; Posey & McDougle, 2000). However, concerns about troubling side effects from conventional neuroleptics have limited their use in the treatment of ASD (Campbell et al., 1997).

The atypical neuroleptic medications, which have effects on both the serotonin (5-HT2) and dopamine (D2) systems, have increasingly replaced the typical neuroleptics due to their favorable side-effect profile and their beneficial therapeutic effects related to social withdrawal. Until recently, only one controlled trial of an atypical neuroleptic (risperidone) in the treatment of adults with ASD has been published (McDougle et al., 1998). Three open-label studies with olanzapine, another atypical neuroleptic, in children have been published and suggest that this medication is similarly effective (Krishnamoorthy & King, 1998; Malone, Maislin, Choudhury, Gifford, & Delaney, 2002; Potenza, Holmes, SJ, & McDougle, 1999). Ziprasidone is reported to improve symptoms of aggression, agitation, and irritability in people of all ages with ASD, without causing significant weight gain in a case series of 12 patients (McDougle, Kem, & Posey, 2002).

Risperidone has been reported in five open-label trials to be effective and safe when used in relatively low doses for the treatment of symptoms associated with ASD in children (Findling, Maxwell, & Wiznitzer, 1997; Masi, Cosenza, Mucci, & De Vito, 2001; McDougle et al., 1997; McDougle et al., 2002; Nicolson, Avad, & Sloman, 1998). More recently, 22 children (M age = 7.1 years) with ASD had significant clinical improvement overall as measured by the CGI and the Children's Psychiatric Rating Scale at 1 month and 6 months at 1.2 mg per day. No child developed dyskinesia, although 2 developed mild, reversible withdrawal dyskinesia (Malone et al., 2002), and 8 of 10 participants with ASD between the ages of 3 and 6 years (M = 4.7 years) who completed a trial demonstrated significant improvement on the CGI and the Childhood Autism Rating Scale after 16 weeks (Masi et al., 2001).

Most recently, a large, multisite, double-blind, 8-week controlled study of 101 children (5–17 years old) with ASD treated with risperidone found that it was effective and well tolerated for the treatment of irritability, stereotypy, hyperactivity, tantrums, and aggression (Research Units on Pediatric Psychopharmacology Autism Network, 2002). Dosage ranged from 0.5 mg to 3.5 mg per day. Side effects included weight gain (M = 2.7 kg), fatigue, and drooling. Two-thirds of the children maintained a positive response at 6 months. Although this is the only double-blind, placebo-controlled study showing efficacy and safety in a population of children with ASD, other atypical neuroleptics and combinations of agents are still worth considering when the effect and side-effect profile fit a particular individual with ASD. Further controlled research will likely find other agents to be beneficial as well.

MOOD STABILIZERS

Anticonvulsants are another category of medications that are frequently prescribed to individuals with ASD. The high rate of epilepsy in this population is one reason. It has been estimated that approximately a third of individuals with ASD have various types of seizure disorders and approximately half have abnormal electroencephalograms (EEGs) whether or not they have a seizure disorder. It has also been reported that individuals with seizure disorders tend to have lower IQ scores and a worse long-term prognosis. Another reason for prescribing anticonvulsants is that individuals with ASD and their first-degree relatives are reported to have a significant rate of mood disorders, including bipolar disorder (DeLong et al., 2002; Hollander, Dolgoff-Kaspar, Cartwright, Rawitt, & Novotny, 2001; Lainhart & Folstein,

1994). Also, disruptive, aggressive behaviors could simply be part of ASD and anticonvulsants have been known to help with these behaviors.

Despite their widespread use, we are not aware of any double-blind, placebo-controlled studies in which anticonvulsants were used to treat irritability and behavioral difficulties in individuals with ASDs. Hollander and colleagues (2001) published results of an open, retrospective trial of divalproex sodium in 14 participants with ASD. Of the 14, 12 were male and 2 were female, 4 had abnormal EEGs and 3 had seizure disorders, and 10 were children or adolescents and 4 were adults (ages 5–40). Ten met *Diagnostic and Statistical Manual of Mental Disorders* (4th ed. [*DSM–IV*]; APA, 1994) criteria for autism, 2 met the criteria for Asperger's Syndrome, and 2 were diagnosed as PDD NOS. Several of them also had comorbid mood, anxiety, and impulse control disorders. Ten of the 14 subjects were rated as responders. Improvement was seen in the core ASD symptoms and in affective instability, aggression, and impulsivity. All patients with histories of seizures or abnormal EEGs were rated as responders.

A study of 50 children and adolescents treated with lamotrigine for intractable epilepsy has been reported (Uvebrant & Bauziene, 1994). Lamotrigine was added to preexisting medication. Thirteen of these patients were also diagnosed with autism, and autistic symptoms decreased in 8 of them. Three cases of young children who had autism and abnormal EEGs but no seizures were reported as much improved during a trial of valproic acid (Plioplys, 1994). Another report describes a set of 3-year-old twins with autism and absence seizures who markedly improved on a trial of valproic acid (Childs & Blair, 1997).

Lithium carbonate, a mood stabilizer, has also been used to treat patients with ASD. Again, as with the anticonvulsants, there are no double-blind, placebo-controlled studies of the use of lithium in children with ASD. In fact, the data in the literature are fairly scant. Four severe cases of autism with associated manic symptomatology were reported to have responded very well to lithium (Kerbeshian, Burd, & Fisher, 1987; Steingard & Biederman, 1987). In both reports the authors commented on how difficult it can be to make the diagnosis of a bipolar disorder in patients who are very limited historians and have severe developmental delay.

STIMULANTS

The ADHD-like symptoms associated with ASD often seriously interfere with the effectiveness of functioning and the ability to utilize behavioral and educational interventions in the ASD population. Therefore, it is not surprising that many of the pharmacologic agents used in the treatment of ADHD are frequently tried in this population. In one survey, 12% of 7- to 13-year-olds in this population were on a stimulant, indicating it was among the most popular type of agent used at the time (Aman, VanBourgondien, Wolford, & Sarphare, 1995). Despite this, the number of controlled studies examining the safety and efficacy of stimulant medications is surprisingly small. Since 1980, in all studies, open and controlled, the total number of participants has been less than 40 (Aman & Langworthy, 2000). Whereas the earlier studies might have indicated stimulants were relatively contraindicated in this population and more likely to produce increased irritability and stereotypic behaviors, recent data have been more positive.

In an early study, Campbell et al. (1972) compared thyroid hormone to dextroamphetamine in 16 boys and girls aged 3 to 6 years in a psychiatric inpatient facility. This was a diagnostically mixed group where 2 of the children had autism, 10 had schizophrenia, and the remaining 4 were diagnosed with chronic brain syndromes. Of the 2 children with autism, 1 was reported as worse and 1 as slightly improved on the dextroamphetamine. Using a double-blind, crossover design, Campbell et al. (1976) compared levodopa and levoamphetamine in 12 children age 3 to 6 years and 9 months, 11 of whom were diagnosed as having schizophrenia with autistic features (Campbell et al., 1976). These children reportedly corresponded diagnostically to the classic description of Early Infantile Autism by Kanner (1943). It is interesting to note that autism at this time was not yet a distinct entity from schizophrenia and the PDD category would not enter the *DSM* until later with the development of the third edition. Of the children receiving levoamphetamine, 2 showed minimal improvement, 2 showed no change, 7 showed minimal behavior worsening, and 1 was transferred to a residential treatment center and did not receive levoamphetamine. However, of the 7 children who showed hyperactivity at baseline, this symptom improved in 5, but negativism worsened in 8 of the 11. Overall, the assessment was that any improvements were minor, and usually outweighed by the concomitant worsening in most cases.

An uncontrolled study by Hoshino and colleagues in 1977 reported results that were somewhat more promising (Hoshino, Kumashiro, Kaneko, & Takahashi, 1977). Fifteen children with autism were treated with methylphenidate and 9 of them improved in terms of their ADHD symptoms. The side effects were anorexia, irritability, insomnia, and aggression, all of which improved with a reduction in dosage. Then in 1981, Geller and colleagues reported two cases of ASD with associated ADHD symptoms including aggressive and disruptive behaviors, which responded well to dextroamphetamine without worsening the ASD symptoms (Geller, Guttmacher, & Bleeg, 1981). One of these cases had been previously unresponsive to a trial of methylphenidate at doses of up to 50 mg per day. Case reports also suggested benefits from methylphenidate for associated ADHD symptoms, without worsening core symptoms of autism (Vitriol & Farber, 1981).

In 1988, Strayhorn and colleagues reported a randomized, single-case trial with a 6-year-old boy with autism, mental retardation, and associated ADHD symptoms including inattention, high activity level, and impulsivity, which included destroying objects (Strayhorn, Rapp, Donina, & Strain, 1988). Methylphenidate significantly improved concentration, hyperactivity, destructiveness, disobedience, verbal behavior, and stereotypies. However, the methylphenidate did appear to worsen sadness and temper tantrums. In this same report, the authors noted a second autistic child who then received an open trial of methylphenidate with apparently similar results. Also in 1988, Birmaher and colleagues reported an open study evaluating the safety and efficacy of methylphenidate in 9 children with autism who had ADHD symptoms (Birmaher, Quintana, & Greenhill, 1988). The dosage range was 10 to 50 mg per day. Eight of the 9 children showed significant improvement in their ADHD symptoms and 1 did not show any changes. No major side effects were seen and there was no exacerbation of stereotypies. However, a few case reports (Realmuto, August, & Garfinkel, 1989; Schmidt, 1982; Sporn & Pinkster, 1981; Volkmar, Hoder, & Cohen, 1985) totaling 5 patients indicated stimulants were associated with hyperactivity, anxiety, rapid pulse, agitation, aggression, tics, and fragmented thinking.

Quintana et al. (1995) evaluated methylphenidate treatment for ADHD symptoms in 10 children with autism, ages 7 to 11, in a double-blind, placebo-controlled crossover study. None of these children had been on methylphenidate previously, nor was there history of any major neurological or medical illness. If they had been on psychotropics, they were off these medications for at least a month before starting the study, thus decreasing the likelihood of any withdrawal dyskinesias that could confound the study. During the study, the patients only received methylphenidate in either low or high doses (10 or 20 mg bid, respectively). Statistically significant improvement was shown for methylphenidate over placebo. This improvement was described as modest and no statistically significant difference was found between the two doses. Likewise, there were no statistically significant differences in side effects between the treatment and control groups, or between doses.

Handen, Johnson, and Lubetsky (2000) reported an additional study evaluating the efficacy of methylphenidate in children with ASDs and symptoms of ADHD. This was another double-blind, placebo-controlled crossover study with 13 children ages 5 to 11 years. Two different doses were used, 0.3 and 0.6 mg per kg per dose, which were given two or three times per day, depending on the individual's symptoms. The authors had three hypotheses in this study. The first was that the methylphenidate would be significantly efficacious and the rate of improvement would be similar to that found in the mental retardation and ADHD population but less than that seen in children with ADHD without major developmental delays. They also hypothesized that as in the mental retardation and ADHD population they would also see a higher rate of side effects. Finally, they hypothesized that core features of autism would not be significantly effected. Eight of the 13 children demonstrated significant improvement on the methylphenidate, with 7 of the 8 showing gains on the lower dose (0.3 mg per kg per dose). This included improvement in attention, activity level, and aggression. The 61% response rate was very similar to what has been reported previously for children with mental retardation and ADHD symptoms. As predicted, the rate of adverse effects was somewhat higher than that seen in children with ADHD who do not have these major developmental difficulties. Side effects included irritability, tantrums, tearfulness, social withdrawal, aggression, and skin picking. One child had to drop out of the study at the lower dose and two at the higher dose due to side effects. There was also some evidence that stereotypic behavior and inappropriate language might also improve with methylphenidate, but this might be explained by the improved attention and concentration.

In summary, early studies and some case reports indicated little, if any, benefit from the stimulants, but rather they seemed to be associated with a number of adverse effects including increased irritability, stereotypies, and hyperactivity. Again, these studies were very small and they had multiple limitations (i.e., size of study, heterogeneous diagnoses, other medications). Nevertheless, the stimulants developed an early reputation for being contraindicated in the ASD population. Although data are still quite limited, it appears the more recent studies are better controlled, are more informative, and suggest that stimulants can provide effective adjunctive treatment for children with ASD who have ADHD symptoms. However, the rate of adverse effects might be increased and very careful monitoring is warranted. Given the fairly widespread use of stimulant medications in the autism spectrum population, further research is clearly indicated.

ALPHA ADRENERGIC AGONISTS

The alpha adrenergic agonists clonidine and guanfacine are frequently used to treat symptoms such as aggression, impulsivity, hyperactivity, inattention, and distractibility. These medications are centrally acting agents that decrease sympathetic tone through a negative feedback mechanism. Both have been used in the treatment of children with ADHD and Tourette's Syndrome. Clonidine is also known for being useful in the treatment of hypertension and opiate withdrawal. These agents have become fairly commonly used for treating symptoms associated with ASD. Only two small studies regarding the use of alpha adrenergic agonists in ASD have been published. Both studies used clonidine and both suggested it might be useful for symptoms such as irritability and hyperactivity.

In the first study, Fankhauser, Karumanchi, German, Yates, and Karumanchi (1992) reported on the use of transdermal clonidine in 9 males with autism, ages 5 to 35. This was a double-blind, placebo-crossover study, with each trial lasting 4 weeks with a 2-week washout between treatment phases. The authors reported that clonidine was effective in decreasing hyperarousal and improving social relatedness.

Studying 8 boys with autism and associated ADHD symptoms, Jaselskis, Cook, Fletcher, and Leventhal (1992) compared clonidine and placebo in a placebo-controlled crossover study. Each was given for 6 weeks in a crossover design. Overall, clonidine was described as modestly effective for irritability and hyperactivity in some of the children. Drowsiness and sedation from clonidine were reported in both of these studies.

Thus, there is a small, limited body of evidence that clonidine might be helpful with hyperarousal in children with ASD. Clonidine has been known to cause sedation, irritability, hypotension, headache, and EKG changes. There has also been debate about it being associated with sudden death in combination with methylphenidate (Popper, 1995; Wilens, Spencer, Swanson, Connor, & Cantwell, 1999). Accordingly, careful monitoring is required. Guanfacine has a longer half-life and is known to be less sedating. It appears to be gaining more widespread use in the ASD population as well. Thus far, we are not aware of any studies involving guanfacine in individuals with ASD.

OTHER MEDICATIONS

Two studies of amantadine hydrochloride suggest that it might have limited usefulness in the treatment of ASD. Because amantadine acts as an indirect dopamine agonist as well as an N-methyl-D-aspartate receptor agonist, an open trial was undertaken for the treatment of impulse control disorders in children. Four out of 7 children with developmental disabilities and impulsiveness showed improvement (King et al., 2001).

A controlled study with children with autism did not evidence significant response on parental ratings, but did so on clinician ratings. A high placebo response rate was also reported (Owley et al., 2001).

Levetiracetam, a nootropic (cognitive enhancer) reported to improve cognition, memory, and language function in a number of conditions, was studied in 10 boys with ASD. Inattention, hyperkinesis, and impulsivity scores showed statistically significant improvement, as did measures of mood instability, but there did not appear to be a nootropic effect (Rugino & Samsock, 2002). Donepezil, a cholinesterase inhibitor, was used to openly treat 8 patients (age 11 ± 4.1 years) with *DSM–IV*-defined autism who were also on other medications (Hardan & Hardan, 2002). Four of these patients (50%) demonstrated significant improvement on the Aberrant Behavior Checklist and the CGI, with only 1 child experiencing gastrointestinal disturbances and another reporting mild irritability.

Naltrexone treatment of ASD demonstrated modest improvements in behavior, and moderate improvement in hyperactivity and restlessness. However it was not effective in reducing self-injurious behavior and there was no increase in learning (Willemsen-Swinkels, Buitelaar, van Berckelaer-Onnes, & van Engeland, 1999; Williams, Allard, Sears, Dalrymple, & Bloom, 2001).

Vancomycin has been tried for treatment of ASD when there are associated gastrointestinal symptoms (Finegold et al., 2002). In an uncontrolled series of cases, 9 out of 11 children improved in terms of both behavior and gastrointestinal symptoms, but all had some relapse after the initial reports of a good response (Sandler et al., 2000).

Famotidine (Pepcid) is a histamine-2 receptor antagonist and has been used for the treatment of children with ASD who have gastrointestinal symptomatology. Four out of 9 children with ASD showed behavioral improvement in a placebo crossover study (Linday, Tsiouris, Cohen, Shindledecker, & DeCresce, 2001).

In a widely circulated abstract not published in a peer-reviewed journal (Chez et al., 2002), an amino acid with antioxidant properties, l-Carnosine, was reported to improve language and behavior in 31 children diagnosed with ASD after 1 to 8 weeks, and to have few side effects.

Finally, a small body of literature and popular belief among parents of children with autism suggest that secretin is an effective treatment for ASD, or at least for a subpopulation of children with ASD. However, a number of controlled trials did not show an improvement in measured symptoms compared with placebo (see Patel, Yeh, Sheperd, & Crimson, 2002, for a recent comprehensive review).

POTENTIAL AGENTS

Clinical researchers are working to link biologic findings in ASD with pharmacologic treatments that might result in improvement in target symptoms. For instance, oxytocin and the closely related peptide, vasopressin, are known to play a role in social and repetitive behaviors. A recent study of a randomized, double-blind oxytocin and placebo infusion with 15 adults with autism or Asperger's Syndrome demonstrated significant reductions in repetitive behaviors following oxytocin infusion compared with placebo infusion (Hollander et al., 2003). Genetic studies linking the gamma-aminobutyric acid receptor to "insistence on sameness" in autism is another example of how a biomarker might someday be used to guide medication interventions.

PSYCHOPHARMACOLOGIC COMBINATION TREATMENTS

Symptoms associated with ASD in children often respond best to a combination of interventions including behavioral and psychopharmacologic treatments. When using pharmacologic interventions it might be necessary to use more than one medication to address multiple target symptoms, using different mechanisms of action and potential drug–drug synergy.

In the past, pharmacologic treatment of ASD has often started with a stimulant because of confusion about the symptoms of ASD resembling ADHD. This might have resulted in side effects, partial or no response, and hesitancy to try other pharmacological approaches. Recently, treatment with psychotropic medication more likely starts with an SSRI because of experience using them, their safety profile, and published studies of their beneficial effects. Although the symptoms of many children with ASD respond to SSRI treatment, others do not respond or respond only partially. In some cases, intolerable side effects limit the use of the SSRI. When this happens, an atypical neuroleptic might be substituted or added in combination with the SSRI. In addition to the frequently used combination of an SSRI and an atypical neuroleptic, other combinations of pharmacologic agents include a stimulant and an SSRI to address distractible inattention and impulsivity; a stimulant and an atypical neuroleptic to address poor executive function and disorganized behavior; and a mood stabilizer and an SSRI to address affective instability and impulsivity. At times, three or even four medications might be used in combination to address multiple target symptoms or to achieve maximal results when there is only a partial response in target symptoms. At times, anxiolytics, alpha adrenergic agonists and some of the medications mentioned in the "Other Medications" section might also be added.

There are no reported trials of combination pharmacology in the treatment of ASD in children and adolescents. One uncontrolled study examined clomipramine versus haloperidol in the treatment of 36 participants with ASD between the ages of 10 and 36 years randomly assigned to one treatment or the other. Clomipramine proved comparable to haloperidol in terms of significant improvement in baseline symptoms, but fewer participants were able to complete the clomipramine trial due to side effects (Remington et al., 2001).

Combination treatments can lead to confusion about what is a target symptom and what is a medication side effect due to each of the medications being used, or to drug interactions. Several principles should be utilized when using more than one medication: (a) identify and monitor target symptoms from the beginning of treatment; (b) start any new medication on a lower test dose to see how it is tolerated before gradually titrating up, and if possible maximize the dose of a medication before discontinuing it as ineffective or adding another medication; (c) change and adjust the dosage of only one medication at a time and leave sufficient time for response or side effects to develop before making further changes; (d) carefully monitor side effects; and (e) when the condition stabilizes, try gradually tapering and finally discontinuing the drug of least benefit if it is clinically tolerated.

CONCLUSION

Psychotropic medications can be an important part of an effective treatment plan for individuals with ASD. Generally, a comprehensive treatment plan involves behavioral interventions, education for the family, special education services, and sometimes speech, occupational therapy, and other services as well. Improvement in symptoms as a result of these interventions plus pharmacotherapy can result not only in symptomatic improvement, but also in better responses from the environment, leading to additional gains for the youngster with ASD. However, although psychiatric medications are widely used in the ASD population, they have not been systematically studied in great detail. Careful monitoring of their use by experienced practitioners and further research are warranted.

REFERENCES

Alcami Pertejo, M., Peral Guera, M., & Gilaberta, I. (2000). Open study of fluoxetine in children with autism. *Actas Espanolas de Psiquiatria, 28,* 353–356.

Aman, M., & Langworthy, K. (2000). Pharmacotherapy for hyperactivity in children with autism and other pervasive developmental disorders. *Journal of Autism and Developmental Disorders, 30,* 451–459.

Aman, M., VanBourgondien, M., Wolford, P., & Sarphare, G. (1995). Psychotropic and anticonvulsant drugs in subjects with autism: Prevalence and patterns of use. *Journal of the American Academy of Child and Adolescent Psychiatry, 34,* 1672–1681.

American Psychiatric Association. (1994). *Diagnostic and statistical manual of mental disorders* (4th ed.). Washington, DC: Author.

Anderson, G., Freedman, D., Cohen, D., Volkmar, F., Hoder, E., McPhedran, P., et al. (1987). Whole blood serotonin in autistic and normal subjects. *Journal of Child Psychology and Psychiatry, 28,* 885 –900.

Anderson, L., Campbell, M., Adams, P., Small, A., Perry, R., & Shell, J. (1989). The effects of haloperiodol on discrimination learning and behavioral symptoms in autistic children. *Journal of Autism and Developmental Disorders, 19,* 227–239.

Anderson, L., Campbell, M., Grega, D., Perry, R., Small, A., & Green, W. (1984). Haloperidol in the treatment of infantile autism: Effects on learning and behavioral symptoms. *American Journal of Psychiatry, 141,* 1195–1202.

Birmaher, B., Quintana, H., & Greenhill, L. (1988). Methylphenidate treatment of hyperactive autistic children. *Journal of the American Academy of Child and Adolescent Psychiatry, 27,* 248–251.

Brasic, J., Barnett, J., Sheitman, B., & Tsaltas, M. (1997). Adverse effects of clomipramine. *Journal of the American Academy of Child and Adolescent Psychiatry, 36,* 1165–1166.

Brodkin, E., McDougle, C., Naylor, S., Cohen, D., & Price, L. (1997). Clomipramine in adults with pervasive developmental disorders: A prospective open-label investigation. *Journal of Child and Adolescent Psychopharmacology, 7,* 109–121.

Buchsbaum, M., Hollander, E., Haznedar, M., Tang, C., Spiegel-Cohen, J., Wei, T.-C., et al. (2001). Effect of fluoxetine on regional cerebral metabolism in autistic spectrum disorders: A pilot study. *International Journal of Neuropsychopharmacology, 4,* 119–125.

Buitelaar, J., & Willemsen-Swinkels, S. (2000). Medication treatment in subjects with autistic spectrum disorders. *European Journal of Child and Adolescent Psychiatry, 9* (Suppl. 1), 185–197.

Campbell, M., Anderson, L., Meier, M., Cohen, I., Small, A., Samit, C., et al. (1978). A comparison of haloperiodol and behavior therapy and their interaction in autistic children. *Journal of the American Academy of Child and Adolescent Psychiatry, 17,* 640–655.

Campbell, M., Armenteros, J., Malone, R., Adams, P., Eisenberg, Z., & Overall, J. (1997). Neuroleptic-related dyskinesias in autistic children: A prospective, longitudinal study. *Journal of the American Academy of Child and Adolescent Psychiatry, 36,* 835–843.

Campbell, M., Fish, B., David, R., Shapiro, T., Collins, P., & Koh, H. (1972). Response to triiodothyronine and dextroamphetamine: A study of preschool schizophrenic children. *Journal of Autism and Child Schizophrenia, 2,* 343–358.

Campbell, M., Small, A., Collins, P., Friedman, E., David, R., & Genieser, N. (1976). Levodopa and levoamphetamine: A crossover study in young schizophrenic children. *Current Therapy Research, 19,* 70–86.

Chez, M., Buchanan, C., Aimonovitch, M., Becker, M., Schaefer, K., Black, C., et al. (2002). Double-blind, placebo-controlled study of L-carnosine supplementation in children with autistic spectrum disorders. *Journal of Child Neurology, 17,* 833–837.

Childs, J., & Blair, J. (1997). Valproic acid treatment of epilepsy in autistic twins. *Journal of Neuroscience Nursing, 29,* 244–248.

Chugani, D., Muzik, O., Rothermel, R., Janisse, J., Lee, J., & Chugani, H. (1999). Developmental changes in brain serotonin synthesis capacity in autistic and non autistic children. *Annals of Neurology, 45,* 287–295.

Cohen, I., Campbell, M., Posner, D., Triebel, D., Small, A., & Anderson, L. (1980). A study of haloperidol in young autistic children: A within-subjects design using objective rating scales. *Psychopharmacology Bulletin, 16,* 63–65.

Cook, E., Rowlett, R., & Jaselskis, C. (1992). Fluoxetine treatment of children and adults with autistic disorder and mental retardation. *Journal of the American Academy of Child and Adolescent Psychiatry, 31,* 739–745.

Couturier, J., & Nicolson, R. (2002). A retrospective assessment of citalopram in children and adolescents with pervasive developmental disorders. *Journal of Child and Adolescent Psychopharmacology, 12,* 243–248.

Croonenberghs, J., Delmeire, L., Verker, K., Lin, A., Meskal, A., Neels, H., et al. (2000). Peripheral markers of serotonergic and noradrenergic function in post-pubertal, Caucasian males with autistic disorder. *Neuropsychopharmacology, 22,* 275–283.

Damore, J., Stine, J., & Brody, L. (1998). Medication-induced hypomania in Asperger's disorder. *Journal of the American Academy of Child and Adolescent Psychiatry, 37,* 248–249.

DeLong, G., Ritch, C., & Burch, S. (2002). Fluoxetine response in children with autism spectrum disorders: Correlation with familial major affective disorder and intellectual achievement. *Developmental Medicine and Child Neurology, 44,* 652–659.

DeLong, G., Teague, L., & McSwain, K. (1998). Effects of fluoxetine treatment in young children with idiopathic autism. *Developmental Medicine and Child Neurology, 40,* 551–562.

Fankhauser, M., Karumanchi, V., German, M., Yates, A., & Karumanchi, S. (1992). A double-blind, placebo-controlled study of the efficacy of transdermal clonidine in autism. *Journal of Clinical Psychiatry, 53,* 77–82.

Fatemi, S., Realmuto, G., Kahn, L., & Thuras, P. (1998). Fluoxetine in the treatment of adolescent patients with autism: A longitudinal open trial. *Journal of Autism and Developmental Disorders, 28,* 303–307.

Findling, R., Maxwell, K., & Wiznitzer, M. (1997). An open clinical trial of risperidone monotherapy in young children with autistic disorder. *Psychopharmacology Bulletin, 33,* 155–159.

Finegold, S., Molitoris, D., Song, Y., Liu, C., Vaisanen, M., Bolte, E., et al. (2002). Gastrointestinal microflora studies in late-onset autism. *Clinical Infectious Diseases, 35*(Suppl. 1), S6–S16.

Fukuda, T. Sugie, H., Ito, M., & Sugie, Y. (2001). Clinical evaluation of treatment with fluvoxamine, a selective serotonin reuptake inhibitor in children with autistic disorder. *No To Hattatsu, 33,* 314–318.

Geller, B., Guttmacher, L., & Bleeg, M. (1981). Coexistence of childhood onset pervasive developmental disorder and attention deficit disorder with hyperactivity. *American Journal of Psychiatry, 138,* 388–389.

Gillberg, C. (1998). Asperger Syndrome and high functioning autism. *British Journal of Psychiatry, 172,* 200–209.

Gillberg, C., & Svennerholm, L. (1987). CSF monoamines in autistic syndromes and other pervasive developmental disorders of early childhood. *British Journal of Psychiatry, 151,* 89–94.

Gordon, C., State, R., Nelson, J., & Hamburger, S. (1993). A double-blind comparison of clomipramine, despiramine, and placebo in the treatment of autistic disorder. *Archives of General Psychiatry, 50,* 441–447.

Handen, B., Johnson, C., & Lubetsky, M. (2000). Efficacy of methylphenidate among children with autism and symptoms of attention-deficit hyperactivity disorder. *Journal of Autism and Developmental Disorders, 30,* 245–255.

Hardan, A., & Hardan, B. (2002). A retrospective open trial of adjunctive donepezil in children and adolescents with autistic disorder. *Journal of Child and Adolescent Psychopharmacology, 12,* 237–241.

Hellings, J., Kelley, L., Gabrielli, W., Kilgore, E., & Shah, P. (1996). Sertraline response in adults with mental retardation and autistic disorder. *Journal of Clinical Psychiatry, 57*(8), 333–336.

Hollander, E., Dolgoff-Kaspar, R., Cartwright, C., Rawitt, R., & Novotny, S. (2001). An open trial of divalproex sodium in autism spectrum disorders. *Journal of Clinical Psychiatry, 62*(7), 530–534.

Hollander, E., Kaplan, A., Cartwright, C., & Reichman, D. (2000). Venlafaxine in children, adolescents, and young adults with autism spectrum disorders: An open retrospective clinical report. *Journal of Child Neurology, 15*(2), 132–135.

Hollander, E., Novotny, S., Hanratty, M., Yaffe, R., DeCaria, C., Aronowitz, B., et al. (2003). Oxytocin infusion reduces repetitive behaviors in adults with autistic and Asperger's disorders. *Neuropsychopharmacology, 28*(1), 193–198.

Hoshino, Y., Kumashiro, H., Kaneko, M., & Takahashi, Y. (1977). The effects of methylphenidate on early infantile autism and its relation to serum serotonin levels. *Folia Psychiatry and Neurology Japan, 31,* 605–614.

Jaselskis, C., Cook, E. H., Jr., Fletcher, K., & Leventhal, B. (1992). Clonidine treatment of hyperactive and impulsive children with autistic disorder. *Journal of Clinical Psychopharmacology, 12,* 322–327.

Kanner, L. (1943). Autistic disturbances of affective contact. *Nervous Child, 2,* 217–250.

Kauffmann, C., Vance, H., Pumariega, A., & Miller, B. (2001). Fluvoxamine treatment of a child with severe PDD: A single case study. *Psychiatry, 64*(3), 268–277.

Kerbeshian, J., Burd, L., & Fisher, W. (1987). Lithium carbonate in the treatment of two patients with infantile autism and atypical symptomatology. *Journal of Clinical Psychopharmacology, 7,* 401–405.

King, B., Wright, D, Handen, B., Sikich, L. Zimmerman, A., McMahon, W., et al. (2001). Double-blind, placebo-controlled study of amantadine hydrochloride in the treatment of children with autistic disorder. *Journal of the American Academy of Child and Adolescent Psychiatry, 40,* 658–665.

Klin, A., Volkmar, F., Sparrow, S., Cicchetti, D., & Rourke, B. (1995). Validity and neuropsychological characterizations of Asperger Syndrome: Convergence with nonverbal learning disabilities syndrome. *Journal of Child Psychology and Psychiatry, 36,* 1127–1140.

Krishnamoorthy, J., & King, B. (1998). Open-label olanzapine treatment in five preadolescent children. *Journal of Child and Adolescent Psychopharmacology, 8,* 107–113.

Lainhart, J. E., & Folstein, S. E. (1994). Affective disorders in people with autism: A review of published cases. *Journal of Autism and Developmental Disorders, 24,* 587–601.

Lesch, K. (2001). Variation of serotonergic gene expression: Neurodevelopment and the complexity of response to psychopharmacologic drugs. *European Journal of Neuropsychopharmacology, 11,* 457–474.

Linday, L., Tsiouris, J., Cohen, I., Shindledecker, R., & DeCresce, R. (2001). Famotidine treatment of young children with autistic spectrum disorders: Pilot research using single subject research design. *Journal of Neural Transmission, 108,* 593–611.

Luiselli, J., Blew, P., Keane, J., Thibadeau, S., & Holzman, T. (2000). Pharmacotherapy for severe aggression in a child with autism: "Open label" evaluation of multiple medications on response frequency and intensity of behavioral intervention. *Journal of Behavior Therapy and Experimental Psychiatry, 31*(3–4), 219–230.

Malone, R., Maislin, G., Choudhury, M., Gifford, C., & Delaney, M. (2002). Risperidone treatment in children and adolescents with autism: Short- and long-term safety and effectiveness. *Journal of the American Academy of Child and Adolescent Psychiatry, 41,* 140–147.

Martin, A., Koenig, K., Anderson, G., & Scahill, L. (2003). Low-dose fluvoxamine treatment of children and adolescents with pervasive developmental disorders: A prospective, open-label study. *Journal of Autism and Developmental Disorders, 33,* 77–85.

Martin, A., Scahill, L., Klin, A., & Volkmar, F. (1999). Higher-functioning pervasive developmental disorders: Rates and patterns of psychotropic drug use. *Journal of the American Academy of Child and Adolescent Psychiatry, 36,* 685–693.

Martineau, J., Barthelemy, C., Jouve, J., Muh, J., & Lelord, G. (1992). Monoamines (serotonin and catecholamines) and their derivatives in infantile autism: Age-related changes and drug effects. *Developmental Medicine and Child Neurology, 34,* 593–603.

Masi, G., Cosenza, A., Mucci, M., & De Vito, G. (2001). Risperidone monotherapy in preschool children with pervasive developmental disorders. *Journal of Child Neurology, 16,* 395–400.

McDougle, C., Holmes, J., Bronson, M., Anderson, G., Volkmar, F., Price, L., et al. (1997). Risperidone treatment of children and adolescents with pervasive developmental disorders: A prospective open-label study. *Journal of the American Academy of Child and Adolescent Psychiatry, 36,* 685–693.

McDougle, C., Holmes, J., Carlson, D., Pelton, G., Cohen, D., & Price, L. (1998). A double-blind, placebo-controlled study of risperidone in adults with autistic disorder and other pervasive developmental disorders. *Archives of General Psychiatry, 55,* 633–641.

McDougle, C., Kem, D., & Posey, D. (2002). Case series: Use of ziprasidone for maladaptive symptoms in youths with autism. *Journal of the American Academy of Child and Adolescent Psychiatry, 41,* 921–927.

McDougle, C., Naylor, S., Cohen, D., Volkmar, F., Heninger, G., & Price, L. (1996). A double-blind, placebo-controlled study of fluvoxamine in adults with autistic disorder. *Archives of General Psychiatry, 53,* 1001–1008.

Miller, J. N., & Ozonoff, S. (2000). The external validity of Asperger disorder: Lack of evidence from the domain of neuropsychology. *Journal of Abnormal Psychology, 109,* 227–238.

Namerow, L., Thomas, P., Bostic, J., Prince, J., & Monuteaux, M. (2003). Use of Citalopram in pervasive developmental disorders. *Journal of Developmental and Behavioral Pediatrics, 24*(2), 104–108.

Naruse, H., Nagahata, M., Nakane, Y., Shirahash, K., Takesada, M., & Yamazaki, K. (1982). A multicenter double-blind trial of pimozide, haloperidol, and placebo in children with behavioral disorders using crossover design. *Acta Paedopsychiatrica, 48,* 173–184.

Nicolson, R., Avad, G., & Sloman, L. (1998). An open trial of risperidone in young autistic children. *Journal of the American Academy of Child and Adolescent Psychiatry, 37,* 372–376.

Owley, T., McMahon, W., Cook, E., Laulhere, T., South, M., Mays, L., et al. (2001). Multisite, double-blind, placebo-controlled trial of porcine secretin in autism. *Journal of the American Academy of Child and Adolescent Psychiatry, 40,* 1293–1299.

Ozonoff, S., & Griffith, E. M. (2000). Neuropsychological function and the external validity of Asperger Syndrome. In A. Klin, F. Volkmar, & S. S. Sparrow (Eds.), *Asperger Syndrome* (pp. 72–96). New York: Guilford.

Patel, N., Yeh, J., Shepherd, M., & Crimson, M. (2002). Secretin treatment for autistic disorder: A critical analysis. *Pharmacotherapy, 22,* 905–914.

Peral, M., Alcami, M., & Gilaberte, I. (1999). Fluoxetine in children with autism. *Journal of the American Academy of Child and Adolescent Psychiatry, 38,* 1472–1473.

Plioplys, A. (1994). Autism: Electroencephalogram abnormalities and clinical improvement with valproic acid. *Archives of Pediatric and Adolescent Medicine, 148,* 220–222.

Popper, C. (1995). Combining methylphenidate and clonidine: Pharmacologic questions and news reports about sudden death. *Journal of the American Academy of Child and Adolescent Psychiatry, 5,* 157–166.

Posey, D., Guenin, K., Kohn, A., Swiezy, N., & McDougle, C. (2001). A naturalistic open-label study of mirtazapine in autistic and other pervasive developmental disorders. *Journal of Child and Adolescent Psychopharmacology, 11,* 267–277.

Posey, D., Litwiller, M., Koburn, A., & McDougle, C. (1999). Paroxetine in autism. *Journal of the American Academy of Child and Adolescent Psychiatry, 38,* 111–112.

Posey, D., & McDougle, C. (2000). The pharmacotherapy of target symptoms associated with autistic disorder and other pervasive developmental disorders. *Harvard Review of Psychiatry, 8,* 45–63.

Potenza, M., Holmes, J., SJ, K., & McDougle, C. (1999). Olanzapine treatment of children, adolescents, and adults with pervasive developmental disorders: An open-label pilot study. *Journal of Clinical Psychopharmacology, 19,* 37–44.

Quintana, H., Birmaher, B., Stedge, D., Lennon, S., Freed, J., Bridge, J., et al. (1995). Use of methylphenidate in the treatment of children with autistic disorder. *Journal of Autism and Developmental Disorders, 25,* 283–294.

Realmuto, G., August, G., & Garfinkel, B. (1989). Clinical effect of buspirone in autistic children. *Journal of Clinical Psychopharmacology, 9,* 122–125.

Remington, G., Sloman, L., Konstantareas, M., Parker, K., & Gow, R. (2001). Clomipramine versus haloperidol in the treatment of autistic disorder: A double-blind, placebo-controlled, crossover study. *Journal of Clinical Psychopharmacology, 21,* 440–444.

Research Units on Pediatric Psychopharmacology Autism Network. (2002). Risperidone in children with autism and serious behavioral problems. *New England Journal of Medicine, 347,* 314–321.

Rugino, T., & Samsock, T. (2002). Levetiracetam in autistic children: An open-label study. *Developmental and Behavioral Pediatrics, 23*(4), 225–230.

Sanchez, L., Campbell, M., Small, A., Cueva, J., Armenteros, J., & Adams, P. (1996). A pilot study of clomipramine in young autistic children. *Journal of the American Academy of Child and Adolescent Psychiatry, 35,* 537–544.

Sandler, R., Finegold, S., Bolte, E., Buchanan, C., Maxwell, A., Vaisanen, M., et al. (2000). Short-term benefit from oral vancomycin treatment of regressive-onset autism. *Journal of Child Neurology, 15,* 429–435.

Scahill, L., & Koenig, K. (1999). Pharmacotherapy in children and adolescents with pervasive developmental disorders. *Journal of Child and Adolescent Psychiatric Nursing, 12*(1), 41–43.

Schmidt, K. (1982). The effect of stimulant medication in childhood-onset pervasive developmental disorder: A case report. *Journal of Developmental and Behavioral Pediatrics, 3,* 244–246.

Sporn, A., & Pinkster, H. (1981). Use of stimulant medication in treating pervasive developmental disorder. *American Journal of Psychiatry, 138,* 997.

Steingard, R., & Biederman, J. (1987). Lithium responsive manic-like symptoms in two individuals with autism and mental retardation. *Journal of the American Academy of Child and Adolescent Psychiatry, 26,* 932-935.

Steingard, R., Zimnitzky, B., DeMaso, D., Bauman, M., & Bucci, J. (1997). Sertraline treatment of transition-associated anxiety and agitation in children with autistic disorder. *Journal of Child and Adolescent Psychopharmacology, 7,* 9–15.

Strayhorn, J., Rapp, N., Donina, W., & Strain, P. (1988). Randomized trial of methylphenidate for an autistic child. *Journal of the American Academy of Child and Adolescent Psychiatry, 27,* 244–247.

Szatmari, P., Bryson, S. E., Streiner, D., Wilson, F., Archer, L., & Ryerse, C. (2000). Two-year outcome of preschool children with autism or Asperger's Syndrome. *American Journal of Psychiatry, 157,* 1980–1987.

Szatmari, P., Merette, P., Bryson, S., Thivierge, J., Roy, M., Cayer, M., et al. (2002). Quantifying dimensions in autism: A factor-analytic study. *Journal of the American Academy of Child and Adolescent Psychiatry, 41,* 467–474.

Uvebrant, P., & Bauziene, R. (1994). Intractable epilepsy in children: The efficacy of lamotrigine treatment, including non-seizure-related benefits. *Neuropediatrics, 25,* 284–289.

Vitriol, C., & Farber, B. (1981). Stimulant medication in certain childhood disorders. *American Journal of Psychiatry, 138,* 1517–1518.

Volkmar, F. (2001). Pharmacological interventions in autism: Theoretical and practical issues. *Journal of Clinical Child Psychology, 30,* 80–87.

Volkmar, F., Hoder, E., & Cohen, H. (1985). Inappropriate uses of stimulant medications. *Clinical Pediatrics, 24,* 127–130.

Wilens, T., Spencer, T., Swanson, J., Connor, D., & Cantwell, D. (1999). Combining methylphenidate and clonidine: A clinically sound medication option. *Journal of the American Academy of Child and Adolescent Psychiatry, 38,* 614–619.

Willemsen-Swinkels, S., Buitelaar, J., van Berckelaer-Onnes, I., & van Engeland, H. (1999). Brief report: Six months continuation treatment in naltrexone-responsive children with autism: An open-label case-control design. *Journal of Autism and Developmental Disorders, 29,* 167–169.

Williams, P., Allard, A., Sears, L., Dalrymple, N., & Bloom, A. (2001). Brief report: Case reports on naltrexone use in children with autism: Controlled observations regarding benefits and practical issues of medication management. *Journal of Autism and Developmental Disorders, 31,* 103–108.

Yokoyama, H., Hirose, M., Haginoya, K., Munkata, M., & Iinuma, K. (2002). Treatment with fluvoxamine against self-injury and aggressive behavior in autistic children. *No To Hattatsu, 34,* 249–253.

PART II

Children

Chapter 5

Cognitive Assessment of Preschool and Elementary School Students

Teresa Bolick
Nashua, New Hampshire, and Westford, Massachusetts

Cognition—the process of knowing or perceiving.

—*Webster's New Twentieth Century Dictionary* (1983, p. 352)

Asperger's Syndrome has been associated with cognitive strength since Hans Asperger first described the disorder in the 1940s. When he wrote of children who sounded like "little professors," Dr. Asperger (1944/1991) was describing not only their pedantic tone but also their cognitive abilities. The assumption of adequate cognitive skill was reiterated when the *Diagnostic and Statistical Manual of Mental Disorders (DSM–IV)* stated that individuals with Asperger's Syndrome show "no clinically significant delay in cognitive development" (American Psychiatric Association, 2000, p. 84).

Although children with Asperger's Syndrome are thought to show no general cognitive delay, there is actually a great deal of variability in the specific abilities of individuals. In spite of mass media suggestions that individuals with Asperger's Syndrome grow up to be scientists or software engineers, we do not yet have data to support this connection. Similarly, despite the frequently described co-occurrence of Asperger's Syndrome and the nonverbal learning disability profile (e.g., Rourke, 1995), this association has not yet been fully investigated in epidemiological research. The bottom line is that we do not yet have sufficient data on Asperger's Syndrome in children to conclude that there is one characteristic cognitive profile (or even a few variations).

The goal of this chapter is to provide a framework for understanding cognitive development in children with Asperger's Syndrome. This framework certainly is not the only way in which to organize cognitive data, and the list of assessment tools is far from exhaustive. Instead, the framework and instruments are discussed as "leads" that the clinician can pursue in making sense of these complicated children.

THE COMPLEX PROCESS OF COGNITIVE ASSESSMENT

Given the state of the research, the purpose of cognitive assessment of children with Asperger's Syndrome is not to make the diagnosis, but rather to investigate the child's unique profile of strengths and challenges. As such, the cognitive assessment is seldom conducted in isolation. Ideally, cognitive skills will be evaluated in the context of other developmental functions and in relation to the family and school environments.

The Story of Doug

Six-year-old Doug entered the office, found the Matchbox vehicles, and announced the make, model, and years of each one. Although the examiner could not confirm the accuracy of the labels, Doug's father indicated that things sounded "right" to him. Doug also regaled the adults with facts about dinosaurs, cloud formations, and professional basketball scores. He sounded like one of Dr. Asperger's "little professors."

Doug was having a terrible time in kindergarten, though. The process of putting outerwear into his cubby often ended in tears. He reported that he "stunk at color-cut-glue." Doug usually left a "trail" behind him, as he dropped paper, writing tools, books, blocks, or whatever he had in his hands. Although he could remember virtually every detail of any book read during circle time, Doug was not able to predict what might happen next in the story. Incredibly attentive and persistent when he had "the floor," Doug struggled to follow class discussions. His teacher became increasingly concerned, especially when Doug started calling himself "stupid."

Comprehensive cognitive, communication, and occupational therapy evaluations revealed a great deal about Doug's neurodevelopmental profile:

- Despite his remarkable verbal expression skills, Doug had trouble understanding what another person "meant" in the midst of a fast-paced conversation or discussion.
- Although Doug could provide verbal information about locations and routes, certain visuospatial skills were rather inefficient. He lost his be-

---

> longings, and he was perplexed by puzzles and construction toys such as Legos. And, as he had told us initially, he had an awful time with "color-cut-glue."
>
> - Doug was quite skilled in repeating stories or play sequences from books or videos, but his own stories and play schemes seldom were creative.
> - Doug's attentional processes were easily compromised in situations that required rapid verbal and nonverbal processing. As a result, he lost track of what was happening, became anxious about "not knowing," and was at risk for silliness and other rule violations.

Doug's story is not atypical for young children with Asperger's Syndrome. The remarkable verbal skills and general information of many children with Asperger's Syndrome allow them to "ace" early academic screening instruments used to identify students at risk. Their difficulties in organizing their belongings and materials or awkwardness in fine motor and visual motor skills are often attributed to "immaturity." As a result, the task for evaluation teams is to separate true neurodevelopmental challenges from the substantial and typical developmental variations common in young children.

Evaluation of young children can tax the skills of even the most experienced clinicians. Limited span of attention and effort, preference for other activities, and developmental variations in motor control (especially fine and visual motor) can interfere with the child's demonstration of knowledge and skill. In addition, the predictive validity of most evaluation tools is limited for younger children. Despite the hurdles, though, careful evaluation of the cognitive skills of young children with Asperger's Syndrome is our best insurance against inadvertent development of "splinter skills" built upon a shaky cognitive foundation. In addition, the evaluation can assist in planning interventions that support social and emotional growth.

The elementary school student with Asperger's Syndrome typically presents fewer challenges in terms of motivation during formal testing. In fact, many older children with Asperger's Syndrome prefer testing to the rest of the school day! The challenge for the clinician is one of tailoring an assessment battery that truly "tests" the child's capacity. In fact, with easel booklets that frame the attention of the student, test formats that assist the creation of a response set, and one-to-one interaction with an interested adult, formal testing is a virtually perfect match for the cognitive strengths and challenges for many elementary school students with Asperger's Syndrome.

Fortunately, recent advances in assessment theory and practice have highlighted several principles that are critical to valid evaluation of all children, and particularly pertinent in assessing children with Asperger's Syndrome.

- **Careful observations** should be interwoven with test results to generate and test hypotheses about neurodevelopmental functions.

- Evaluation should be **process-based**, with a focus on how the child arrived at an answer. In this regard, incorrect responses are just as important as correct ones.
- Evaluation should be **dynamic**. If the child does not solve the problem, how can we help him or her be more successful?
- Comprehensive evaluations should involve **cross-battery assessment**. Ideally, we should use broad-brush instruments not as the final results, but as starting points that generate "leads" for in-depth specific assessment.
- Whenever possible, assessment should be **multidisciplinary** and should match the **multitrait, multimethod** standard for assessing human behavior and traits. Convergence of results from different assessment measures and professional disciplines adds to the validity of our findings and recommendations.
- **Cautious interpretation** should be the rule. Too many children and their families have expected the "superior" scores achieved on the highly rote preschool and primary tests to correspond to lifelong cognitive superiority.

A FRAMEWORK FOR COGNITIVE ASSESSMENT

A neurodevelopmental framework of cognition can be quite helpful in understanding the specific and often discrepant cognitive abilities of the child with Asperger's Syndrome. Simply put, we need to answer these questions:

- What neurodevelopmental characteristics support or impede the child's ability to learn and to demonstrate that knowledge on demand?
- What contextual factors (or "load") facilitate or interfere with the child's cognitive functioning?

The remainder of this chapter will describe specific neurodevelopmental domains, discuss challenges in assessment, and provide a partial listing of relevant assessment instruments. We also revisit Doug.

ASSESSMENT OF SPECIFIC NEURODEVELOPMENTAL DOMAINS

Assessment of Attention and the Executive Functions

The foundation skills of attention and executive functions are essential for learning and for the demonstration of knowledge on demand. Careful evaluation of these skills is especially important because so many children with Asperger's Syndrome are initially identified as having attention deficit hyperactivity disorder (ADHD) or other executive challenges. Evaluation of attentional processes and executive functions should include consideration of:

- Deployment (or shifting) of attention from one task or activity to another.
- "Salience determination" (Levine, 1999, 2002) or capacity to decide on and attend to the most critical elements of the situation.
- Inhibition of irrelevant responding.
- Accurate depth of processing.
- Maintenance of attention, even when "bored."
- Establishment and shifting of relevant perceptual and response sets.

In addition, the dynamic, process-based approach will consider the conditions under which each of these processes is more or less efficient.

Given the challenges of formal testing (especially for young children), it is helpful to begin an evaluation of foundation skills by gathering information from parents and teachers. Many clinicians find it helpful to begin this process by interviewing parents and then following up with checklists or rating scales. Information from teachers is often acquired most efficiently by following the reverse of this sequence: Provide checklists or questionnaires and then talk with the teacher about items of concern (or confusion). Adult response bias can be reduced by starting with a more general checklist (such as Achenbach's [2000] Child Behavior Checklist and Teacher's Report Form or the Behavior Assessment System for Children [Reynolds & Kamphaus, 2002]). As the hypothesis testing process begins, the clinician might want to add a more specific instrument, such as the Behavior Rating Inventory of Executive Function (BRIEF; Gioia, Isquith, Guy, & Kenworthy, 2000), or the Conners' Rating Scales–Revised (Conners, 1997). (Both are available in parent and teacher versions.) Formal testing of attention and the executive functions can then proceed from leads generated by parental and teacher report (see Table 5.1).

Traps and Tips.

- Consider test results within the context of both developmental requirements and environmental demand. For example, although a 10-year-old child achieves a scaled score in the "expected" range on the NEPSY Auditory Attention and Response Set test (Korkman et al., 1998), he or she might actually struggle to attend within a fourth-grade classroom when attentional "targets" are less clearly defined and environmental distractors are more plentiful than in the structured testing environment.
- Use clues from the testing environment and task context or format to guide recommendations for the classroom.
- Observe attention and executive functions during play. Does the child move from one toy to another without settling down to play productively? Are board games frequently aborted before completion? Does the kindergarten (or older) student suggest a play scenario and then lose track of the plan? Do extraneous characteristics of the props capture the child's attention and derail him or her from the plan? Behav-

TABLE 5.1

Examples of Tests for Attention and Executive Functions

Test or Subtest	Attention or Executive Function Assessed	Age Range
NEPSY Auditory Attention/Response Set (Korkman, Kirk, & Kemp, 1998)	Auditory verbal attention and inhibition of irrelevant responses; maintenance and shifting of complex response sets	5–12 years
NEPSY Visual Attention	Attention to simple visual stimuli and inhibition of irrelevant responses (3–4 years); attention to simple and complex visual stimuli and inhibition of irrelevant responses (5–12 years)	3–12 years
NEPSY Statue	Motor persistence, inhibition of response to auditory distraction	3–12 years
NEPSY Knock & Tap	Inhibition of responses to visual stimuli that conflict with auditory directions	5–12 years
WPPSI–III Symbol Search (Wechsler, 2002)	Concentration, response inhibition	4 years–7 years, 3 months
WPPSI–III Coding	Visual scanning and attention	4 years–7 years, 3 months
K–ABC Magic Window (Kaufman & Kaufman, 1983)	Attention to visual detail, salience determination	2 years, 6 months– 4 years, 11 months
K–ABC Face Recognition	Attention to visual detail, salience determination	2 years, 6 months– 4 years, 11 months
K–ABC Gestalt Closure	Attention to visual detail	2 years, 6 months– 12 years, 5 months
K–ABC Matrix Analogies	Attention to visual detail, salience determination	5 years–12 years, 5 months
K–ABC Photo Series	Attention to visual detail, salience determination	6 years–12 years, 5 months
WISC–III Arithmetic (Wechsler, 1991)	Freedom from distractibility, auditory attention	6 years–16 years, 11 months
WISC–III Digit Span	Auditory attention	6 years–16 years, 11 months
WISC–III Coding	Visual scanning and attention	6 years–16 years, 11 months

WISC–III Symbol Search	Visual concentration, inhibition	6 years–16 years, 11 months
Conners' Continuous Performance Tests (Conners & Multi-Health Systems Staff, 2000)	Vigilance, impulsivity, sustained attention, deterioration of attention over time (using interactive computer software)	4–5 years (K–CPT) 6 years and up (CPT–II)
WISC–III PI Elithorn Mazes (Kaplan, Fein, Kramer, Delis, & Morris, 1999)	Inhibition, maintenance of response set	8 years–16 years, 11 months
NEPSY Tower (Korkman et al., 1998)	Inhibition, maintenance of response set, spatial planning	5–12 years
D–KEFS Tower (Delis, Kaplan, & Kramer, 2001)	Inhibition, maintenance of response set, spatial planning	8 years and up
D–KEFS Color–Word Interference	Inhibition of verbal responding, cognitive switching	8 years and up
D–KEFS Verbal Fluency	Letter and category fluency, cognitive shifting (during category fluency)	8 years and up
D–KEFS Design Fluency	Design fluency, visual-motor response inhibition, cognitive flexibility	8 years and up
NEPSY Design Fluency	Design fluency, visual-motor response inhibition, cognitive flexibility	5–12 years
D–KEFS Trail Making	Visual scanning, motor inhibition, cognitive switching	8 years and up
Rey–Osterrieth Complex Figure Developmental Scoring System (Berstein & Waber, 1996)	Organization and self-monitoring of visual motor perceptual task, management of complexity	5–14 years

Note. NEPSY = NEPSY Developmental Neuropsychological Assessment; WPPSI–III = Wechsler Preschool and Primary Scale of Intelligence–3rd edition; K–ABC = Kaufman Assessment Battery for Children; WISC–III = Wechsler Intelligence Scale for Children–III; D–KEFS = Delis Kaplan Executive Function System iors apparent during play can signal that intervention is warranted to address real-world inefficiency.

Doug's Attention and Executive Functions

When reevaluated as an 11-year-old, Doug's attention to topic remained dogged when he was pursuing a special interest. Yet his parents and teachers rated him within the clinical range on the Attention Problems factor of the Achenbach checklists. Items such as "frequently fails to complete assignments" were consistently checked on report cards and behavior checklists.

Doug's score on the Auditory Attention and Response Set test of the NEPSY was 11, but this average score was actually quite deceiving—Doug scored 14 on the Auditory Attention portion of the test but only 9 on the Response Set portion. On Wechsler Intelligence Scale for Children–III (WISC–III) PI Elithorn Mazes, Doug repeatedly worked his way into "blind alleys" with impulsive responding. In play and in the classroom, Doug was famous for blurting out answers before considering their relevance. Testing results converged with naturalistic observations to suggest that Doug's "attentional problems" were quite specific, reflecting his challenges in salience determination (deciding the critical elements of a situation) and inhibition of irrelevant responding.

Assessment of Memory Processes

If attention and executive functions are the "hardware" of mental processing, then memory can be thought of as the "software." Memory processes are involved in every aspect of daily functioning, but the details of how they all work remain some of the most vehement controversies in the cognitive sciences. Given the complexity of memory processes in general, it is not surprising that memory in children with Asperger's Syndrome is a mixed bag. There is no doubt that many individuals with Asperger's Syndrome demonstrate prodigious storage and recall of certain types of information. Yet children with Asperger's Syndrome can also show challenges in memory storage and retrieval processes.

Comprehensive assessment of memory processes in children with Asperger's Syndrome should proceed according to the principles of dynamic, process-based assessment outlined earlier in this chapter. It also goes without saying that any measure of memory should be considered in light of whether the child was able to deploy attention adequately to the task at hand. In addition, the evaluator should be aware that our common notions about memory influence reports about a child's functioning. When we ask parents about their child's memory, they typically consider the ability to recall facts or events. Some parents and teachers do consider the ability to recall directions long enough to follow them (working memory), but they often attribute this skill (or limitation) to attention. Although these aspects of memory are important, they are far from the whole story in memory processing. Moreover, consideration of just these aspects of memory puts us at risk for seeing only the memory strengths of the child with Asperger's Syndrome and missing some of the limitations.

Current research points to the importance of assessing at least the following elements of memory processing in children (see Table 5.2):

- Working memory (the ability to "hold" information in short-term memory stores while performing simultaneous mental operations).
- Short-term memory.
- Long -term memory.
- Differences in memory associated with input modality (e.g., visual vs. auditory).
- Cross-modal memory.
- Memory for procedures (habit memory).

Traps and Tips.

- Try to "tease out" the contributions of various memory processes to the child's performance. For example, compare performance on the free recall trial of a story memory task with cued recall of the same story. Then consider whether initial recall was diminished because the information was not encoded (stored) in a framework that would assist retrieval, because the memory trace was sufficiently strong for recognition but not for free recall, and/or because the child simply could not organize the information for oral recall. For many children with Asperger's Syndrome and other social communication disorders, the encoding process is inefficient simply because the child does not know what to expect of the task. These children often do better on the second story of the subtest.
- Use a variety of tests to zero in on the "guilty" function. Sometimes what looks like a memory failure is related to inefficient output processes (such as oral expression or motor skill). On the other hand, we are sometimes left with the realization that the culprit is what Levine, Reed, and Hobgood (2000) called the "junction between functions."
- Take care to assess memory within different input or output modalities, especially if the child shows inefficiency in other types of processing within a given modality. A child with strong verbal skills and more challenged visuospatial abilities, for example, might do quite nicely on "span" tests that utilize verbal information but then struggle with spatial span tasks. Another child with intact visual memory skills but poor graphomotor abilities might score within the average range on the recognition trial of the Rey Complex Figure Test (RCFT; Meyers & Meyers, 1995) despite below average performance on recall trials that require drawing.

TABLE 5.2

Examples of Tests for Memory Functions

Test or Subtest	Memory Functions Assessed	Age Range
NEPSY Memory for Faces (Korkman et al., 1998)	Immediate and delayed recognition memory for faces	3–12 years
WRAML Picture Memory (Sheslow & Adams, 1990)	Immediate memory for meaningful complex visual stimuli	5–17 years
WPPSI–III Coding (Wechsler, 2002)	Short-term visual memory, graphomotor response	4 years–7 years, 3 months
WISC–III Coding (Wechsler, 1991)	Short-term visual memory, graphomotor response	6 years–16 years, 11 months
WISC–III PI Coding-Incidental Recall (Kaplan et al., 1999)	Incidental recall of visual information under paired associate and free recall conditions, graphomotor response	8–16 years
WISC–III PI Coding-Incidental Recall (Kaplan et al., 1999)	Incidental recall of visual information under paired associate and free recall conditions, graphomotor response	8–16 years
WRAML Design Memory (Sheslow & Adams, 1990)	Immediate memory for abstract complex visual stimuli, graphomotor response	5–17 years
WRAML Finger Windows	Short-term memory for visuospatial sequences	5–17 years
WISC–III PI Spatial Span Forward and Backward	Short-term memory for visuospatial sequences, working memory for backward spatial span	6–16 years
WRAML Visual Learning	Visuospatial paired associate learning of locations and complex abstract stimuli (immediate and delayed)	5–17 years
NEPSY Memory for Names	Visual-verbal paired associate learning (immediate and delayed, faces and names)	5–12 years
WRAML Sound-Symbol	Visual-verbal paired associate learning (immediate and delayed; abstract symbols and nonsense syllables)	5–17 years
WRAML Number/Letter Memory	Auditory short-term memory for nonmeaningful information	5–17 years

WISC–III Digit Span Forward and Backward	Verbal short-term memory for nonmeaningful information; Digits Backward also assesses working memory	6 years–16 years, 11 months
WISC–III PI Letter Span	Auditory short-term memory for nonmeaningful information	6 years–16 years, 11 months
WISC–III Arithmetic	Auditory working memory	6 years–16 years, 11 months
NEPSY Sentence Repetition	Verbal short-term memory for meaningful material	3–12 years
WRAML Sentence Memory	Verbal short-term memory for meaningful material	5–17 years
NEPSY Narrative Memory	Verbal short- and long-term memory under free and cued recall conditions, organization of recall	3–12 years
WRAML Story Memory	Verbal short- and long-term memory under free and recognition memory conditions, organization of recall; inclusion of second story allows child to establish cognitive set for task	5–17 years
NEPSY List Learning	Verbal learning, response to interference, active rehearsal strategies (semantic chunking), primacy, recency	5–12 years
WRAML Verbal Learning	Verbal learning, response to interference, active rehearsal strategies (semantic chunking), primacy, recency	5–17 years
K–ABC Magic Window (Kaufman & Kaufman, 1983)	Visual short-term memory	2 years, 6 months–4 years, 11 months
K–ABC Hand Movements	Visual sequential short-term memory, motor response	2 years, 6 months–12 years, 5 months
K–ABC Gestalt Closure	Retrieval from visual long-term memory	2 years, 6 months–12 years, 5 months
K–ABC Spatial Memory	Visuospatial short-term memory	5 years–12 years, 5 months

(continued on next page)

TABLE 5.2 (continued)

Test or Subtest	Memory Functions Assessed	Age Range
K–ABC Word Order	Cross-modal integration (auditory stimulus/visual motor response)	4 years–12 years, 5 months
Rey–Osterrieth Complex Figure Developmental Scoring System (Bernstein & Waber, 1996)	Immediate and delayed recall of visual spatial information, use of configuration to aid recall, graphomotor response	5–14 years
Rey Complex Figure Test and Recognition Trial (Meyers & Meyers, 1995)	Delayed recognition of visual information, no graphomotor response	6 years and up

Note. NEPSY = NEPSY Developmental Neuropsychological Assessment; WRAML = Wide Range Assessment of Memory and Learning; WPPSI–III = Wechsler Preschool and Primary Scale of Intelligence–3rd edition; WISC–III = Wechsler Intelligence Scale for Children–III; K–ABC = Kaufman Assessment Battery for Children

- Check for active rehearsal strategies. Because of their strong rote memories, children with Asperger's Syndrome might not have acquired efficient rehearsal strategies (such as repetition or chunking). They continue to rely on rote strategies (memorization) even after amount or type of information exceeds the usual capacity of short-term memory or when the task format is less familiar. Order of recall during list learning tasks or visual perceptual tasks are helpful clues regarding rehearsal.
- Any task that assesses the child's fund of information, academic skills, or general problem-solving abilities can be assumed to involve some degree of retrieval from long-term memory.
- Evaluate procedural (or habit) memory, which allows us to accomplish the more mundane tasks of life without utilizing conscious "brain power." Unfortunately, many children with Asperger's Syndrome have not yet achieved "automaticity" on such tasks. They have to work harder and longer to accomplish a task, sometimes losing track of belongings (and finished work) and "forgetting" the directions that were given while they were thinking about how to write their name and date on the worksheet. Careful observation of the child's behavior and cautious (nonleading) questioning of parents and teachers allow the examiner to assess the functional impact of inadequate habit memory.
- Do not forget working memory. This complex process bridges short-term and long-term memory (such as by "holding" the question in mind while

we search for the answer) and allows us to plan a sequence of actions (such as by "holding" our goal in mind while deciding what steps to use to get there). For children with working memory deficits, lists, task cards, and other written (or picture) directions can enhance productivity and reduce frustration immensely.

Doug's Memory Processes

By report, Doug had an exceptionally strong memory for facts and events. Performance on formal memory tasks, though, revealed that his encoding and retrieval processes were actually less developed than would be expected. On the Rey–Osterneth Complex Figure Test (ROCF), Doug carefully copied each line segment, without appreciating the overall configuration of the design. On early teaching trials of the NEPSY List Learning subtest, Doug repeated the first several words in the order in which they were presented (primacy effect) and then the last few words (recency effect) rather than grouping the words in conceptual categories. It was not surprising, then, that when asked to recall either visual or verbal information after a delay, Doug recalled bits and pieces without any inherent organizational structure.

Within the real world, Doug's subtle challenges in information retrieval became more and more apparent in upper elementary school. If he did not remember something automatically, he did not have efficient ways of finding the "lost" information. Once his teachers taught Doug to use mnemonic strategies and graphic organizers to emphasize concepts and relationships, his understanding and application of knowledge improved.

Assessment of Visuospatial Processing

Spatial processing allows us to create order in a complex world. We perceive incoming visual information, organize that information in ways that facilitate storage and retrieval, and utilize the material to understand interrelationships between and among the parts and whole. Inefficient visuospatial processing has long been associated with learning disorders. Spatial processing even affects social development, as a function of its impact on facial recognition and "reading" nonverbal communication.

Assessment of spatial processing has a long history, dating to the early works of Bender (1956) and Frostig (1964; Frostig and Maslow, 1973). Virtually every modern cognitive assessment battery now includes measures of visuospatial abilities. As with other aspects of cognitive assessment, though, we must take care to go beyond the child's scores to determine exactly what is wrong (or right) in the visuospatial domain (see Table 5.3).

TABLE 5.3

Examples of Tests of Visuospatial Processing

Test or Subtest	Visuospatial Processes Assessed	Age Range
NEPSY Design Copying (Korkman et al., 1998)	Integration of visuospatial skills and graphomotor coordination	3–12 years
Beery–Buktenica Developmental Test of Visual Motor Integration (VMI; Beery & Buktenica, 1997)	Integration of visuospatial skills and graphomotor coordination	3 years
Rey–Osterrieth Complex Figure (ROCF)-Developmental Scoring System (Bernstein & Waber, 1996)	Complex visuospatial organization and graphomotor coordination	5–14 years
Rey Complex Figure Test and Recognition Trial (RCFT; Meyers & Meyers, 1995)	Complex visuospatial organization and graphomotor coordination, motor-free recognition trial	6 years and up
NEPSY Arrows	Visualization of spatial relationships, judgment of direction, distance, and orientation in space, motor-free	5–12 years
NEPSY Route-Finding	Understanding of visuospatial relationships, visual analogous representation	5–12 years
Motor-Free Visual Perception Test–Revised (Colarusso & Hammill, 1996)	Spatial relationships, visual closure, visual discrimination, figure ground discrimination, visual memory	4–11 years
Test of Visual-Perceptual Skills–Revised (Gardner, 1996)	Visual discrimination, visuospatial relationships, visual form constancy, visual closure, motor-free	4–17 years
WPPSI–III Coding (Wechsler, 2002)	Visual perception, visual-motor speed and coordination, graphomotor response	4 years–7 years, 3 months
WISC–III Coding (Wechsler, 1991)	Visual perception, visual-motor speed and coordination, graphomotor response	6 years–16 years, 11 months
WPPSI–III Symbol Search	Visual discrimination, visual-motor coordination, simple graphomotor response	4 years–7 years, 3 months

WISC–III Symbol Search	Visual discrimination, visual-motor coordination, simple graphomotor response	6 years–16 years, 11 months
WISC–III Mazes	Visual-motor organization and planning, capacity for motor delay	6 years–16 years, 11 months
WISC–III PI Elithorn Mazes (Kaplan et al., 1999)	Visual-motor organization and planning, capacity for motor delay, maintenance of cognitive set	8–16 years
WPPSI–III Picture Completion	Visual perception and organization, visual recognition of objects and details, visualization of "ideal" stimulus; motor-free	4 years–7 years, 3 months
WISC–III Picture Completion	Visual perceptual organization, visual recognition, visualization and differentiation of essential details, motor-free	6 years–16 years, 11 months
K–ABC Magic Window (Kaufman & Kaufman, 1983)	Simultaneous visuospatial processing, part–whole relationships, motor-free	2 years, 6 months–4 years, 11 months
K–ABC Face Recognition	Simultaneous processing of facial information, motor-free	2 years, 6 months–4 years, 11 months
K–ABC Gestalt Closure	Visual perceptual organization, part–whole relationships, motor-free	2 years, 6 months–12 years, 5 months
K-ABC Matrix Analogies	Visual perceptual organization, visual analogies, motor-free	5 years–12 years, 5 months
K–ABC Photo Series	Visuospatial organization of meaningful stimuli (photos of people, things); essentially motor-free	6 years–12 years, 5 months
K–ABC Triangles	Visual analysis and organization of part–whole relationships (nonverbal concept formation), visual-motor coordination	4 years–12 years, 5 months
WPPSI–III Block Design	Analysis and synthesis of abstract visual stimuli (nonverbal concept formation), visual observation and matching, visual-motor coordination, no time bonuses	

(continued on next page)

TABLE 5.3 (continued)

Test or Subtest	Visuospatial Processes Assessed	Age Range
WISC–III Block Design	Analysis and synthesis of abstract visual stimuli (nonverbal concept formation), spatial visualization, visual-motor coordination and speed	6 years–16 years, 11 months
WISC–III PI Block Design Multiple Choice	Visual-perceptual organization, closure, and speed, visual discrimination, inhibition, motor-free	6 years–16 years, 11 months
WPPSI–III Object Assembly	Visual-perceptual organization, part–whole relationships, visual-motor coordination; no time bonuses	2 years, 6 months– 7 years, 3 months
WISC–III Object Assembly	Visuospatial organization, visualization, part–whole relationships, visual-motor coordination and speed	6 years–16 years, 11 months
NEPSY Block Construction	Visualization and understanding of three-dimensional spatial relations, understanding of negative space, visual-motor coordination and speed	3–12 years

Note. NEPSY = NEPSY Developmental Neuropsychological Assessment; WPPSI–III = Wechsler Preschool and Primary Scale of Intelligence–3rd edition; WISC–III = Wechsler Intelligence Scale for Children–III; K–ABC = Kaufman Assessment Battery for Children

Traps and Tips.

- Recognize the "load" associated with copying, drawing, or writing. Because many children with Asperger's Syndrome have visual motor inefficiencies, it is important to contrast performance on visuospatial measures that include a motor component with performance on motor-free measures.
- Do not assume that appreciation and discrimination of visual detail is equivalent to visuospatial processing. Some children with Asperger's Syndrome are so attentive to visual detail that they lose sight of the overall configuration of the information or the purpose of the task. Assess both discrimination and processing.
- Attend carefully to the process by which the child solves a visual problem. It is not at all unusual for a bright child with visuospatial challenges to do quite well on the first several designs of Block Design (Wechsler, 1991) as these include the grid lines and facilitate what is essentially a sequential left-to-right, top-to-bottom approach. When the grid is removed and/or

when the items require a 3×3 configuration, this child is likely to falter. Use of the Block Design PI (Kaplan et al., 1999), which allows the placement of a transparency with grid lines on the stimulus figures, allows us to confirm the child's visuospatial processes and to identify modifications and teaching strategies for the future.

- Compare performance on circumscribed tasks such as Block Design with that on more open-ended tasks such as Object Assembly (Wechsler, 1991; especially the horse, soccer ball, and face puzzles). A child with Asperger's Syndrome may approach the task in a logical sequential or part-oriented manner (such as by trying to match individual lines) and lose track of the gestalt of the figure. Not surprisingly, older elementary school students who use a part-oriented approach to Block Design and Object Assembly (Wechsler, 1991) tasks also seem to persist in a similar approach to the ROCF (Bernstein & Waber, 1996) long after their peers have begun to appreciate the organizing configuration of the Rey design.
- Children who have difficulties in visuospatial processing of tests and academic tasks also tend to miss the forest for the trees in social interactions. Not only do they err in interpretation of facial expression or body language, but they also neglect social information conveyed by physical proximity and location. We might go so far as to suggest that social interaction represents the ultimate visuospatial processing challenge.
- Ironically, carefully designed visual (graphic) organizers can facilitate academic performance in children with visuospatial inefficiencies. Unlike oral input that "disappears" as soon as it leaves the speaker's lips, visuospatial information can be captured in pictures, diagrams, or charts that remain static. Use the assessment process to identify the nature or format of spatial input that is most helpful for a child and then to formulate recommendations for modifications and interventions (e.g., whether to present math computation problems on graph paper or what type of graphic organizer is most likely to reinforce the child's understanding of a concept or cause–effect relationship).

Doug's Spatial Processing

As a 6-year-old, Doug actually scored within the superior range (14) on the Wechsler Intelligence Scale for Children–III (WISC–III) Block Design subtest. He did not receive bonus points for speed on timed tests, but his conscientious approach allowed him to solve items that prove quite difficult for many children his age. As an 11-year-old, Doug's score was within the average range (10) on the same test. Again, he was accurate but rather slow. Was this a "loss" of skills? Probably not. Instead this rather common finding illustrates how changes in developmental expectations affect our assessment of a child's skills.

Doug's spatial challenges were relatively mild. However, his spatial abilities were highly vulnerable to load: When complexity or time demands increased, Doug's performance suffered.

Assessment of Sequential Processing

By imposing sequential (serial) order on our experiences, we organize our understanding of the world as well our own responses. Imagine trying to brush your teeth without some appreciation of the sequence of movements involved. Inefficient sequential processing can also lead to confusion over time concepts (even those such as *before* and *after*), difficulties with the so-called automatized sequences (days of the week, months of the year), trouble with multistep directions and explanations, disorganized telling or retelling of stories and experiences, and poor motor planning.

Some of our most important information about sequential processing emerges from observation and careful history taking. How well does the child understand and use time-laden vocabulary? Did the child master the automatized sequences (days of week, months of year, letters in alphabet) by the age of 8? How well does the child remember and follow multistep directions? Can the young child put together a sequence of actions to activate a favorite toy or electronic device? Can the child tell a story in a reasonably correct order? Does the older child still struggle with familiar motor sequences (see Table 5.4)?

Traps and Tips.

- Formal testing of sequential processing should include evaluation across input and output modalities. Look for discontinuities of performance—such as when the child easily manages sequences of meaningful auditory information (such as words) but struggles with nonmeaningful sequences (such as numbers or letters). Another example of useful comparison is between a task requiring oral repetition of a sequence of words and the task of touching pictures in the same order in which the corresponding words were stated.
- Given the tendency of children with Asperger's Syndrome to show motor awkwardness, it is also critical to assess fine and gross motor sequencing. If possible, assess the child's motor output in response to different types of sequential input (e.g., oral directions, written directions, live demonstration).
- Sequential processing works hand in hand with various attentional and memory processes. If a child scores low on sequential processing tasks, take care to assess attention and memory functions for similar types of information to determine whether the information was registered and encoded in the first place.
- For some children with Asperger's Syndrome, sequential processing of auditory verbal information is intact, by virtue of their strong rote verbal

TABLE 5.4

Examples of Tests for Sequential Processing

Test or Subtest	Sequential Processes Assessed	Age Range
WISC–III PI Spatial Span Forward and Backward (Kaplan et al., 1999)	Sequential processing and active working memory for visuospatial sequences	6–16 years
WISC–III Digit Span Forward & Backward (Wechsler, 1991)	Verbal short-term memory for nonmeaningful information; Digits Backward also assesses working memory	6 years–16 years, 11 months
WISC–III PI Letter Span	Auditory short-term memory for nonmeaningful information	6–16 years
K–ABC Hand Movements (Kaufman & Kaufman, 1983)	Visual motor sequencing, motor imitation	2 years, 6 months–12 years, 5 months
NEPSY Manual Motor Sequences (Korkman et al., 1998)	Visual motor sequencing, motor imitation	3–12 years
NEPSY Fingertip Tapping Sequential Tapping Task	Motor sequencing and planning	3–12 years
NEPSY Oromotor Sequences	Sequential production of speech sounds	3–12 years
K–ABC Word Order	Cross-modal sequencing (auditory stimulus/visual motor response)	4 years–12 years, 5 months
WISC–III Picture Arrangement	Visual sequencing of meaningful material (line drawings of social situations)	6 years–12 years, 11 months
WISC–III PI Sentence Arrangement	Sequencing of visual representations of words	8–16 years

Note. WISC–III = Wechsler Intelligence Scale for Children–III; K–ABC = Kaufman Assessment Battery for Children; NEPSY = NEPSY Developmental Neuropsychological Assessment

memory. Some children with Asperger's Syndrome, however, fail to appreciate sequences beyond the level of simple repetition. For example, an upper elementary student might not recognize that the sequence of action in a story carries meaning or that the sequence of a joke conveys much of the humor. These examples emphasize the important of assessing sequential processing beyond the level of mere repetition of sequences.

- When relative strength in sequential processing and a preference for approaching problems in a "logical sequential" manner are identified in the dynamic assessment process, teach the child to use sequential problem-solving processes to circumvent inefficiencies in other cognitive processes.

Doug's Sequential Processing

Doug could recite almost every book and video he had ever seen. He also easily mastered lists of information (days, months, ABCs, numbers to 1,000) by the time he was 5.

Doug was less skilled with motor and visual motor sequences (certainly a contribution to his snowpants struggles). Although he scored high on tests of auditory sequencing, he was baffled by motor sequencing tasks (such as Hand Movements). In the classroom, even as an 11-year-old, he struggled with the motor components of multistep tasks.

Doug's motor and visual motor sequencing improved when his teachers began to write down the steps in a task. Doug committed these to (verbal) memory and mentally "ticked off" each step as he completed it.

Assessment of Language-Based Comprehension and Expression

As noted throughout this chapter, language represents a relative strength for many children with Asperger's Syndrome. Whether a 4-year-old with a passion for blue objects and an encyclopedic memory for state capitals and interstate routes or a 9-year-old who recites sports statistics to anyone who will listen, the child with Asperger's Syndrome usually considers words "friends." These children typically perform well on verbal tests of rote learning and vocabulary and demonstrate developmentally appropriate grammar and syntax. It is not unusual for young children with Asperger's Syndrome to show age-level abilities on standardized speech and language testing, a finding that can sometimes hinder the diagnosis and intervention process.

Speech and language testing and *DSM–IV* (American Psychiatric Association, 2000) criteria aside, the examiner is cautioned against assuming that the language comprehension and expression skills of the individual child are "just fine." Careful history taking and observation often reveal difficulties in pragmatic communication (using and understanding language in social context) and abstract language. Children with Asperger's Syndrome are also likely to misinterpret communication that requires simultaneous consideration of both the verbal and nonverbal elements of the message. Challenges in shifting cognitive set (an executive function) might hinder comprehension of multiple-meaning words, figures of speech, and humor. Thus, any comprehensive evaluation of language-based comprehension and expression should include observation of the child in the real world of classroom, cafeteria, playground, and (if possible) home. In addition, formal testing provides valuable sources of data on language comprehension and expression.

TABLE 5.5

Examples of Tests for Language Comprehension and Expression

Test or Subtest	Language Processes Assessed	Age Range
NEPSY Phonological Processing Part A (Korkman et al., 1998)	Word segmentation, formation of auditory verbal gestalt	3–12 years
NEPSY Phonological Processing Part B	Phonological segmentation and recombination	5–12 years
NEPSY Speeded Naming	Rapid naming of familiar visual stimuli, establishment of verbal patterns	5–12 years
NEPSY Repetition of Nonsense Words	Phonological decoding of nonsense words, encoding and articulation	5–12 years
NEPSY Comprehension of Instructions	Receptive understanding of oral directions (pointing response)	3–12 years
NEPSY Verbal Fluency	Word retrieval within semantic categories (ages 3–12; oral response); word retrieval within phonemic categories (ages 7–12; oral response)	3–12 years
D–KEFS Verbal Fluency (Delis et al., 2001)	Word retrieval within letter or semantic category (oral response)	8 years and up
WPPSI–III Information (Wechsler, 2002)	Retention and retrieval of verbal information (oral response)	2 years, 6 months–7 years, 3 months
WISC–III Information (Wechsler, 1991)	Retention and retrieval of verbal information (oral response)	6–16 years, 11 months
WISC–III PI Information Multiple Choice (Kaplan et al., 1999)	Retention and recognition of verbal information (oral or pointing response)	8–16 years
WPPSI–III Receptive Vocabulary	Comprehension of oral directions, word knowledge, integration of auditory input and visual perception (pointing response)	2 years, 6 months–7 years, 3 months

(continued on next page)

TABLE 5.5 (continued)

Test or Subtest	Language Processes Assessed	Age Range
WISC–III PI Picture Vocabulary	Comprehension of oral directions, word knowledge, integration of auditory input and visual perception (pointing response)	9–16 years
WPPSI–III Picture Naming	Word retrieval, association of visual stimulus with verbal label (oral response)	2 years, 6 months– 7 years, 3 months
WPPSI–III Vocabulary	Word knowledge and verbal concept formation, oral formulation skills	4 years–7 years, 3 months
WISC–III Vocabulary	Word knowledge and verbal concept formation, oral formulation skills	6 years–16 years, 11 months
WISC–III PI Vocabulary Multiple Choice	Recognition of word meaning (oral or pointing response)	9–16 years
WISC–III PI Sentence Arrangement	Recognition and construction of meaning at the sentence level (motor response)	8–16 years

Note. NEPSY = NEPSY Developmental Neuropsychological Assessment; D–KEFS = Delis Kaplan Executive Function System; WPPSI–III = Wechsler Preschool and Primary Scale of Intelligence–3rd edition; WISC–III = Wechsler Intelligence Scale for Children–III

Standardized tests can identify linguistic strengths and weaknesses relative to the child's agemates, illustrate how a child uses language to solve different types of problems, and reveal how the child's language skills help or hinder social interaction (see Table 5.5). (Language-based tests typically administered by psychologists are often supplemented by instruments commonly employed by speech and language pathologists.)

Traps and Tips.

• When a child performs below expectations on a language-based task, investigate contributing factors from other domains. Was the child insufficiently interested or attentive? Was the student able to determine the salience of verbal information, to know what to listen for? Was the child unable to retain questions and relevant information in working memory long enough to formulate a relevant answer? Was the child sidetracked by extraneous information to the extent that a response was incomplete? Was the child unable to shift cognitive sets to provide a second explanation or association on comprehension or multiple meaning tests?

- Assess mastery of complex and abstract language. Can the child interpret what others "mean"? Is the child able to identify the gist of spoken or written communication? Can the older student read a test question and identify what the teacher is asking? Is the child able to provide oral or written responses that fit "the audience"?

- Most children with Asperger's Syndrome thrive on scripts and routines, and we can teach them to use these tools to compensate for other inefficiencies. For example, if the child has trouble identifying relevant and irrelevant information in a math word problem, assess whether a list of key words and the corresponding arithmetic operations is helpful. Throughout the dynamic assessment process, identify the routines, scripts, or tips that facilitate performance.

- Investigate whether story maps, paragraph templates, and concept and cause–effect maps help a child organize language understanding and expression.

- Always remember to compare the child's social language with that of his or her peers. Watch for developmental as well as "neighborhood" variations of "normal."

Doug's Language Comprehension and Expression Skills

Doug's superior scores on the WISC–III Verbal Comprehension Index as a 6-year-old held up when he was retested at age 11. What became even more apparent, however, was Doug's difficulty with the pragmatic language. Most commonly, Doug did not seem to know when he had said enough.

In addition, Doug tended to talk excessively when stressed by a task. In the midst of one visual sequencing subtest, he launched into lengthy descriptions of the characters and favorite passages in the Harry Potter books. Such attempts to regain topic control are reportedly Doug's common response to "performance anxiety." Needless to say, Doug's teachers and classmates find this strategy perplexing and annoying.

Assessment of Higher Order Thinking

Higher order thinking reflects the ability to "put it all together." Processes involved in higher order thinking include concept formation, problem solving, rule development and application, classification, recognition of similarities and differences, creativity, and metacognition (Levine, 1999). Higher order cognition is not only important as the "pinnacle" of complex human thought, but also as a mechanism that frees up other brain functions. For example, if a student has acquired critical concepts about rainforest habitat, he or she can make reasonable predictions about whether a penguin could survive there. A 7-year-old who has learned to use an "inside voice" in his or her school library is likely to infer a similar rule about the public library in town.

If Asperger's Syndrome is truly a disorder of the integration of complex information from multiple sources, we would expect many children with Asperger's Syndrome to be inefficient in higher order thinking. In fact, family members and educators frequently report that the inability to "get it" is one of the most confounding aspects of living with or teaching a child with Asperger's Syndrome. In evaluating the cognitive skills of children with Asperger's Syndrome, then, it is important to assess not only whether they know something, but also how well they use the information or skill in novel or unfamiliar contexts (see Table 5.6).

Traps and Tips.

- Higher order thinking is highly vulnerable to weaknesses in "lower" cognition. For example, inefficient inhibitory processes (attention and executive functions) can lead a child to respond impulsively to a situation rather than considering an alternative solution.
- A child with a strong memory and fund of knowledge might not have developed higher order skills because he or she "knew" the answer without having to figure it out. Be sure to assess higher order skills in sufficiently novel context.
- Higher order thinking, especially in younger children, is quite sensitive to opportunity. Before assuming that a child is not "creative," consider whether the environment reinforced divergent thinking or rote, rule-bound knowledge.
- Particularly with younger children, formal tests of concept formation, classification, and problem solving might actually reflect the child's learned mastery of facts, concepts, and rules. Strong performances on the tasks in the preschool and primary years might or might not hold up under the more abstract demands of upper elementary school and beyond.
- Some of our most useful data emerges from systematic observation of the child. Does the child use basic concepts (appropriate to age) to organize new information? How easily does the preschooler apply prior knowledge to new toys? Is problem solving systematic or "hit or miss"? Has the preschooler begun to use internalized rules (e.g., "walking feet," "criss-cross applesauce" for legs in circle time)? Is the primary grade student beginning to make inferences about unstated rules? If the child does not know how to do something, what strategies does he or she use to find out? Has the child's symbolic play evolved from lining up or arranging toys to multistep scenarios? Does the child's cause–effect reasoning support a developmentally appropriate understanding of events and emotions?

TABLE 5.6

Examples of Tests for Higher Order Thinking

Test or Subtest	Higher Order Processes Assessed	Age Range
K–ABC Riddles (Kaufman & Kaufman, 1983)	Integration of auditory verbal information, conceptual inference, classification (oral response)	3 years–12 years, 5 months
WPPSI–III Word Reasoning (Wechsler, 2002)	Verbal reasoning and concept formation, integration and synthesis of verbal information (oral response)	4 years–7 years, 3 months
D–KEFS Word Context (Delis et al., 2001)	Deductive reasoning, integration of multiple bits of verbal information (oral response)	8 years and up
WPPSI–III Picture Concepts	Abstract, categorical reasoning (pointing response)	4 years–7 years, 3 months
WPPSI–III Matrix Reasoning	Visual pattern completion, classification, analogical reasoning, serial reasoning (pointing response)	4 years–7 years, 3 months
D–KEFS Sorting	Rule generation and recognition, initiation of problem solving (motor response)	8 years and up
D–KEFS Twenty Questions	Abstract verbal reasoning, verbal formulation	8 years and up
WPPSI–III Similarities	Verbal reasoning and concept formation, associative thinking, oral formulation skills	4 years–7 years, 3 months
WISC–III Similarities (Wechsler, 1991)	Verbal reasoning and concept formation, associative thinking, oral formulation skills	6 years–16 years, 11 months
WPPSI–III Comprehension	Verbal reasoning and conceptualization, application of knowledge and experience, oral formulation skills	4 years–7 years, 3 months
WISC–III Comprehension	Application of social knowledge and judgment, oral formulation skills	6 years–16 years, 11 months
Boehm Test of Basic Concepts (Revised and Preschool; Boehm, 1986a, 1986b)	Knowledge of concepts of time, quantity, space	Preschool–8 years

Note. K–ABC = Kaufman Assessment Battery for Children; WPPSI–III = Wechsler Preschool and Primary Scale of Intelligence–3rd edition; D–KEFS = Delis Kaplan Executive Function System; WISC–III = Wechsler Intelligence Scale for Children–III

- For many children with Asperger's Syndrome, these higher-order skills are markedly less developed than their fund of knowledge or academic abilities. For some, higher order thinking improves when inefficiencies in self-regulation and other cognitive processes are addressed successfully. For others, the leap to abstract thinking is made only with substantial assistance from parents and teachers.
- Do not neglect what might be the greatest challenge for children with Asperger's Syndrome—that of the "hidden curriculum." This term refers to a mind-boggling higher order task that permits the successful student to "just know." How do you please a teacher or parent? How "neat" is "neat"? When can you run in the halls? What is the teacher likely to put on the test? Although there are no norms for mastery of the hidden curriculum, anyone who spends time in school can identify the students who "know." It is rare for the child with Asperger's Syndrome to be in that group. Observe children to determine what aspects of the hidden curriculum still elude them and then to specify which of these "rules" should be taught directly and concretely.

Doug's Higher Order Thinking

As a precocious reader, Doug learned in preschool that he could find virtually any answer in a book (or later, on the Internet). He developed classification skills because he was fascinated with the "Outlines of Knowledge" in the encyclopedia. He became skilled in analogous thinking because his parents enjoyed playing "thinking games" at dinner.

Doug could quote the rules for virtually any situation in preschool and elementary school, but he did not seem to be able to recognize unwritten rules or expand previously learned rules for novel situations (especially in math or cooperative learning activities). Whether in play, creative writing, or brainstorming, Doug's thinking remained rigid and unimaginative. Over time, his inflexibility interfered with his capacity to take another person's point of view and to understand behavior and emotions.

INTEGRATION OF COMPLEX INFORMATION
FROM MULTIPLE SOURCES

The value of any assessment ultimately rests upon its usefulness for the child, family, and team. Typically, this is determined largely by the examiner's ability to integrate the complex information derived from a multitude of sources and to answer the referral questions. The evaluation report needs to tell the story of the child and to answer the questions posed at the beginning of this chapter:

- What neurodevelopmental characteristics support or impede the child's ability to learn and to demonstrate that knowledge on demand?
- What contextual factors (or "load") contribute to or interfere with the child's cognitive functioning?

Excerpts From Doug's Reports

At age 6—Doug exhibits superior intellectual abilities in several domains, notably verbal comprehension and well-circumscribed visual perceptual skills ... He has a remarkable memory for detail and a strong capacity to attend to topics that intrigue him. He is less efficient in deploying attention on demand and in understanding and recalling the gestalt or gist of a situation ... Despite his strengths in intellectual domains, Doug struggles with more abstract problem solving, especially that required for social/emotional functioning. His interactions have been aided greatly by his parents' ability to pre-teach social scripts. He also benefits from the interest that adults and older children show in his fund of information. However, Doug's ability to respond flexibly is taxed in interactions with agemates who continue to stymie him with their spontaneity.

At age 11—When faced with most visual perceptual challenges, Doug is bright enough that he arrives at a solution eventually. However, both his accuracy and his efficiency of problem solving are less than would be expected for a child with his overall intellectual ability ... It is essential to remember that Doug's inefficiency in visual perceptual organization and reasoning becomes even more pronounced when the nonverbal dilemma takes on a social/emotional cast ... Doug's most significant cognitive challenge lies in his inefficiency in determining what a task is and is not. He is constrained in his ability to deploy attention and effort to the most salient elements of a task and is at risk for being distracted by less relevant information ... He has trouble moving flexibly between problem solving strategies ... He is most successful when relevant information is explicitly defined at the outset and when the requirements of the finished product are clear-cut.

Labor-intensive integration of information typically leads fluidly to recommendations for modifications and interventions for home and school. Most important, the dynamic, process-based approach allows us to recognize, celebrate, and utilize the strengths of the individual child.

REFERENCES

Achenbach, T. M. (2000). *Achenbach System of Empirically Based Assessment (ASEBA)*. Burlington, VT: Research Center for Children, Youth, & Families.

American Psychiatric Association. (2000). *Diagnostic and statistical manual of mental disorders* (4th ed.). Washington, DC: Author.

Asperger, H. (1991). Autistic psychopathy in childhood. In U. Frith (Ed. & Trans.), *Autism and Asperger Syndrome* (pp. 37–92). Cambridge, England: Cambridge University Press. (Original work published 1944)

Beery, K. E., & Buktenica, N. A. (1997). *Beery Buktenica Developmental Test of Visual Motor Integration*. Parsippany, NJ: Modern Curriculum Press.

Bender, L. A. (1956). *Psychopathology of children with organic brain disorders*. Springfield, IL: Thomas.

Bernstein, J. H., & Waber, D. P. (1996). *Developmental scoring system for the Rey–Osterrieth Complex Figure (ROCF)*. Odessa, FL: Psychological Assessment Resources.

Boehm, A. E. (1986a). *Boehm Test of Basic Concepts—Preschool version*. San Antonio, TX: Psychological Corporation.

Boehm, A. E. (1986b). *Boehm Test of Basic Concepts—Revised*. San Antonio, TX: Psychological Corporation.

Colarusso, R. P., & Hammill, D. D. (1996). *Motor-Free Visual Perceptual Test–Revised*. Novato, CA: Academic Therapy.

Conners, C. K. (1997). *Conners' Rating Scales–Revised (CRS–R)*. North Tonawanda, NY: Multi-Health Systems.

Conners, C. K., & Multi-Health Systems Staff. (2000). *Conners' Continuous Performance Test II (CPT II)*. North Tonawanda, NY: Multi-Health Systems.

Delis, D., Kaplan, E., & Kramer, J. H. (2001). *Delis–Kaplan Executive Function System*. San Antonio, TX: Psychological Corporation.

Frostig, M. (1964). *Developmental Test of Visual Perception*. Palo Alto, CA: Consulting Psychologists Press.

Frostig, M., & Maslow, P. (1973). *Learning problems in the classroom*. New York: Grune & Stratton.

Gardner, M. F. (1996). *Test of Visual-Perceptual Skills–Revised*. Burlingame, CA: Psychological and Educational Publications.

Gioia, G. A., Isquith, P. K., Guy, S. C., & Kenworthy, L. (2000). *BRIEF: Behavior Rating Inventory of Executive Function*. Odessa, FL: Psychological Assessment Resources.

Kaplan, E., Fein, D., Kramer, J., Delis, D., & Morris, R. (1999). *WISC–III as a Process Instrument (WISC–III PI)*. San Antonio, TX: Psychological Corporation.

Kaufman, A. S., & Kaufman, N. L. (1983). *Kaufman Assessment Battery for Children (K–ABC)*. Circle Pines, MN: American Guidance Services.

Korkman, M., Kirk, U., & Kemp, S. (1998). *NEPSY: A developmental neuropsychological assessment*. San Antonio, TX: Psychological Corporation.

Levine, M. (1999). *Developmental variation and learning disorders* (2nd ed.). Cambridge, MA: Educators Publishing Service.

Levine, M. (2002). *A mind at a time*. New York: Simon & Schuster.

Levine, M., Reed, M., & Hobgood, A. (2000). *A table of neurodevelopmental constructs*. Cambridge, MA: Educators Publishing Service.

Meyers, J. E., & Meyers, K. R. (1995). *Rey Complex Figure Test and Recognition Trial*. Odessa, FL: Psychological Assessment Resources.

Reynolds, C. R., & Kamphaus, R. W. (2002). *BASC: Behavior Assessment System for Children*. Circle Pines, MN: American Guidance Service.

Rourke, B. R. (1995). Introduction: The NLD syndrome and the white matter model. In B. R. Rourke (Ed.), *Syndrome of nonverbal learning disabilities: Neurodevelopmental manifestations* (pp. 1–26). New York: Guilford.

Sheslow, D., & Adams, W. (1990). *Wide Range Assessment of Memory and Learning (WRAML)*. Wilmington, DE: Wide Range.

Webster's New Twentieth Century Dictionary (2nd ed.). (1983). Nashville, TN: Word Publishing.

Wechsler, D. (1991). *Wechsler Intelligence Scale for Children–Third Edition (WISC–III)*. San Antonio, TX: Psychological Corporation.

Wechsler, D. (2002). *Wechsler Preschool and Primary Scale of Intelligence–Third Edition (WPPSI–III)*. San Antonio, TX: Psychological Corporation.

Chapter 6

Supporting Elementary School Students

Teresa Bolick
Nashua, New Hampshire, and Westford, Massachusetts

Elementary school children with Asperger's Syndrome possess remarkable strengths and challenges that can confound parents, teachers, and other professionals. Intervention planning can be equally confounding, since it is anything but a "one-size-fits-all" proposition.

Yet intervention can make a huge difference—in the child's growing social awareness and skill, in the capacity to regulate emotions and behavior, and in the demonstration of knowledge and skill on demand. Perhaps most important, intervention during the elementary school years may be our best insurance against anxiety, depression, and low self-esteem in adolescence and adulthood.

CHALLENGES FOR THE CHILD WITH ASPERGER'S SYNDROME

Asperger's Syndrome has been defined largely in terms of social and communicative challenges, but children with Asperger's Syndrome struggle with other aspects of development as well. In the sections that follow, we explore how "glitches" in particular developmental domains signal the need for intervention.

Self-Regulation and "The Four As"

All of us strive to develop self-regulatory strategies to help us settle down or perk up, to control our attention and our behavior, and to modulate and/or disguise our emotions. Children with Asperger's Syndrome are no different from the rest of us in using self-regulatory strategies. They get in trouble, though, because their strategies are often inefficient, socially inappropriate, or both.

Challenges in self-regulation are among the earliest concerns identified for many children with Asperger's Syndrome. Intervention is warranted when the child's inefficiencies go beyond those of other children at a similar developmental level or when the inefficiencies interfere with development in other domains. Examples of self-regulatory challenges that warrant the need for intervention include:

- Disturbances of sleep and eating that interfere with daily functioning.
- Excessive difficulty in settling down after becoming upset or excited.
- Under- or overreactivity to sensory input.
- Inefficiencies in deploying attention (in comparison to peers).
- Inability to inhibit (or stop) behavior (again, in comparison to agemates).
- Intense reactions to change.
- All-encompassing preoccupation with specific objects or topics.
- Repetitive behavior or rigid adherence to routines.
- Emotional outbursts ("meltdowns" or "tantrums") that exceed developmental norms for frequency, intensity, or duration.
- Persistent expressions of anxiety, sadness, or self-deprecation.
- Behavior that injures the child or others.

Social Competence

Just as self-regulation is a lifelong endeavor, so is the acquisition of social competence. All of us know the young child who says "the darnedest things." Children with Asperger's Syndrome persist in saying "the darnedest things," though, long after their agemates have learned the "rules of the social road." Intervention for poorly developed social competence is warranted when the child shows significant differences from developmental expectations, such as:

- Frequent misunderstandings of the social communication of others.
- Lack of empathy or perspective taking.
- Limited ability to engage in reciprocal interaction.
- Poorly developed play skills.
- Violations of developmental norms for manners or personal space.
- Frequent conflicts with others, especially peers and siblings.
- Being the target of teasing or harassment.
- Bullying or threatening behavior.

- Naiveté regarding age-appropriate social norms.

Cognitive and Academic Development

By definition, students with Asperger's Syndrome demonstrate "no clinically significant delay in cognitive development" (American Psychiatric Association, 2000, p. 84). In other words, the child with Asperger's Syndrome is thought to have overall intellectual ability within the low average range or above.

Despite this expectation of adequate cognitive ability, students with Asperger's Syndrome actually demonstrate a broad range of cognitive skills. Some present strong (if not precocious) verbal skills that far outstrip their visuospatial (nonverbal) abilities. (Asperger's Syndrome has been compared to nonverbal learning disability or NLD, but this association has not yet been confirmed by extensive research.) Some students with Asperger's Syndrome read long before they enter first grade; others have difficulties with the acquisition of sound–symbol association. Some exhibit significant strengths in mathematics and sciences, whereas others show marked difficulties in math calculation and application. Intervention is warranted for:

- Specific cognitive or academic weaknesses (such as difficulties in working memory, reading comprehension, or math computation).
- Difficulties in abstract reasoning or other forms of higher order thinking (relative to classmates).
- Inefficiency in demonstrating knowledge on demand (orally or in writing).
- Problems in organization, sequencing, or "materials management" (again, relative to classmates).
- Missed deadlines, lost assignments, and other lapses in "follow through."

In early elementary school, it is not unusual for teachers and parents to dismiss the student's challenges with abstraction and organization as a function of age (e.g., "Most second graders have trouble with that"). Early intervention is important, however, because it is unlikely that these skills will evolve naturally for the child with Asperger's Syndrome. In addition, early intervention allows the child to acquire "templates" for problem solving before the productivity demands explode in the adolescent years.

Closing Thoughts About Asperger's Syndrome and the Need for Intervention

Because Asperger's Syndrome is a disorder that interferes with the integration of complex information from multiple sources, intervention is never simple. Additionally, the "match" between the child's neurodevelopmental profile and life's demands will change over time. Self-management, social, and academic skills that are adequate for the primary grades might be insufficient for upper elementary school and preadolescence. As such, interventions should be adjusted not just for the child's "profile" but also for the demands that he or she faces at a given point in time.

To be effective, intervention for elementary school students with Asperger's Syndrome must be comprehensive; integrated across home, school, and community; developmentally appropriate; and flexible. In the remainder of this chapter, I describe some of the interventions that have been helpful for elementary school students with Asperger's Syndrome. The reader is cautioned, however, that any intervention is only as effective as its match with the individual child and its integration with other aspects of the child's program.

HISTORY OF INTERVENTIONS

The very factors that have made definition and diagnosis of Asperger's Syndrome so perplexing have also limited our investigation of the effectiveness of interventions. Fortunately, though, we are able to apply many of the intervention approaches that have been successful for children with related difficulties. We have also learned to build skills that are likely to reduce the negative impact of the child's neurodevelopmental makeup. The following sections describe specific interventions that build regulatory, social, and cognitive skills and limit (or sometimes eliminate) the "downsides" of Asperger's Syndrome. In the interest of clarity, these interventions are divided loosely into the categories of neurodevelopmental, behavioral, developmental and social pragmatic, and educational strategies. The reader is cautioned to remember, however, that there is no such thing as a "pure" intervention for Asperger's Syndrome, just as there is no such thing as a "prototypic" child with Asperger's Syndrome.

INTERVENTIONS FOR ELEMENTARY STUDENTS WITH ASPERGER'S SYNDROME

Neurodevelopmental Interventions

Most neurodevelopmental interventions are designed to address the child's sensory and regulatory challenges. They rest upon the assumption that no one is available for learning or social interaction when besieged by overwhelming input from the external environment or from within oneself.

Sensory integration (SI) refers to the processes that the nervous system uses to perceive, interpret, connect, and organize incoming sensations. Many professionals and parents have come to believe that differences in sensory processing are common in individuals with Asperger's Syndrome and that SI interventions might facilitate the student's "availability" for learning, but well-designed research on effectiveness remains sparse. Additional information regarding SI theory and practice can be found in chapter 10, "Sensory Integration" and in *Sensory Integration and the Child* (Ayres, 1979).

The *Alert Program* ("How Does Your Engine Run?"; Williams & Shellenberger, 1996) combines knowledge about self-regulation and sensory integration with cognitive behavioral strategies. It is based on the assumption that children with neurodevelopmental challenges often employ self-regulatory techniques that are ineffective, situationally inappropriate, or both. The program teaches children to identify their own levels of arousal or alertness in terms of engines that are running too high, too low, or just right. Initially, adults provide cues regarding engine states and potential remedies for too high or too low. Over time, however, many children independently identify their level of arousal or alertness and choose adaptive remedies. Although designed for children over 8 (and with adequate language and cognitive abilities), elements of the program have been used with children as young as 5. As with SI techniques in general, the Alert Program has not yet been tested and replicated in controlled scientific research. From a clinical perspective, however, its child-friendly descriptions of behavior and internal states and its concrete and adaptive strategies have been useful for many children. Like SI interventions, the Alert Program should not be implemented without the consultation of a professional trained in its use.

Relaxation techniques (including breathing, muscle relaxation, and imagery) have been used with children and adults for many years. Although these techniques have not been evaluated specifically for children with Asperger's Syndrome, their effectiveness in managing anxiety, reducing stress levels, improving immune system functioning, and promoting an overall sense of well-being for people in general is well recognized. They can be used to reduce the high levels of arousal or affect experienced by many children with Asperger's Syndrome. Older children might find deep breathing, muscle relaxation, or imagery helpful in preventing performance anxiety. Relaxation techniques are also important components of the exposure and response prevention techniques used for obsessions and compulsions (March & Mulle, 1998). Relaxation techniques are essential to behavioral and cognitive-behavioral interventions such as systematic desensitization, prolonged exposure, habit reversal, and modeling (Schroeder & Gordon, 2002). An excellent (but dated) manual for teaching relaxation techniques to children was written by Cautela and Groden (1978). Young children also enjoy the story and imagery of *A Boy and a Bear* (Lite, 1996). One caution: Some older children with Asperger's Syndrome resist relaxation techniques because they consider them "dumb" or "babyish." The more "scientific" of these children might be swayed by research on relaxation strategies, immune system functioning, and academic performance (see the work of Herbert Benson and The Mind Body Medical Institute at www.mbmi.org).

From a less clinical perspective, do not overlook the potential that *physical exertion and the arts* offer as "neurodevelopmental" interventions. Martial arts, swimming, singing in a chorus, and blowing a woodwind or brass instrument require controlled breathing and muscular control and, as such, often serve as efficient and adaptive regulatory strategies. (They also avoid many of the motor planning pitfalls embedded in ball sports.) These interventions also introduce children to activities that might serve as hobbies and/or coping strategies. Moreover, they tend to introduce children to peers who share similar "kinds of minds." Involvement in sports or the arts in the elementary grades can then serve as a "springboard" for social connections in adolescence and adulthood.

In summary, neurodevelopmental interventions are most likely to be used in conjunction with other treatment strategies. They should not be overlooked, however, as they often facilitate the child's readiness for other interventions. As components of the self-regulatory repertoire, these interventions also tend to give children, parents, and professionals the confidence that there is *something* they can *do* when life feels overwhelming. This advantage alone justifies inclusion of neurodevelopmental interventions in the overall treatment package.

Behavioral Interventions

Behavioral supports for students with Asperger's Syndrome run the gamut from the general to the specific, with goals of building adaptive responses and/or eliminating problematic behaviors. Choice of behavioral techniques depends, of course, on the unique strengths and challenges of the child. Across students, though, two components of behavioral intervention appear necessary for virtually any "best practices" program—the use of functional analysis of behavior and the creation of positive behavioral support plans.

Functional analysis of behavior is an ongoing process that involves:

1. Definition and identification of observable target behaviors, including their frequency, intensity, course, and duration.
2. Identification of setting events, antecedents, and consequences of the target behaviors.
3. Formation of a hypothesis about the function or purpose of the behavior.
4. Consideration of adaptive alternatives (or replacement behaviors) already within the child's behavioral repertoire.
5. Development of a plan that includes modifications and accommodations (to reduce the impact of setting events) and direct teaching and reinforcement of adaptive behavior.
6. Evaluation of treatment effects and "fine tuning" of the program (Powers, 1997).

There is a wealth of clinical research regarding functional analysis for children with autism. The use of functional analysis of behavior for children with Asperger's Syndrome is less extensively documented, but certainly offers great promise. From a practical standpoint, functional analysis of behavior is essential to intervention with children with Asperger's Syndrome in two interrelated ways: in identifying skills that are not yet developed and in understanding the reasons for less adaptive behavioral responses. The case of Melanie might be a useful example.

> Melanie, a fifth-grader with Asperger's Syndrome, repeatedly responded to her teachers' assistance by "snapping" at them ("Leave me alone." "Can't you see that you're disturbing me?") Her teachers and parents were torn between acceding to Melanie's rebuffs and "forcing" academic assistance on her. Functional analysis revealed that Melanie was most likely to "snap" during classes in which several "high-status" peers were known to roll their eyes or snicker when other students answered incorrectly. Her teachers and parents also noticed that she was more prone to snapping when she had stayed up late the previous night. Even these setting events were unlikely to lead to snapping unless certain antecedents occurred: the classwork included math calculation, multiple-choice responding, or extensive handwriting; the teacher or paraprofessional approached Melanie from behind; or the adult touched Melanie. Common consequences of the snapping were the retreat of the adult and Melanie's completion of the assignment at home.
>
> The team determined that the function of Melanie's snapping was at least twofold: to remove the aversive experience of feeling incompetent and to have the chance to do the work in the less overwhelming environment of home. Although Melanie did possess the adaptive alternative of saying, "No, thank you," politely when help was offered, she seldom had access to this response under conditions of high "load."

The functional analysis of behavior leads logically to the development of a *positive behavioral support plan*. Positive behavioral supports (PBS) have been used with individuals who struggle with a variety of developmental challenges (e.g., Carr et al., 2002; Dunlap & Fox, 1999; Florida Department of Education, 1999; National Research Council, 2001). Positive behavioral support plans consider not only the skills to be taught, but also the modifications of the physical and interpersonal environment necessary to support adaptive skills and quality of life. Positive behavioral supports for students with Asperger's Syndrome have not been evaluated extensively in controlled research studies. However, the data on their effectiveness with other populations are compelling enough to warrant inclusion of PBS in the Asperger's Syndrome intervention toolkit. Melanie's positive behavioral support plan included recommendations such as these:

> *Modifications and Accommodations*
>
> - At the beginning of next school year, Melanie's class will complete *The Mind That's Mine* program developed by the All Kinds of Minds Institute.

- Staff members will refrain from approaching Melanie from the back and from touching her without warning or permission.
- The team and other critical school personnel will be cautioned not to interpret snapping as an indication of disrespect. Any such behavior will be handled by Melanie's case manager and not through typical school disciplinary policy.
- Melanie will be given a choice of completing assignments in a quiet place outside of the classroom.
- Melanie's fatigue will be addressed by setting an upper limit on homework each night. If Melanie's parents will sign off on "good faith efforts," the assignment will be considered complete.

Direct Teaching

- Melanie will be taught to shake her head discreetly if she does not want assistance at a given time. She will place a yellow card on her desk to signal that she does want help.
- Melanie will be taught at least three "polite refusals" to use when she does not want or need help (e.g., "No, thank you," or "I'm fine right now, thanks").
- Appropriate use of these adaptive behaviors will be recorded on daily point sheet, with a "trade-in" of points at the end of each week.

Discrete trial teaching is a highly structured subset of applied behavioral analysis that has been used extensively with young children with autism. It is especially effective in teaching the foundations of learning (such as attending, imitation, matching, sorting) as well as early academic skills (McEachin, Smith, & Lovaas, 1993; Smith, Eikeseth, Klevstrand, & Lovaas, 1997). This method breaks skills into small "chunks," teaches and reinforces one chunk at a time until it is mastered, teaches the child to combine the chunks into sequences of skill or action, fades out the prompts for the skills, and then assists in the generalization of the skills across environments. Initial stages of teaching occur within carefully controlled settings to ensure that the child learns to discriminate the most salient elements of the discriminative stimulus, the response, and the resulting feedback. For children with Asperger's Syndrome, discrete trial teaching can be especially helpful for skills that have not been acquired in more "naturalistic" learning contexts. *A Work in Progress* (Leaf & McEachin, 1999) provides a comprehensive and systematic guide to discrete trials teaching, with many programs that are useful for elementary school students with Asperger's Syndrome.

As mentioned, behavioral interventions for children with Asperger's Syndrome may also include interventions that are known to reduce the frequency of problematic behavior in other groups of children. For example, a child with Asperger's Syndrome and repetitive thoughts and behaviors might benefit from the *exposure and response prevention* (E/RP) model of cognitive-behavioral therapy for obsessive–compulsive behavior. Within E/RP, a child works with his or her parents and therapists to identify target behaviors and to create a hierarchy of situations that elicit the problematic thoughts or actions. The child is then purposefully "exposed" to the situations, beginning with the least threatening situation. During the exposure, the child prevents himself or herself from engaging in the target behavior and learns to tolerate the resulting anxiety. Individualized reinforcement is used to increase the likelihood of the child's participation. In addition, most children find immense intrinsic reinforcement in the realization that they have "power" over their emotions and behavior. For some children, anxiety management techniques such as relaxation training and imagery are combined with standard E/RP to facilitate the child's tolerance for the anxiety associated with blocking the usual responses. A detailed protocol for E/RP can be found in March and Mulle (1998).

Other behavioral strategies that might be helpful in reducing the frequency of interfering behaviors in children with Asperger's Syndrome include *systematic desensitization* (in which relaxation training is combined with gradual exposure to feared objects or situations), *habit reversal* (in which the child is reinforced for performing a behavior that is incompatible with the problematic response), and *contingency management* (in which antecedents and consequences of the behavior are carefully assessed and controlled to ensure reinforcement of adaptive responses). For children with Asperger's Syndrome who have a strong need for "completion," *backward chaining* is a behavioral strategy that teaches the last step in a multistep sequence first and then works backwards until the sequence is mastered. Whether in activities of daily living (ADLs) or in the arts-and-crafts tasks common to the primary grades, backward chaining can avoid many tears.

Experienced clinicians and educators have undoubtedly used a whole host of additional behavioral strategies for students with Asperger's Syndrome. Teams are encouraged to consider the full range of these tools. Only one caveat remains: Always start with a sound assessment of the behavior's function and with a clear understanding of the supports necessary for optimal functioning.

Developmental/Social Pragmatic Interventions

Developmental/social pragmatic interventions include a variety of techniques that target the communicative, social, and emotional development of the child. These interventions emerged from several sources: the play therapy tradition, developmentally appropriate practice in preschools and kindergartens, and social-pragmatic language therapy. Most developmental/social pragmatic approaches share a number of common elements, including a focus on relationships, communication, "teachable moments," and naturalistic reinforcement. Developmental/social pragmatic approaches also posit that children learn best in contexts that are natural, meaningful, and fun.

An Example of Developmental/Social Pragmatic Intervention

For several sessions, Joe played "Arthur and DW" (from the TV show) with his psychologist and dictated what both characters should do and say. Finally, Arthur (the psychologist) protested. DW (Joe) responded by hitting Arthur. A firm believer in rules, Joe spontaneously took DW to a "time-out corner." After a moment in time out, DW promised not to hit again and emerged from the corner. Of course, DW hit again and the time-out sequence was repeated. Arthur (the psychologist) then wondered aloud, "I can't figure out why DW keeps hitting me." DW (Joe) replied, "The rule is 'no hitting.' If I hit, I have to go to time out."

For weeks, Joe (DW) was unable to explain why the hitting continued. After many more time outs, Joe began to make sense of the event–emotion connections. "You won't do it my way!" DW told Arthur. Arthur replied that he got mad when DW always told him what to say. DW then said, "But you don't do it right." Arthur then explained that friends allow each other to talk for themselves.

DW (Joe) began to experiment with new "scripts"—"What do you want to play, Arthur?" "Arthur, do you want to go first or do you want me to go first?" Joe was acquiring new skills for flexible interaction and learning to consider the "mental state" of his play partner!

Floor time and the DIR model refer to a developmental/social pragmatic intervention strategy that evolved from the play therapy traditions of the 1950s (e.g., Axline, 1969; Moustakas, 1959) and subsequent advances in child-directed psychotherapy. Within this model, all learning is assumed to reflect the child's capacities for regulation and shared (joint) attention, warm engagement with caretakers, intentional two-way (reciprocal) communication ("circles of communication"), interactive problem solving (at the nonverbal as well as verbal level), functional use of ideas (including words and gestures), and making connections between ideas (Greenspan & Wieder, 2000; Interdisciplinary Council on Learning Disorders, 2001). Disruption of any of these abilities is thought to result in impaired learning and social competence. (This model would suggest that Joe's continued hitting reflected the disruption of interactive problem solving, functional use of ideas, and making connections between events and ideas or emotions.) Originally designed as a largely child-directed intervention, floor time now includes the child-directed spontaneous interaction; a semistructured component in which the adult creates opportunities for learning by presenting materials that the child enjoys; and a series of physical activities to address gross motor and perceptual motor functioning as well as spatial processing.

Although research support for the effectiveness of floor time remains limited, there is little doubt from a clinician's perspective that floor time techniques lend themselves well to the expansion of social and emotional skills. For children with Asperger's Syndrome, floor time can be particularly helpful in freeing the child from rule-bound, "black-and-white" thinking and in improving the capacity to take another person's perspective. Clinicians often find that floor time techniques, used in the office and at home, teach the child many of the symbolic play skills that are employed so readily by peers. In other words, a clear advantage of floor time is that it teaches a child to play!

Within the school setting, the "philosophy" of floor time is compatible with speech and language and occupational therapies, counseling sessions, and adult facilitation during "choice" or "center" time. Even when the classroom environment does not support play per se, a focus on joint attention, reciprocity, and making connections between ideas, feelings, and events can be incorporated into the day. For example, instead of sitting silently as the child with Asperger's Syndrome eats his or her snack and his or her tablemates chat about weekend activities, the teacher can comment to the child with Asperger's Syndrome, "Janet and Joe went to *Harry Potter* over the weekend. I wonder what they thought of it." This cues the child with Asperger's Syndrome to establish joint attention with his or her classmates and, perhaps, to engage with them in reciprocal interaction. With floor time and other developmental/social pragmatic approaches, the essential task of the adult is to encourage joint attention, reciprocal interaction, and (eventually) the building of connections between and among events, thoughts and ideas, and emotions.

The most recent version of intervention pioneered by Barry Prizant and Amy Wetherby, *SCERTS* (Social/Communication, Emotional Regulation and Transactional Support) combines the principles of floor time with naturalistic applications of contemporary applied behavioral analysis and positive behavioral supports (Prizant, 1983; Prizant, Wetherby, & Rydell, 2000). This model emphasizes the importance of initiation, spontaneity, and modeling for the development of social communication. Although this approach has not been evaluated for children with Asperger's Syndrome, its integration of developmental, social pragmatic, and behavioral interventions actually mirrors many of the real-world interventions that are utilized within a best practices model.

Peer-mediated social interaction refers to interventions in which an adult facilitates interactions between the child with Asperger's Syndrome and typically developing peers by supporting the children's efforts to maintain (and repair) interaction, and then fading out adult assistance (e.g., McTarnaghan, 1998; Strain & Kohler, 1998; Wolfberg, 1999). Peer mediation often includes giving peers an understanding of the challenges of their classmate. ("The Sixth Sense II" by Gray [2002] is a useful class lesson.) Many parents and professionals have found that simple tips such as "She's still listening even if she isn't looking at you" or "He really likes dinosaurs, but he'll talk about something else if you just tell him you want to change the subject" go a long way in terms of encouraging typically developing peers to press on in their interactional efforts. Many school teams have also found that the "Circle of Friends" strategy not only encourages interactions at school but also extends them into the community.

An Example of "Circle of Friends"

Ken was a fourth-grader who regularly astounded his teachers and class-mates with his factual knowledge. Despite his strengths, Ken was never in-vited for play dates. Classmates thought Ken was trying to prove that he was smarter than everyone else. They viewed his frequent conversations with adults as evidence that he did not like other kids.

After securing permission from all of the involved parents, Ken's speech and language pathologist and school counselor talked with a small group of fourth-graders about Asperger's Syndrome. The children agreed that they would like to help Ken learn to be "cool." In weekly meetings, the group (in-cluding Ken) talked about their plans. The first plan was to revamp Ken's wardrobe (get some cool T-shirts, exchange the sweatpants for warmup pants). Finding success in the dress department, the group agreed that they would signal Ken when he got going on a monologue.

As the group's efforts continued, all of the children became more adept in their social communication. They began to get together on the weekends for movies or bowling—with Ken included.

A frequent and valid criticism of the developmental/social pragmatic interven-tions is that their effectiveness has not been assessed thoroughly via well-designed scientific research. Although there are a few outcome studies (e.g., Delprato, 2001; Greenspan & Wieder, 1997; Rogers & DiLalla, 1991), the bulk of evidence rests upon anecdote and case report. As with sensory integration strategies, though, the attraction of these interventions for many parents and professionals is that they feel "right" and that the children have fun. And, as Greenspan has frequently noted, few of us learn well unless we are "affectively engaged" in our endeavors.

Educational Strategies

As reported earlier, it is apparent that there is no such thing as a "typical" intellec-tual profile for children with Asperger's Syndrome. Many parents and educators have found the All Kinds of Minds model to be quite helpful in understanding the unique strengths and challenges of children. Levine and his colleagues created a user-friendly framework of neurodevelopmental functions that allows a team to develop interventions that address specific learning challenges at a given point in time (and/or to develop enrichment opportunities for areas of "giftedness"; Levine, 1999, 2002; Levine, Reed, & Hobgood, 2000).

Although not yet "proven" in the epidemiological research, many clinicians and educators have also observed that elementary students with Asperger's Syndrome tend to have difficulty in "showing what they know." Several strategies appear to be helpful in helping the elementary student with Asperger's Syndrome show knowledge and skill on demand.

1. Identify the purpose of the activity for *this* student (e.g., is the purpose to demonstrate understanding of the plot and characters of the story, to write grammatical sentences, or to write neatly?). Then "offload" any elements of the task that are not essential to the purpose.
2. Once identified, label the purpose of the activity for the student (e.g., "I just want you to jot down your ideas about the characters. Don't worry about complete sentences or handwriting").
3. Use "frames" for the student's visual and auditory attention. For example, use an overhead projector to emphasize where to look during a math lesson. Similarly, you can announce, "We're going to watch a video about bats. Listen carefully to find out what makes a bat a mammal and not a bird").
4. Teach "zoom in–zoom out" (Bernstein, 1995) strategies to ensure that the student processes information at the appropriate level of detail. After demonstrating with a camera lens, help students decide which tasks require "zooming in" (such as editing) versus "zooming out" (such as brainstorming).
5. Use graphic organizers and other visual supports to help the student understand what a lesson is "about." Ideally, these should be introduced at the beginning of a lesson or unit to ensure that the student encodes the information in a usable framework.
6. Whenever possible, assess prior knowledge at the beginning of a unit or lesson. Many students with Asperger's Syndrome have a great deal of information, but few organizing concepts or principles. Be sure to correct misconceptions!
7. Provide guided reading questions for stories and nonfiction passages. Teach the student how to use text conventions to ease his or her search for specific information.
8. Do not require the student to copy off the board or to copy questions before answering them. The student with Asperger's Syndrome is likely to expend so much effort in copying that he or she loses sight of the critical information.
9. Expand the space allotted on math worksheets. If possible, copy computation problems onto graph paper. This is especially helpful for the student with visual spatial or graphomotor challenges.
10. When the student has difficulty demonstrating knowledge in writing, have a student–teacher conference. Take notes as the student talks (bulleted notes

are particularly helpful). Then, using the notes as a visual support, debrief about what the student said. Correct any misconceptions or omissions.

Elementary school teams will find additional intervention "gems" in the work of Myles and Simpson (1998), Tanguay (2002), and Thompson (1997).

Educational strategies at the elementary school level should not be focused solely on academic competence, as many students with Asperger's Syndrome find their greatest challenges in the social milieu of the classroom, hallway, playground, and cafeteria. These students not only need the social experience afforded by behavioral and developmental/social pragmatic interventions; they also need instruction in the "what" and "how" of social interaction.

Perhaps the best known strategy for increasing social knowledge is the *social story* (e.g., Gray, 2000). Social stories can alleviate anxiety associated with upcoming events, teach the perspective of others, and (often) ward off the interfering behaviors that occur when a student does not know what to do. Although often written about situations that are novel and potentially problematic for a child, social stories can also be used quite effectively to highlight what a student did well in a given circumstance.

A SOCIAL STORY about TALKING in THIRD GRADE

I like third grade. We learn cool things. We read good stories. At morning meeting, we get to talk about things we like. Everyone tries to be quiet in third grade. They listen quietly to the teacher when she is reading a story or giving directions. If a third grader wants to talk, he remembers to raise his hand. When the teacher calls his name, then he can talk in an inside voice. An inside voice is not too loud and not too soft.

Now that I'm in third grade, I'll try to raise my hand. I'll try to wait for the teacher to call my name. Then I can say what I want in an inside voice. If she doesn't see me, I'll whisper to a grown-up that I need help.

Central to the effectiveness of a social story is the avoidance of "lecturing." Gray (2000) suggested using no more than one "directive" statement for every two to five "descriptive" or "perspective" statements in a story. Even though the social story strategy has not been evaluated extensively in controlled research, it is widely considered an essential element of the intervention toolkit of the elementary school team. Many teams also find the companion technique of "Comic Strip Conversations" helpful in debriefing about social situations (Gray, 1994).

Another remarkably helpful (but not yet fully researched) strategy is the Power Card (Gagnon, 2001). Akin to the social story, the Power Card approach identifies a "hero" within the student's special interest and then attributes desirable characteristics to that person. Once the student has learned (through a story) that the hero promotes certain actions, he or she can carry the Power Card in a pocket or purse as a reminder of the desirable behavior. The following Power Card was written for an 11-year-old boy who admired the men of the WWF.

"The Rock" reminds you:

1. Stop and listen to what your friend is saying. Repeat it in your mind so you remember.
2. Even if you're not interested, act like you are.
3. Let your friends talk about their interests as often as you talk about yours.
4. Learn to talk about more topics.

In addition to strategies that teach the "what" of social development, there are a few resources to guide parents and professionals through the maze of teaching the "how" of social skills (Freeman & Dake, 1997; McAfee, 2002; Moyes, 2001). These programs break down social skills into smaller chunks than do the social skills curricula that are usually employed within the elementary school classroom. One cautionary note: Many students with Asperger's Syndrome can "talk the talk" during social skills training. Do not assume that they can "walk the walk" in spontaneous social interactions with peers. One of the benefits of using a specialized program is that the foundations of social and emotional competence are solidly established and then generalized to a multitude of contexts. This ensures that the child will have portable and functional skills for everyday life.

A Few Closing Thoughts About Interventions for Elementary Students

Given that our work with children with Asperger's Syndrome is truly in its infancy, parents and professionals are well advised to consider interventions along several dimensions:

- Is there research to support using this intervention with children with Asperger's Syndrome?
- Is there research to support using this intervention with challenges similar to those seen in my child?
- Is there evidence that this intervention will build the skills that my child needs?
- If there is insufficient research for this intervention, is it considered useful by individuals who are considered experts in the field?
- Can I rest assured that this intervention will not harm my child or interfere with other intervention efforts?

If the answer to any of the first four questions is "yes," and there is no apparent harm or interference, it is reasonable to proceed with a cautious trial of the intervention. Remember, though, to assess benefit (and harm) objectively at regular intervals along the way.

WHERE CAN WE GO FOR HELP?

Asperger's Syndrome remains largely unfamiliar to many professionals within the medical, mental health, and education disciplines. In fact, very few professional training programs devote substantial time to Asperger's Syndrome. There are several promising avenues for assistance, however. Parents and educational teams are encouraged to make use of:

- Referrals from the child's physician or school.
- Local support groups (for Asperger's Syndrome, autism, or nonverbal learning disabilities).
- Workshops for parents and professionals.
- Word of mouth (as long as the source is considered carefully).
- Resources available through special education consortia and professional associations.
- The Internet (for information about Asperger's Syndrome and intervention and also for upcoming conferences and workshops)

WHAT'S NEXT?

Some of the best minds in the world are attempting to answer our nagging questions about Asperger's Syndrome and its treatment in school-aged children. In particular, multidisciplinary, multisite research teams are addressing questions related to the criteria for diagnosis, the overlap between Asperger's Syndrome and other disorders, and the effectiveness of particular intervention strategies.

In the meantime, the rest of us should remember several "dos and donts" of intervention:

- **DO** work as a team. Interventions that span home, school, and community are the most likely to be effective and long lasting.
- **DO** leverage strengths and passions to help the child overcome the more challenging aspects of everyday life.
- **DO** think developmentally and practically. How do the child's current skills and concerns match the demands of everyday life?
- **DO** remember that there are many roads to the same end. Many of the most effective interventions occurred in the least expected ways.
- **DON'T** sweat the small stuff.
- **DON'T** lose your sense of humor.
- **DO** remember that our ultimate goal is for the child to "own" strategies that can be used spontaneously and independently. Our best measure of success is when we work ourselves out of a job!

REFERENCES

American Psychiatric Association. (2000). *Diagnostic and statistical manual of mental disorders* (4th ed.). Washington, DC: Author.

Axline, V. (1969). *Play therapy.* New York: Ballantine.

Ayres, A. J. (1979). *Sensory integration and the child.* Los Angeles: Western Psychological Services.

Bernstein, J. H. (1995, July). *Clinical assessment of children: The neurodevelopmental systems perspective.* Workshop presented at the Cape Cod Institute, Eastham, MA.

Carr, E., Dunlap, G., Horner, R., Koegel, R., Turnbull, A., Sailor, W., et al. (2002). Positive behavior support: Evolution of an applied science. *Journal of Positive Behavioral Interventions, 4*(1), 4–16, 20.

Cautela, J., & Groden, J. (1978). *Relaxation: A comprehensive manual for adults, children, and children with special needs.* Champaign, IL: Research Press.

Delprato, D. J. (2001). Comparisons of discrete-trial and normalized behavioral language intervention for young children with autism. *Journal of Autism and Developmental Disorders, 31,* 315–325.

Dunlap, G., & Fox, L. (1999). A demonstration of behavioral support for young children with autism. *Journal of Positive Behavioral Interventions, 1*(2), 77–87.

Florida Department of Education. (1999). *Facilitators guide: Positive behavioral support.* Tallahassee, FL: Bureau of Instructional Support and Community Services.

Fouse, B., & Wheeler, M. (1997). *A treasure chest of behavioral strategies for individuals with autism.* Arlington, TX: Future Horizons.

Freeman, S., & Dake, L. (1997). *Teach me language: A language manual for children with autism, Asperger's syndrome and related developmental disorders.* Langley, BC, Canada: SKF Books.

Gagnon, E. (2001). *Power cards: Using special interests to motivate children and youth with Asperger Syndrome and autism.* Shawnee Mission, KS: Autism Asperger Publishing.

Gray, C. (1994). *Comic strip conversations.* Arlington, TX: Future Horizons.

Gray, C. (2000). *The new social story book: Illustrated edition.* Arlington, TX: Future Horizons.

Gray, C. (2002). *The sixth sense II: A revised and expanded version of the original 1993 lesson plan.* Arlington, TX: Future Horizons.

Greenspan, S. I., & Wieder, S. (1997). Developmental patterns and outcomes in infants and children with disorders in relating and communicating: A chart review of 200 cases of children with autistic spectrum diagnoses. *Journal of Developmental and Learning Disorders, 1,* 87–142.

Greenspan, S. I., & Wieder, S. (2000). Principles of clinical practice for assessment and intervention. In Interdisciplinary Council on Developmental and Learning Disorders, *Clinical practice guidelines* (pp. 55–82). Bethesda, MD: ICDL Press.

Interdisciplinary Council on Developmental and Learning Disorders. (2001). *Training videotape series: Floor time techniques and the DIR model for children and families with special needs: A guide.* Bethesda, MD: ICDL Press.

Leaf, R., & McEachin, J. (Eds.). (1999). *A work in progress.* New York: DRL Books.

Levine, M. (1999). *Developmental variation and learning disorders* (2nd ed.). Cambridge, MA: Educators Publishing Service.

Levine, M. (2002). *A mind at a time.* New York: Simon & Schuster.

Levine, M., Reed, M., & Hobgood, A. (2000). *A table of neurodevelopmental constructs.* Cambridge, MA: Educators Publishing Service.

Lite, L. (1996). *A boy and a bear: The children's relaxation book.* Plantation, FL: Specialty Press.

March, J. S., & Mulle, K. (1998). *OCD in children and adolescents: A cognitive-behavioral treatment manual.* New York: Guilford.

McAfee, J. (2002). *Navigating the social world: A curriculum for individuals for Asperger's Syndrome, high functioning autism, and related disorders.* Arlington, TX: Future Horizons.

McEachin, J. J., Smith, T., & Lovaas, O. I. (1993). Long-term outcome for children with autism who received early intensive behavioral treatment. *American Journal on Mental Retardation, 97,* 359–372.

McTarnaghan, J. (1998). *Circle of friends.* Unpublished training manuscript; Community Autism Resources, Fall River, MA.

Moustakas, C. E. (1959). *Psychotherapy with children: The living relationship.* New York: Harper & Row.

Moyes, R. A. (2001). *Incorporating social goals in the classroom: A guide for teachers and parents of children with high-functioning autism and Asperger Syndrome.* London: Jessica Kingsley.

Myles, B. S., & Simpson, R. L. (1998). *Asperger Syndrome: A guide for educators and parents.* Austin, TX: Pro-Ed.

National Research Council. (2001). *Educating children with autism* [Committee on Educational Interventions for Children with Autism, Division of Behavioral Sciences and Education]. Washington, DC: National Academy.

Powers, M. (1997). Behavioral assessment of individuals with autism. In D. J. Cohen & F. R. Volkmar (Eds.), *Handbook of autism and pervasive developmental disorders* (pp. 448–459). New York: Wiley.

Prizant, B. (1983). Language acquisition and communicative behavior in autism: Toward an understanding of the "whole" of it. *Journal of Speech and Hearing Disorders, 48,* 296–307.

Prizant, B., Wetherby, A. M., & Rydell, P. J. (2000). Communication intervention for children with autism spectrum disorders. In A. M. Wetherby & B. M. Prizant (Eds.), *Autism spectrum disorders: A transactional developmental perspective* (pp. 193–224). Baltimore: Brookes.

Rogers, S. J., & DiLalla, D. (1991). A comparative study of a developmentally based preschool curriculum on young children with autism and young children with other disorders of behavior and development. *Topics in Early Childhood Special Education, 11,* 29–48.

Schroeder, C. S., & Gordon, B. N. (2002). *Assessment and treatment of childhood problems* (2nd ed.). New York: Guilford.

Smith, T., Eikeseth, S., Klevstrand, M., & Lovaas, O. I. (1997). Intensive behavioral treatment for preschoolers with severe mental retardation and pervasive developmental disorder. *American Journal on Mental Retardation, 102,* 238–249.

Strain, P., & Kohler, F. (1998). Peer mediated social intervention for children with autism. *Seminars in Speech and Language, 19,* 391–405.

Tanguay, P. B. (2002). *Nonverbal learning disabilities at school: Educating students with NLD, Asperger Syndrome, and related conditions.* London: Jessica Kingsley.

Thompson, S. (1997). *The source for nonverbal learning disorders.* East Moline, IL: LinguiSystems.

Williams, M. S., & Shellenberger, S. (1996). *"How does your engine run?" A leader's guide to the Alert Program for self-regulation.* Albuquerque, NM: TherapyWorks.

Wolfberg, P. J. (1999). *Play and imagination in children with autism.* New York: Teachers College Press.

PART III

Adolescents

Chapter 7

Counseling Adolescents

Kate Sofronoff
University of Queensland

Adolescents with Asperger's Syndrome face both the typical problems of adolescence and those associated with being different. Although they can be difficult to engage in therapy, teachers or parents refer them because they can foresee the potential benefits. The adolescent might resist, doubting the advantages, and worrying about the stigma of seeing a mental health professional. Their resistance can be challenging, but this transitional period between childhood and adulthood might be the last window of opportunity for helping them navigate the neurotypical world.

A cognitive-behavioral approach, which focuses on correcting thought patterns and developing new and effective behaviors, is particularly helpful for individuals with Asperger's Syndrome. Whereas traditional therapies rely on "insight" and the ability to make inferences about interpersonal behaviors, this more pragmatic approach is directly applicable to issues and problems faced by this population. It capitalizes on the adolescent's most prominent strength: the ability to use intellectual analysis to break down and solve problems. In addition, cognitive behavioral therapy that makes use of scripts and visual cues is particularly tailored to adolescents with Asperger's Syndrome.

INFORMATION ON WORKING WITH ADOLESCENTS

Unlike adult clients who are often self-referred, adolescents might not clearly understand why they have been directed to see a mental health professional. Problematic behaviors or parental concerns might not be obvious to the young person who can misinterpret an appointment with a psychologist as punishment. If possible, when arranging the appointment for the young person, discuss with the parent how they will explain the visit both in terms of the reason for coming and what they can expect to occur. Many parents will not be clear about how an interview with a psychologist will progress and might need to be coached about how to best present this to the young person. An adolescent will often not be motivated to discuss personal issues with a psychologist and it could take some time and skill to establish rapport sufficient for a working relationship to develop.

Young people with Asperger's Syndrome might not have good insight into the problems that they are experiencing, particularly if those problems concern emotions and emotional regulation. The process of building rapport will benefit from a sound explanation of the purpose of the visit as well as the likely benefits that could occur for the adolescent. It is important to emphasize that confidentiality will be respected, but safety issues are paramount and any information about potentially harmful situations will be shared with the appropriate adult. It is important not to patronize the adolescent and it is also important to avoid trying to be "cool." I generally find that if I am open and clear and can demonstrate the benefits of engaging in the process of therapy, even if only on a trial basis, the vast majority of adolescents are willing to talk about themselves.

THE ADOLESCENT WITH ASPERGER'S SYNDROME

Adolescence is a major transition period for all adolescents. It is a period of physical and emotional change when a whole range of factors can interact to cause distress and discomfort. Most notably, adolescence is a time when peer relationships assume great importance. This is significant for the adolescent with Asperger's Syndrome because it means that an even greater focus will fall on an area of functioning in which they are least competent. The result for many adolescents is that they suffer increasing stress, increasing anxiety, and in some cases increasing depression. The adolescent at this time might exhibit more rigid behaviors, an increased amount of time engaged with a special interest, more stereotypic behaviors, and more anger or aggressive outbursts.

The basis of many adolescent friendships is a sharing of similar beliefs, values, and interests. Adolescents group together to engage in activities, to demonstrate their move toward adulthood, and to show that they belong together as a group. The sense of belonging is often demonstrated by wearing similar clothes, familiarity with similar music, avowing and expressing similar views, and sharing experiences that can be retold and worn as a badge of group membership.

Adolescents are very astute at recognizing those who do belong and those who do not. Often those who do not belong are targeted and labeled with epithets that cause great discomfort. The act of labeling someone else as an outsider is yet another way adolescents demonstrate that they know what is required to belong. The common labels directed at young people who do not fit the current notion of what is required to belong include "weirdo," "psycho," "loser," "nerd," "geek," and "gay." At a time when a majority of adolescents are feeling confused and unsure about themselves in relation to their bodies, their emotions, and their place in society, how much more difficult is it to withstand the idea that "there is something very wrong with me?"

When an adolescent with Asperger's Syndrome presents with difficulties, the most beneficial mode of intervention will often be a small group of adolescents with Asperger's Syndrome experiencing similar or related difficulties. There are multiple benefits in using the small-group format including, importantly, the clear demonstration that the adolescent is not alone and there are others with similar issues. It is also possible that the young people might have interests in common and that friendships and supportive relationships might develop. Finally, many young people with Asperger's Syndrome will not be able to generalize information and skills learned in a therapy session to other situations. This is especially likely to be the case when practicing a skill occurs only with an adult therapist. In a group situation, skills can be rehearsed with multiple partners using different scenarios and alternate outcomes.

Unfortunately, it is not always possible to provide the ideal mode of intervention. Small groups run infrequently, the age group needs to be appropriate, and the problems need to be similar. Therefore, many adolescents will receive individual therapy when difficulties arise. For individual therapy with an adolescent with Asperger's Syndrome to be successful, it is necessary to be mindful of how typical interventions might need to be modified to accommodate the characteristics of the disorder. Cognitive behavior therapy (CBT) is one approach that lends itself well to this population and the case studies outlined in this chapter all use CBT as the basis of the intervention.

CASE STUDY 1

Samantha was 15 years old when she first presented at the clinic. Her parents had sought the referral because they were concerned that she was becoming increasingly depressed and that her behavior was deteriorating both at school and at home. Samantha was increasingly engaged in repetitive behaviors, found relationships with teachers very stressful, and had spoken on several occasions of harming herself.

Samantha's parents reported that at age 4 she had been given a diagnosis of autism. Her parents had sought assistance from a wide variety of sources but had put in a great deal of work themselves to work with Samantha in areas of deficit. Samantha had attended a mainstream primary school where she had been considered of below average intelligence and naughty.

As Samantha developed, she acquired relatively normal speech, and with one-to-one coaching she achieved adequate grades and entered high school with her same age cohort. By the time I encountered Samantha her speech was appropriate and she was achieving good grades at school (B+ average). At this time

Samantha met criteria for Asperger's Syndrome. Samantha had learned to mimic the conversations of the girls in her class and to change her facial expression to accommodate whatever she believed to be appropriate at the time. For the most part she was able to get by in social situations but she admitted that she really did not follow many of the conversations. Samantha also said that things that her "friends" said to her frequently dismayed her. She described how she would take offense and become angry only to be told later that it was normal joking around and that she had misinterpreted the situation. These types of occurrences were relatively frequent (three or four times a week) and created feelings of distress and awkwardness. After talking with Samantha over several sessions it became apparent that she was finding the school situation so stressful that she had few resources left by the time she arrived home at the end of the day.

Samantha's special interest was archaeology and she was determined that she would go to university to undertake further study in her chosen field. The teachers were concerned that she had set herself an extremely high standard, that there was a possibility that she would not achieve this standard, and that her feeling of pressure to achieve high grades caused great anxiety and led to unfortunate interactions with teachers. Whenever Samantha felt that she had not fully grasped a concept or an instruction she would call out to the teacher concerned and demand that an explanation be given immediately. On several occasions she had spoken extremely rudely to teachers and caused offense. Following these incidents Samantha could not understand why the teacher might be offended.

At home Samantha had several strategies she used to relax. One of these was to listen to the same piece of music repeatedly, another was to read about archaeology, and a third was to jump on the trampoline. Unfortunately, these strategies caused further distress because she was unable to regulate the time she spent engaged in them and would lose hours of valuable study time. She would then feel angry and depressed because she had failed to complete the work she had intended. It was at these times that she would contemplate harming herself.

Working With Samantha

Samantha was not a difficult client to engage although she revealed information slowly over time as trust built up. Following the initial sessions that were devoted to gathering information and building a relationship, we mapped out a plan for working together. Samantha identified her priorities as decreasing her need to engage in what she described as time-wasting activities and increasing her ability to understand social situations. We also included repairing relationships with teachers and learning how to work within the school framework. Samantha agreed that she would like to attend the clinic initially on a weekly basis for a trial period of 12 weeks.

We began by monitoring the frequency of the activities that eroded Samantha's study time in terms of hours and minutes spent. At baseline across 7 days she was spending 40 minutes per day jumping on the trampoline, 1 hour and 20 minutes per day reading archaeology, and 50 minutes per day listening to the same songs repeatedly. Following these activities, Samantha would try to do her homework and study and would find that she was too tired. Negative interactions were occurring with peers an average of six times per week. Negative interactions were occurring with teachers an average of two or three times per day.

We spent some time talking about stress, anxiety, and feelings of depression to establish a framework and a level of understanding about how the different things bothering Samantha could be related. It was also important to negotiate where to start working to effect a change both in behavior and distress level. Samantha initially wanted to work only on reducing her time-wasting activities, but on reflection she came to realize that she might better be able to control these behaviors if her time at school was not so distressing.

It was also important, with consent from Samantha and her parents, to make contact with the school and spend some time with teaching staff to educate them about Asperger's Syndrome and management of the behaviors that caused them concern. It is important to recognize that many teachers are not familiar with the characteristics and presentation of Asperger's Syndrome. In this instance, teachers attributed Samantha's behaviors to excessive egocentricity, rudeness, and poor parenting. These attributions implied that Samantha should know how to behave appropriately. When this misunderstanding occurs, as it often does, the young person is frequently punished for the disorder over which he or she has no control.

By Session 4 we were working together on specific incidents that had occurred at school. We used an electronic whiteboard to draw cartoon representations of salient interactions to highlight what had occurred, what had been said, and what the motivations of individual participants might have been. This is the technique developed by Gray (1994a) known as comic strip conversations and is very useful for accessing events from the perspective of the young person. It allows us to see clearly why an event or comment might have been misinterpreted. Once we are able to see the event from the young person's perspective we can then replay it differently using a problem solving approach. See Fig. 7.1 and the accompanying commentary for an outline of this approach. When we initially began using the strategy, Samantha needed a lot of help generating motives for other people's comments and actions. Over several weeks she began to recognize that there was more than one possible interpretation of an event or comment and she was keen to role play alternative ways of responding. We developed a series of scripts that could be used in different situations to respond to comments or questions. By using the electronic whiteboard, Samantha was always able to take away a copy of whatever we had discussed. This can also be achieved using butcher's paper, but it is very important for such records to be kept and for the young person to have a clear record of what occurred so that he or she can process it further in his or her own time.

One comic strip that Samantha and I developed involved a recent altercation she had experienced with her math teacher. We began by revisiting the setting, who was

FIG. 7.1   A comic strip conversation example for Samatha.

there, and what was happening. We established that Samantha was anxious from the outset because she was concerned about the possible grade that she would receive.

As the revision session proceeded, Samantha found that she had not entirely understood what the teacher had meant in one explanation. What she had done was to call out "I don't understand!" We further established that Samantha had thought that if she did not clarify the explanation immediately, she would possibly miss some marks on the test.

Samantha then reported that the teacher did not respond to her initial statement and so she called out again with "You'll have to help me with this now!"

A picture now emerged of what had taken place in the classroom and it was somewhat different from Samantha's first description that her math teacher had refused to give her any help with revision.

We then moved on to the more difficult aspect of the situation: trying to establish what the teacher might have been thinking or feeling during this exchange. It is often necessary to generate this for the young person in the first instance.

We then progressed through the sequence of events that led to Samantha leaving the room and the teacher reporting her to the principal for rudeness.

Following this process, Samantha engaged in a role play in which I took her part and she tried to be her teacher. This allowed her to feel the frustration from the other point of view. We then started to problem solve how Samantha could achieve what she needed without having to resort to behavior that would annoy her teacher.

We developed a script for Samantha to approach the teacher to apologize for her behavior and to explain why she was so anxious in the class. We also worked out several suggestions of times that Samantha could approach the teacher outside of class time to ask for assistance (this would reduce her anxiety about missing information in class). We also rehearsed and scripted how and when she should ask for help in class.

This situation was resolved very positively for both Samantha and the teacher.

Samantha was highly motivated and was very willing to role play solutions to problems with both peers and teachers in an experimental framework (i.e., let's try this and then analyze the outcome). We formulated a good generic script for asking teachers for help, identified appropriate times to do this, and rehearsed strategies to overcome the anxiety of not having a teacher's attention immediately. Samantha repaired relationships with two teachers over three sessions and came to an agreed time schedule for her to ask for assistance. Once this system was in place she no longer had a reason to call out in class or be rude. Samantha found the teachers to be very reasonable when approached in the manner that we had rehearsed. The fact that teachers had been included in the intervention from the outset made this a win–win situation.

In many ways the activities that Samantha referred to as her time-wasting activities were her outlet from stress and we did not want to eliminate these entirely. The focus of our efforts centered on giving Samantha a sense of control over the time she spent engaged in the activities. It is very easy for a person with Asperger's Syndrome to lose track of time and this is what was occurring for Samantha. We agreed that she would still use the trampoline but that she would use it only at specific times—just before dinner so that someone would call her or just before dark so that she would be aware of the time passing. She also agreed to use a timer that would buzz loudly when her specified time had elapsed.

We incorporated her special interest in archaeology as a reward for achieving other goals. So, for example, when Samantha had completed a section of study she would reward herself with 20 minutes of reading about archaeology and she would use a timer to indicate when the time was finished and she needed to return to other work. We found that this process was also helpful in allowing Samantha to organize her work schedule more clearly and create discrete blocks of time in which specific goals were achieved. The visual cue created by the schedule meant that Samantha had tangible evidence of her achievement and she could see that she had earned her reward.

Although many adolescents have music playing while they study, young people with Asperger's Syndrome might not be able to do this. Samantha could either listen to music or complete schoolwork; she could not do both simultaneously. We decided to use her favorite music as an additional reward that she could select on completion of discrete sections of work. Again, she used a timer to indicate when she needed to return to other work. In conjunction with this we decided to try to increase her repertoire of listening and each week she would bring along another song that she was willing to listen to.

Samantha is continuing to do well at school and still has an ambition to work in archaeology. From time to time she encounters difficulties and I see her approximately every 6 weeks to talk through social situations, to rehearse new scripts and strategies, and to problem solve any other thoughts or behaviors that might be causing distress either to Samantha herself or to others. Educating teaching staff about Asperger's Syndrome and negotiating strategies with individual teachers has had a significant impact on their ability to manage problem situations. This has also led to a significant reduction in stress for Samantha in the school setting and eased the problems occurring at home.

CASE STUDY 2

Ben is a 16-year-old who was initially diagnosed with Asperger's Syndrome when he was 10 years old. His parents reported that until the year of presentation he had always achieved very well at school and there had been an expectation that he would attend university to study either computer science or music. His parents were concerned that he was no longer interested in his schoolwork, his marks had deteriorated, he was moody and bad tempered, and he did not want to attend school. Ben reported that he had friends at school but his parents explained that the friends were two other boys with significant difficulties. Ben described the students in his year group as either "high status" or "low status" and said that he was a low-status student although there was one high-status boy who spent time with him outside of school. This friendship was based on the fact that Ben was a talented musician who could help the high-status boy with his own musical aspirations.

Ben was confused and agitated by what he was currently experiencing at school. He could not understand why his friend, Mark, would spend time with him outside of school but at school would join in with other students in name-calling and put downs directed at Ben. Ben's two school friends were ill equipped to support him when this occurred and on occasion would even join in. The content of the jibes directed at Ben included the suggestion that he was gay as well as the suggestion that he was a psycho. Ben believed that there must be something really wrong with him for people to say these things and was distressed by the idea that he was gay. Ben also said that he was desperately unhappy, wanted to leave school, and wanted to get a full-time job as an attendant at a fast-food outlet.

Ben's parents had tried to talk with him about the school situation and in one of their conversations his mother had said, "I don't care if you are gay, I love you anyway!" Ben had taken this comment, intended to be positive, as further proof that even his parents believed he was gay.

Working With Ben

Ben had come willingly to the clinic at his parents' suggestion and agreed to speak with me for a trial period of six sessions. Although Ben was quite competent in describing the interactions that occurred with peers, he had little insight into why these interactions might occur. On assessment, Ben presented as depressed with serious confusion about his sexual orientation. He was also unable to clearly identify a range of emotions within himself. He could describe an occasion on which he had been happy and many occasions on which he had been sad or angry, but nothing in between.

We agreed to work together on several levels. It was important to Ben to tackle the issue of sexuality, even though he found this profoundly embarrassing to discuss. We also agreed to examine the social interactions at school to try to identify why they were occurring and what we might be able to put in place to help. Finally, Ben agreed to consider engaging in some work on emotions.

We tackled the issue of sexuality initially as a project designed to find out what it would be like if Ben were gay, (i.e., how would he know this, what physiological indications there would be, etc.). We spent a session talking about the topic, using the whiteboard to record information, and looking for evidence both for and against the possibility. Some of the items included:

FOR	AGAINST
Peers call me gay	Not attracted to other boys
I feel different from others	Not physically aroused by males
I don't have a girlfriend	I would like a girlfriend
Never experienced sex with a girl	Sometimes become aroused by girls

We also examined instances of other students who had been labeled gay to see what the similarities and differences were. Ben was able to name three other students, one of whom was openly gay. He was also able to say quite clearly that he was different from this boy. The others were students who, for various reasons, did not belong in the mainstream group. Ben came to the realization for himself that calling a boy gay often just means that he is different from the group and that it might have little to do with his sexual orientation. The process of exploration, finding evidence, looking at the perspectives of others, and forming a conclusion allowed Ben to decide for himself that he was not gay. He came to realize that he was the subject of name-calling because he was different from the others and they did not have a better adjective to use to describe him. We also talked about why people—and often young people—have difficulty with others who are different from themselves—why it should be the case that friendships are based on sameness and why differences can be threatening. Ben found this discussion to be intellectually interesting; once again it contains the perspective of others that he did not have access to naturally.

We used the comic strip conversation format to illustrate examples of the social interactions Ben was having at school. It became apparent that in many instances Ben was demonstrating social behavior that his peers were finding difficult to understand. He was, for example trying to turn schoolyard conversations to topics with which he was comfortable and familiar (classical music and computer technology). One example involved a conversation about the upcoming Red Hot Chili Peppers concert. Ben had attempted to divert this topic to discussion of a

Rachmaninov concerto. This was not well tolerated by his peer group and the general consensus was that the perpetrator of such an indiscretion must be gay.

It further became apparent that there had been a number of occasions on which he had misinterpreted colloquialisms, leading to added evidence of his "weird" status. When asked if he had ever had a "stiffy" (Australian slang for an erection) he replied that he thought that Mr. Smith, the math teacher, gave him one this morning. Ben had actually thought he understood the colloquial expression of a stiff problem—he could not understand why his "friends" not only fell about laughing but also took this as an admission of blatant homosexuality.

To decrease the likelihood of these problems recurring, we started a dictionary of slang terms and double or even triple meanings for words. We also established rules for topics of conversation. Rules included these: When someone else starts a conversation it is good to ask several questions about that topic. What sort of questions could you ask? Write these out and rehearse. Find out if people are interested in classical music or computers before introducing the topic. How can you do this? Write out and rehearse. In the early stages, we developed a series of scripts to help with this and used a number of case scenarios to role play the interactions. We also wrote out and rehearsed a number of clarification probes that Ben could use in conversations if he got lost or stuck and did not know what people were talking about. Ben practiced using these instead of his usual strategy of switching the conversation to classical music or computers. He reported almost immediately that this worked quite well and that he felt more comfortable in casual conversations. We continued to expand his repertoire of topics.

The final component of our work involved increasing Ben's awareness of his own emotional state. If he could identify a range of different emotions within himself and describe degrees of emotion then he could learn several things. He could learn that *happy* has a very wide range and if you are not as happy as you were when your new computer arrived then it does not mean that you are sad. It might mean, however, that you are contented or relaxed and this is also a positive thing. It was also possible to learn that there are degrees of sadness or upset and it is okay to feel a little down from time to time. Likewise, there will be times when we are mildly irritated and times when we are absolutely furious. These states should not be caused by the same events. Once a young person is able to identify emotional states themselves, they can then look for situations, people, or interactions that trigger the emotions. This is a step in the chain toward learning to manage or regulate emotions more successfully.

We used a series of strategies to identify emotions and degrees of emotion in Ben. Some of these strategies included creating a feelings diary in which Ben started with happiness and built up a collection of entries describing incidents, situations, and people that made him happy. He then rated each entry for the degree of happiness elicited and gave it a descriptor (e.g., contented, satisfied, amused, interested, calm). Ben included activities such as running with his dog, taking his bike and going for a long ride, listening to Rachmaninov, playing the trumpet, talking with his dad, helping his brother, and so on. Ben said that he had never really thought about these activities as positive or happy things before, they had just seemed neutral to him. The idea of the feelings diary came from the work of Attwood (Attwood, 1998; Sofronoff & Attwood, 2003) and was very effective in this case. The diary is further used as a tool when the young person is feeling sad or angry; he or she can turn to it to alleviate negative feelings by looking for strategies that have worked in the past.

Following Ben's growing ability to identify positive emotions and associate activities with these emotions, we then agreed to tackle negative emotions and the associated events and interactions. Ben was able to identify a range of events that had occurred at school and had caused him distress. We further examined these events to create a hierarchy to illustrate more or less distress associated with each event. Ben was able to recognize that he did not discriminate among these events, rather he saw them all as equally devastating and rated his distress as extreme in each case. To Ben's credit he did not immediately accept the position that he should not feel so distressed by some events. He was quick to point out that it was his distress and if he felt the distress then it was real and the event (however minor) had indeed caused it. The "what I feel is real and therefore justified" argument is not uncommon and occurs frequently when working with adolescents. It is important to validate the reality of the feeling for the young person: "Yes, I acknowledge your feelings; what we are looking at is the adaptiveness of the feelings." So, the question is, "Do you like feeling this way?" and "Would you prefer to control these feelings?"

Ben suggested that he would like to control the reactions he had to events and interactions but said that he did not believe he was capable of doing that. I introduced Ben to the cognitive-behavioral model: the suggestion that the way we think about events and situations influences the way we feel. It is easy to demonstrate that two people can think differently about the same event or situation and as a result will feel very differently; one might feel distressed or angry, whereas the other might feel neutral or even positive. Although Ben could accept the rationale presented, he still maintained that this would probably not work for him.

We moved on to trying to capture some of Ben's thoughts in situations that occurred at school. Remember, we had already challenged some of these thoughts in relation to his being gay so Ben was familiar with the strategy but he could still not see how it might generalize to other situations. Slowly, over several sessions we began to challenge some of Ben's thoughts associated with "being stupid" and "being a psycho." We replaced these thoughts with more reality-based interpretations: "I see things slightly differently," "This is not bad, it is just different," "It is okay to be different," or "People who are a bit different sometimes scare others."

Another strategy that worked well for Ben was to imagine someone else in a situation and to think through how he or she would handle that situation. This gave Ben another perspective, a different way to handle situations, and role models to evaluate and imitate if helpful. He began to develop an interest in observing people and taking note of how they reacted in various situations. Ben developed a system for recording how different people he knew managed a variety of situations. He included situations that he found quite comfortable as well as situations that were difficult for him. Over time he chose to change some of his interactions and to use a style copied from someone else. In some of our sessions we discussed why people behave differently in similar situations; this gave Ben information about the different motives of various people.

Ben has continued to do well; the last time I saw him he told me that he had two new friends, that they had similar interests, and that he felt he was getting the hang of social interactions. He said that he still needed to think things through very carefully and there was a lot that he still did not really understand, but he thought he would continue to learn about all of this social stuff. He does this by continuing to observe and take notes that he brings to sessions, as well as maintaining his diary and list of "difficult" expressions. Ben had originally contracted to see me for 6 sessions, but at the conclusion of these initial sessions he extended the contract to 14 sessions. We currently have an agreement that Ben will contact me for a session whenever he feels overwhelmed or confused. I still see him on this basis about once every 3 months.

CASE STUDY 3

Jake was 13 years old when his mother appeared at the clinic in distress. Jake had been diagnosed with Asperger's Syndrome at age 5. He was the youngest child of parents whose other children were adult and had left home. When Jake was 2 years old his father had also left the family and his mother, Denise, had tried to raise the boy on her own. Denise had come to the clinic at this time because of a series of events that had occurred in the past month.

Jake had been accepted as a participant in a school-based social skills group but had been asked to leave after assaulting another boy. On another occasion Jake had threatened his mother with a knife when she suggested he should leave the computer and attend to his homework. For the past several weeks Jake had taken to urinating and defecating on his mother's bed when he did not get his own way immediately. His ongoing noncompliance and temper outbursts continued to occur on a daily basis both at home and at school.

The history of Jake's situation was that from an early age (about 2 years) he had sought to get his own way through aggressive behavior. His mother, Denise, reported that if he did not get what he wanted immediately he would tantrum. She described the tantrums as violent and frightening and said that as a consequence people would rush to soothe him and accommodate his wishes. Essentially this meant that Jake received positive reinforcement for his aggressive behavior and was never given the opportunity to learn emotional regulation for himself (i.e., learning to cope with delay of gratification or even that you sometimes cannot have what you want).

Denise also described situations as Jake grew older in which she would threaten consequences for aggressive or noncompliant behavior such as withdrawal of privileges. She said that when the time came to follow through she would nearly always feel sorry for Jake and allow him to have the privilege anyway. Once again, if we look at what Jake has learned we see that there are no negative consequences for his aggression, no responsibility taken. So, as a strategy for Jake, aggressive and violent behavior was very functional.

In other situations Jake was equally aggressive and noncompliant. He attended a local private school but even with maximum aide assistance, the school was only prepared to accept Jake for a few hours a day. He was not attending a school at which the staff had any expertise in the management of Asperger's Syndrome. When Jake was not at school he was in his mother's care. Denise had no respite and no family support. Jake's special interest was computer games and if he were not permitted to engage in these games he would become increasingly aggressive toward Denise. Denise said that she knew she should do something to stop the behaviors but she did not know what to do; furthermore, she was exhausted and did not have the resources to cope. Denise presented as severely clinically depressed and expressed suicidal ideation but with no intention or plan to carry out any suicide attempt.

Jake was not prepared to attend the psychology clinic willingly and Denise was unable to either coax him to attend or insist that he attend. I visited both home and school to observe Jake's behavior. At school he was restless and distracted and generally noncompliant. Staff needed to be constantly vigilant so that he did not assault other children. At home Jake was engaged in computer games and refused to leave the computer to eat lunch. When Denise insisted that he leave the computer he threatened to punch her and began to scream abusively. Denise allowed him to eat his lunch at the computer.

I had come to the home equipped with a new computer game that Jake was eager to play. He agreed to speak with me for 45 minutes if he could then play the new game. Jake had no insight into the effect of his behavior on other people, including his mother. He was able to see events and interactions only from his point of view and espoused the belief that if he behaved badly, that was the fault of the person who "made" him behave like that.

How Did It Get to This Stage?

The behavior that was causing significant problems had begun when Jake was 2 years old. In many instances, parents excuse aggressive and tantruming behavior in a toddler as a stage that the child will outgrow. This is not necessarily the case. It is particularly unlikely to be the case for children who cannot see situations from the perspective of another or to take into account the feelings of others. It is much easier to modify the behavior of a small child, one whose behavior has not been reinforced and rewarded for 10 years or more. Jake had learned that aggressive behavior was successful in accessing the things he wanted; it allowed him to control his environment and accommodate his obsessions. He did not need to suffer the distress of delaying gratification, nor had he ever learned to regulate his own emotions.

What becomes evident from this case study is that behaviors that are accommodated and tolerated in toddlerhood can be the very behaviors that become dangerous and distressing to others in adolescence. At the time that I encountered Jake there were many people, including teachers, neighbors and his mother, who were frightened of what he might do if he did not get his own way.

Working With Jake

Jake agreed to work with me for six sessions on the basis that following those sessions I would give him the computer game that he wanted. I also asked to work with Jake's mother at the same time to teach her management skills and to develop and implement behavioral contracts for both Jake and Denise.

Initially, it was important to limit Jake's access to weapons such as knives, and it was agreed that all sharp implements would be removed from the home. It was important that changes in the environment occur slowly and that they initially be as positive for Jake as possible. Any immediately punitive moves would be likely to result in escalating aggression toward Denise.

The first joint session was presented as a means to increase the possibility of good things occurring for both Jake and Denise, to make it possible for them to do more positive things together, and for Jake to learn some of the skills he would need to be a "smart" adult. Jake saw himself as a highly intelligent young man (superior to others in nearly every way) so it was important to appeal to his sense of what was an intelligent way to proceed. This approach I must also attribute to Dr. Tony Attwood. Because many young people with Asperger's Syndrome do have significant talents, they appreciate being called intelligent far more than they appreciate pleasing a parent, teacher, or other adult.

Some basic ground rules were established to start the process of change in the home. These rules included: first, trying to speak to one another in a polite way (because that makes each person feel good and that is what smart people do); second, trying to respect each person's property (e.g., not damaging his mother's bed and not unplugging the computer) so that each person is less likely to be offended and become angry; third, trying to do something nice for the other person once each day (Jake agreed to set the table and clear the dishes and Denise agreed to cook one of his favorite meals each day in the first week). These ground rules sound simple and straightforward but, in fact, it took a lot of negotiation with Jake to reach an agreement.

It is important to remember that from Jake's point of view, he had relatively little to gain from changing his behavior. It was necessary to rehearse and script each of the rules across a variety of situations. Being an intelligent young man, Jake was able to learn several polite things to say to his mother in response to interactions initiated by her. He also quite liked the idea that positive behavior from him could exert control over situations (i.e., if he did something positive he was more likely to receive something positive in return). Initially this needed to be reinforced on every occasion so that Jake saw the benefit of changing his behavior. Jake also needed the visual cue of having the ground rules (with examples) posted on a notice board in the kitchen in clear view.

I began individual sessions with Jake based on developing strategies to enhance emotional regulation as well as anger management skills. As with many other young people with Asperger's Syndrome, Jake was not good at recognizing his own emotions, and so we followed a similar plan of identifying emotions starting with the positive ones and keeping a record of how these could vary in different situations. Jake was very rigid and restricted in the range of activities that gave him pleasure; computer games were essentially all there was. However, he also enjoyed food, so we were able to use both of these as reinforcers. Nearly every negative outburst from Jake was a response to being told "no" or "later," or being asked to do something in which he had no interest. The obvious question was why Jake should modify his behavior and reduce the number of outbursts when they were currently so effective.

In work with young children it is common to elicit behavioral change by introducing a reinforcement schedule. This works by changing the contingencies for behavior such that rewards are given to increase desirable behaviors, and an absence of rewards, or punishers (e.g., withdrawal of attention, removal of privileges) are used to decrease undesirable behaviors. Even though Jake was an adolescent, we decided to try a reinforcement schedule to modify some behaviors. Denise wanted to increase the time Jake spent on his schoolwork and decrease the amount of time spent playing computer games. A schedule was set up that required school assignments to be completed on weekday afternoons between 12.30 p.m. and 4 p.m. Computer access was limited to between 7 p.m. and 9 p.m. on weekday evenings (i.e., after dinner and washing up). The reward for complying with the new routine was additional computer games on the weekend and a visit to a computer arcade for 2 hours on Saturday afternoon. Jake was initially unwilling to agree to the new routine so I continued to work with him individually for several more weeks before it was possible.

We spent quite some time examining situations during which Jake experienced negative emotions. Using role play and comic strip conversations, Jake came to the conclusion that he did not like it when another person displayed aggressive behavior toward him. Unfortunately, this did not mean that he realized he needed to change his own behavior, but he did agree to rehearse some strategies for managing his own feelings of anger and aggression. I suggested to Jake that developing this skill would indicate real intelligence and prove that he was a person who could take control. We also discussed the fact that this was new and uncharted territory for Jake and we agreed to approach the endeavor as he would approach conquering a new and very difficult computer game (one for which he did not have access to the rules). He agreed that I could be the expert on this particular game until he had mastered it.

We rehearsed many different scenarios. For example, we began with imaginary situations (or real-life situations that had already occurred) in which he was told that he could not do something he wanted to do, or that he must do something that he did not want to do. Jake was able to learn applied breathing techniques to reduce the physical arousal that he felt in these situations. As Jake had a fondness for gadgets, we also used a small biofeedback device on which he placed his hand; it changed color to indicate different levels of arousal. Jake could see his arousal decrease as the color changed and was able to attribute the change to his ability to take control.

In addition, Jake used visual cues to suggest that when someone says "later" that would be like a computer glitch that means you cannot proceed immediately but need to wait for something else to happen first. We created small computer-generated messages to indicate this. We used similar cues for when someone says "no" and generated a computer message to indicate that the move he wanted to make was not possible at this time (e.g., the rules of the game do not allow it or the computer needs more software before you can proceed).

For situations when Jake was asked to do something he did not want to do we created a social story. This is another technique introduced by Gray (1994b) that tailors a story to a specific individual and a specific situation. The story is written according to a precise formula and helps the person develop the social understanding required. It uses sentences that describe the situation (descriptive sentences), sentences that provide the perspective of others and explain the situation (perspective sentences), a sentence that indicates what the young person should try to do in the situation (directive sentences), and possibly a sentence or two that indicates how the person might implement what he or she is trying to do (control sentences). The ratio of sentences in a social story must be five or more descriptive and perspective sentences to one or zero directive and control sentences. The story is meant to provide social understanding, not just direct the person to comply. Here is an example of a social story for Jake.

Doing Homework

Almost every day my teachers give me homework to complete. (descriptive)

Most students find homework fairly boring. (perspective)

Teachers give homework so that we can practice some of the things we have learned in class that day. (perspective)

It is important to complete homework so that we do not fall behind in the work we are doing. (perspective)

My mum often asks me to do my homework. (descriptive)

My mum is concerned that I keep up with the work at school because she knows I am clever and that I want to work with computers. (perspective)

When my mum asks me to start my homework I will try to say, "Okay mum, I will start now" and I will try to start. (directive)

I will try to think of homework as the computer program that I need to develop in order to play a great game. (control)

When I have finished my homework my mum will be pleased and I can then play a game. (perspective)

We will both feel better because we did not have an argument. (perspective)

7 descriptive and perspective sentences

1 directive sentence

1 control sentence

After several sessions, Jake was able to use his strategies within the clinic setting and in the scenarios that we rehearsed. To generalize his use of strategies to other settings, I spent several more sessions at home with Denise as the person saying "no" or asking Jake to comply with requests. It took another 6 weeks of rehearsing and rewarding Jake for efforts expended in the right direction before he once used the strategies in an unrehearsed situation. Progress was slow and gains were small.

Eventually Jake agreed to try the new homework and computer schedule and we negotiated the rewards for his efforts and his successes. Once again, the progress was slow with many setbacks. During this time Denise sought medical assistance for symptoms of depression and made links with several other parents of difficult adolescents with Asperger's Syndrome. She was able to get some respite from the constant burden of caring for a very difficult young man, but she was also able to share many more positive interactions with Jake himself. Denise has become an expert in dealing with Jake's moods and demanding temperament, and is now able to negotiate with him quite effectively.

Jake is a young man who needs ongoing assistance, but on the positive side, he is now willing to work on making some changes. There are still times when he loses his temper and becomes threatening and abusive, but he continues to rehearse strategies and carry his visual cue cards. We are currently working on directing his special interest in playing computer games toward a more extended interest in developing computer games. With this project in mind, it is easier for Jake to understand the relevance of some of his schoolwork. At age 17, he is still mostly home schooled, but attends classes in graphic design and math.

Jake agreed to continue attending the clinic after the initial 6 weeks. He has attended several group programs to work on anger management and social skills. He is generally uninterested in forming friendships with other adolescents and tends to remain aloof within the group context. He is, however, willing to work with an adult who can help him achieve his goals, and to this end he has formed a relationship with a young man who works in computer animation. We are hopeful that with continued effort Jake will be able to follow his dream and lead a productive life.

IN CONCLUSION

It is my opinion that each of the young people described in this chapter will continue to experience a variety of problems as they navigate the transition through adolescence into adulthood. Enormous effort and dedication on the part of parents is pivotal; parents trained as cotherapists are invaluable. In some cases, as with Samantha, there is also a significant advantage to working closely with school staff, both to educate them about the disorder and to teach them effective management strategies for difficult behaviors.

I believe it is also imperative to intervene early with children diagnosed with a disorder such as Asperger's Syndrome. They will face multiple complex difficulties. These might include severe anxiety, obsessive and ritualistic behaviors, temper tantrums and demanding behaviors, violent rages, self-harming behaviors, destructive behaviors, sleep disturbances, eating difficulties, sensory difficulties, speech and language and learning difficulties, and so on.

The benefits of early intervention for the child with Asperger's Syndrome are numerous. First, many difficult behaviors or features of the disorder will be much more easily modified if steps are taken to assist the child early on. Second, many skills and strategies can be introduced when the child is still in primary school and will act as the basis for more sophisticated strategies to be used when the child moves toward adolescence. Third, the sooner parents begin to learn about and work with the disorder, the better equipped they will be to advocate for their child. Fourth, in seeking help for the child it is likely that parents will meet others in similar circumstances and will gain support and comfort from interacting with parents who are confronting similar challenges.

Where to From Here?

We are really at the beginning of developing the knowledge and expertise to work with children, adolescents, parents, and teachers to promote positive outcomes and prevent distress and harm. It is important that we continue to advocate for children with Asperger's Syndrome, that programs be developed and introduced early, and that parents and teachers be trained to work together to promote the best interests of any diagnosed child.

It is also paramount that we continue to validate existing interventions by conducting sound research, and demonstrating techniques and strategies that are effective. It is important to promote continued trials of new and innovative approaches, and to share information with others who work with these children. As knowledge of the spectrum increases, so too should resources and services increase so that everyone can benefit.

REFERENCES

Attwood, T. (1998). *Asperger's syndrome: A guide for parents and professionals*. London: Jessica Kingsley.

Gray, C. (1994a). *Comic strip conversations*. Arlington, TX: Future Horizons.

Gray, C. (1994b). *The new social story book*. Arlington, TX: Future Horizons.

Sofronoff, K., & Attwood, T. (2003). A cognitive behaviour therapy intervention for anxiety in children with Asperger's Syndrome. *Good Autism Practice, 4,* 2–8.

Chapter 8

Supporting Middle and High School Students

Joan S. Safran
Ohio University

How many of us would choose to return to our early high school days—or worse yet, middle school? The transition into adolescence has been considered as the worst of times; according to early adolescent psychologist Gus Hall, a time of "storm and stress." Although prior to the 1960s the woes of adolescence garnered minimal research attention, the last three decades have been marked by massive attempts to investigate, describe, and understand this period. Adolescent years are permeated by anxiety, resistance, confusion, depression, and increased vulnerability to outside forces. Hormones are raging and orientation toward peers skyrockets. Most teens intensely wish to be like everyone else in terms of language, appearance, behaviors, likes, and dislikes. Self-concept, self-esteem, and egocentrism all run amuck. Complications related to family dysfunction, societal upheaval, and the advent of the information age prevail. In the midst of these internal changes, we transform the makeup and focus of school. We move from smaller to much larger settings, to inflexible schedules, more content-specific focus, multiple teachers with different rules, and rigid requirements for fitting in with increasingly important peers.

These are difficult, challenging times for all young people, but for the adolescent with Asperger's Syndrome, this myriad of changes, emphasis on social competence, and explosion of new demands presents additional trials. Identified by Austrian Hans Asperger in 1944, this autistic spectrum disorder went largely unrecognized until the early 1980s, when British researcher Lorna Wing (1981) brought it to the attention of the world. Progressively more prominent in the educational and psychological communities, this neurologically based disorder significantly affects social perception, interactions, language, and nonverbal communication. According to the most recent diagnostic definitions from the American Psychiatric Association (APA) *Diagnostic and Statistical Manual of Mental Disorders* (4th ed., Text Revision [*DSM–IV–TR*]; APA, 2000), Asperger's Syndrome manifests in two primary clusters: qualitative impairment in social interactions and restricted areas of interest with stereotypic behaviors and activities that interfere with normal functioning. Although individuals with Asperger's Syndrome generally perform within the normal range for language development, cognition, and self-help skills, there is some indication that they span the IQ continuum, including persons who are in the mild range of mental retardation (Barnhill, Hagiwara, Myles, & Simpson, 2000; Ehlers et al., 1997). Regardless, Asperger's Syndrome is a continuous, interfering, and lifelong disability.

There are some striking implications in the ways that Asperger's characteristics play out for the adolescent. Although the demands and complexity of the social world intensify, there are fresh options and opportunities that can offset the difficulties. It is essential to note that although the Asperger's Syndrome diagnosis can be beneficial, not all symptoms are present in each individual and there is a wide range of severity. This is not a homogeneous group.

THE BAD NEWS

In the only study specifically addressing social functioning in an adolescent population with Asperger's Syndrome, Green, Gilchrist, Burton, and Cox (2000) concluded that their sample evidenced anxieties, depression, and suicidal ideation similar to a peer group with conduct disorders—but those with Asperger's Syndrome showed significantly more social impairment. These deficits might become more obvious as agemates concentrate on gaining the approval of classmates, finding friends, and fitting in. For example, inability to understand social cues might keep the person with Asperger's Syndrome still talking while others roll their eyes; he or she might not react to deprecating comments or self-monitor what he or she says or does.

Out-of-place behaviors, excused or overlooked in younger children, can prove stigmatizing among younger adolescents, who are more inclined to comply with the social standards of peers. The adolescent who ignores that which is typically embraced by teens (music, clothes, "trends") while promoting his or her own special interest (e.g., Pokemon or train schedules) might find it difficult to fit in with the group. Further, many individuals with Asperger's Syndrome find safety in rigid adherence to routine and rules. The typical adolescent search to stretch the bounds of authority might leave adolescents with Asperger's Syndrome frustrated and confused. They might scold classmates for misleading a substitute teacher, and see no reason to refrain from talking about others' problems or misbehaviors to adults. Although this could make them less susceptible to illegal activity, it will likely set them apart from peers. Oddities and deficits in pragmatics, conversational style, self-regulation, or word usage can also interfere with acceptance. They could have trouble keeping up with teenage slang, leading their language to sound too formal, or even phony or rehearsed. For example, at a memorial service for a classmate who died, a 14-year-old with Asperger's Syndrome remarked, "How fortunate that we can comfort each other during this sad time!" Unlike those with clear cognitive, physical, or sensory disabilities, this person has no obvious explanation for social faux pas and transgressions. Because we anticipate a match between cognitive and social acuity, we are even less prone to make allowances: Given their high intellect, they should know better.

In the context of normal development, individuals engage in social activity and their skills grow: If children with Asperger's Syndrome are excluded from these practice opportunities, they can fall even further behind. Sports participation becomes increasingly based on skill, "play dates" less determined by parents, and parties become more exclusive. I always gave excellent parties for my son, in hopes that he would be invited back. I vividly recall one of the last I held, prior to his diagnosis with moderate to severe Asperger's Syndrome. Seven sixth-grade boys sat around the table eating make-your-own pizza, and their conversation turned to the imminent remarriage of one boy's parent. The boys talked about the discomfort this boy was feeling, and another who had been in a similar situation offered comfort and advice. A few were unable to participate in this intimate kind of conversation, but respectfully listened. Where was my son? As soon as the discussion moved on from the Nintendo craze, he escaped to play video games alone.

In addition, characteristics deemed unattractive in any teens (e.g., motor clumsiness, excessive activity, and varied tics or repetitive behaviors) are often associated with Asperger's Syndrome. Lack of interest, commitment to routine, or for those with acute sensory difficulties, aversion to particular fabrics or fit (see Myles, Cook, Miller, Rinner, & Robbins, 2000) and disregard for common grooming strategies might leave these adolescents outside the all-important fashion trends. Although individual differences among students with Asperger's Syndrome abound, the unique combination of interpersonal, motor, and language characteristics often obscures diagnosis and serves to disconnect persons with Asperger's Syndrome from peers, even those with other disabilities. Lacking both the skills to blend in and the visible distinction that might signal a need for understanding, the individual with Asperger's Syndrome is a natural victim for bullies and at significantly increased risk for depression, additional anxiety disorder, and even suicide. In fact, research (Tantam, 2000) suggests that the incidence and severity of these related conditions are both more serious and prevalent than generally believed.

Signs That We Need to Help

As the child moves from elementary to middle and then high school, parents and professionals need to be alert for signs of deepening isolation from the social community. Earlier friendships driven by proximity or parental support might falter. The old friend might still occasionally visit, but pay little attention to "the nerd" when others are around. In middle school, the lines become further delineated—the popular students from various elementary schools find each other and lunch tables are formed. A common response from students with Asperger's Syndrome to feeling unwelcome at the tables is to eat lunch in the bathroom or hall. Social engagements might move from few to none. One family described their son's seventh-grade year. He was confused by the different styles of his seven teachers, and frequently neglected to match the books he carried home with the subject homework assigned. Frustrated, lonely, and sad, he was further humiliated by bullying in the halls. His unrestrained responses were reinforcing to bullies, so it happened time and again. Although he was unable to explain his feelings, his grades dropped and incidents of temper tantrums and self-destructive behaviors increased in quantity and severity both in school and at home. Any changes in grades, behavior, and activities should therefore be explored as indicators that problems could be getting out of hand.

Role in the Family

Lamarine (2001) described one family's experience with a daughter with Asperger's Syndrome. She was undiagnosed until her later teens, and the author noted that the strain of trying to help and understand this child was largely responsible for her parents' divorce. Certainly many, if not most, families remain intact, but parents commonly report extreme stress, both internal to the family and in their relationship to the external world. All parents of teenagers share the stress of mood swings and emerging independence issues, but the quality and extreme nature of issues for many individuals with Asperger's Syndrome add a unique dimension. Our problems are hard to explain to families with typical teens, who might moan about their taste in music or clothes or need to be like everyone else. How I longed to experience what it would be like to have a child who felt a need to conform!

Parents like Jacqui Jackson (2003) and Liane Holliday Willey (2001, 2003; she is also a self-proclaimed "aspie") recounted the ways in which their adolescent children with Asperger's Syndrome impacted family life. Countless other parents in workshops, support groups and listservs have shared stories of how their children and their parenting are judged and censured by family members and friends who are less forgiving of an older child's flaws. Further, there is a whole new set of concerns: What about sexuality? Safety and legal issues in the wider world? Preparation for adult life? In families with other children, there is the constant effort to balance the needs of the child with the disability and those of typical siblings.

In an attempt to contribute to our understanding of family dynamics, Dellve, Cernerud, and Hallberg (2000) investigated relationships and coping mechanisms through the perspectives of adolescent sisters of boys with deficits in attention, motor control, and perception, Asperger's Syndrome; or both. The researchers found that all 14 respondents described their lives as a "dilemma of requirements and concerns" centered about their disabled siblings. Those who were best informed about the disability generally described a "family-oriented" method of coping and were most empathic and bonded to their brothers; alternately, those most concerned with increasing independence and self-protection were more removed.

THE GOOD NEWS

It is clear that we are in the midst of an information explosion on Asperger's Syndrome. When I first looked for books on Asperger's Syndrome in 1998, Amazon.com had about 12 hits, compared to a May 2003 list of more than 100. Articles are no longer limited to autism-specific journals but appear in general education publications and across related professions: Many entire issues have been devoted to this topic. Autism centers around the country (e.g., Universities of North Carolina and Kansas; Yale University) are allocating time, space, personnel, and funds to study and work with this population. Pharmacological options are growing better, safer, more effective, and more affordable. Preservice teachers are learning about Asperger's Syndrome in classes, and workshops sponsored by publishers, universities, national advocacy groups, and regional special education centers are routinely offered across the country. Internet sites number in the hundreds and advocacy groups are finding their voice. Asperger's Syndrome has been featured in the *New York Times, Wired, Time,* and *Newsweek* magazines; ABC's *Primetime*; and even an episode of NBC's *Law and Order.* We are seeing a resultant swell in public awareness and understanding and tremendous increase in earlier rates of diagnosis. Given the commitment of resources, families, and researchers, our ability to provide appropriate services and supports is exponentially beyond what it was even a few short years ago.

Those adolescents who were identified and received services at a younger age undoubtedly enter their secondary years with advantages. Various therapies have helped them to better manage their behaviors, teachers have built a foundation of effective strategies that can be passed on, and peers have become accustomed to their differences and learned effective ways to communicate. Even those adolescents missed or misdiagnosed can benefit from the variety of options that secondary school affords: There is band, drama club, math club, sports managing, school service, and more. My son discovered a haven in his volunteer work as a high school library aide. If the special interest can be shaped in a socially acceptable direction (e.g., music or Web design), it can transmit status and serve as a connection point to like-minded peers. By 10th grade or so, typical students are becoming more flexible in their judgments and more willing to accept and value difference. Recognition of historical figures like Thomas Jefferson, and other successful individuals who might have the syndrome provides positive role modeling and opportunities for identifying that enhance self-esteem.

Intervention History

There are numerous articles (e.g., J. S. Safran, 2002a, 2002b; S. P. Safran, Safran, & Ellis, 2003; Williams, 2001) and books (e.g., Attwood, 1998; Cumine, Leach, & Stevenson, 1998) offering solid, general intervention strategies, many of which are applicable to adolescents. Although this growing literature on interventions is as yet in its data-based infancy and offers limited adolescent-specific focus, there is a clear move toward addressing these needs. Most data-generating research on adolescence is descriptive in nature (Barnhill et al., 2000; Carrington & Graham, 2001; Connor, 2000; Gilchrist et al., 2001; Koning & Magill-Evans, 2001), but there are a growing number of books (e.g., L. Jackson, 2002; Myles & Adreon, 2001; Willey, 2003) and articles (e.g., Adreon & Stella, 2001; Barnhill, Cook, Tebbenkamp, & Myles, 2002; Gutstein & Whitney, 2002; Marks et al., 1999) offering adolescent-specific strategies regarding individual and group social skills training, speech and language and occupational therapies, classroom practice, and even transitions.

Probably the most widely used intervention strategy involves the use of social stories and comic book conversations, developed by Gray (1995). Success with similar populations has been carefully documented, and teachers indicate that they are both classroom-friendly and applicable to Asperger's Syndrome. Rogers and Myles (2001) described the use of these techniques with an eighth-grader with Asperger's Syndrome, concluding that they seemed to help Tom "understand his social world." There are also models emphasizing the development of friendships with typical peers. Citing other researchers' suggestions, Whitaker, Barratt, Joy, Potter, and Thomas (1998) developed ways to use the Circle of Friends approach specifically for middle and early high school students, intended to engage peers as positive supports for six students with Asperger's Syndrome. They pronounced the efforts successful, crediting the fact that they produced changes in the social culture of the schools, making them more accepting of the students' differences.

We can only speculate about the actual numbers of persons identified with Asperger's Syndrome in schools and how they are being served, but there are some recognizable trends. Although many students remain in regular classes, Asperger's Syndrome is associated with the full continuum of support: Some are provided with one-to-one aides or other significant levels of special education supports; others receive only minimal direction from 504 or individualized education plans (IEPs). Academic achievement ranges from impaired to exceptional, but regardless of cognitive ability, sociocentric intervention is essential to ensure that these students do not fail in other important ways. With careful intervention from informed adults—parents, friends, teachers—who model and advocate acceptance and understanding of this child, the middle and high school years can provide ample opportunity for adolescents to practice and learn the rules for school and life and the move from traditional elementary to middle or junior high school can be shaped toward ensuring success.

STRATEGIES AND SUPPORTS FOR SECONDARY STUDENTS

Transition Planning

Prior to the school year, carefully select teachers and the support person, conduct professional development activities for the full staff (with additional support for classroom teachers), prepare the student, and walk through the schedule.

One way to minimize the impact of moving from one or two to multiple instructors is to seek consistency in teacher characteristics and styles. The most desirable teachers are flexible, patient, and structured; have clear rules, routines, and expectations; and espouse a more student-centered approach. The special educator, school psychologist, or guidance counselor, in some cases conjointly with parents, must provide substantive information and suggestions for these primary teachers. (See J. S. Safran and Safran's [2001] description of the consultation process related to Asperger's Syndrome for more detailed information about the collaborative process.) One of these individuals should also plan to become a primary support person for the child, assuming some responsibility for helping him or her to learn the hidden agenda and unwritten rules of the school, and to be available for comfort or consultation in times of crisis. Leaving the all-day teacher relationship typical in elementary schools, the student needs the comfort of one person to turn to if he or she is particularly upset or overwhelmed. Because the student might react differently or more intensely to some disturbance or unexpected event, this contact person should be available throughout the day to help prevent or defuse a crisis.

It is imperative to educate the full staff, including all teachers, cafeteria and office workers, and so on, to ensure that they can interact effectively with the student outside of scheduled classes, in cafeteria, in the office, and in the hall. One school district addressed the issue of transitioning from elementary to middle school by having a full staff professional development session for one half-day; the next day, the expert was engaged in one-to-one meetings with each subject teacher, assessing the classroom environments and helping to identify appropriate adjustments and supports. The student was primed for the move during the late spring, and his trusted elementary teacher served as a "bridge," introducing him to his new teachers, helping to translate their rules and expectations, and sharing her insights with them. In August, prior to the start of the school year, he walked through his schedule, including locker and homeroom, until some comfort was achieved before the first day of school. The elementary teacher identified a cadre of empathic students who had been kind to him; we looked for congruence in classes and approached various individuals to walk with him from class to class. A more formal buddy system or Circle of Friends (Whitaker et al., 1998) plan can also be put in place. Whenever involving peers, make sure to provide thoughtful, direct information about their role, and encourage them to seek ongoing guidance, suggestions, and support.

Managing the School Day

Build in "quiet time," a safe haven, alternatives to potentially stressful events, and prepare for changes in routine.

Interpersonal interactions are not automatic for students with Asperger's Syndrome. In the company of others, they might perceive themselves as "on stage" and "on alert," constantly preparing to substitute intellectual analysis for natural empathy and insight. Some teenagers with Asperger's Syndrome explain their school day as "the masquerade" (Carrington & Graham, 2001). Social cues that spark an intuitive response in others are processed cognitively instead. One adolescent with Asperger's Syndrome explained his thought processes in this way: "You know how when I'm upset, you just know what to do? Well, if you're upset, I can't do that. I have to look at your face, input the information to my brain—you're crying, you look sad—and then my brain tells me I'm supposed to say, 'what's wrong?'" In sum, social interactions are work.

Each day on my son's return from middle and early high school, he was so on edge that the slightest comment or question I raised could spark a rage. In our attempts to figure out why (was it just because his medication had worn off?), the simplest answer was the truest: He was so worn out from the effort to engage, even minimally, all day, that he had nothing left for even surface conversation once he got home. Building in a "people break" during the school day can mitigate this stress. Access to a quiet, private place where the student can choose to spend lunchtime, study hall, or other free time alone can alleviate the stress that accompanies the constant effort to fit in. If possible, it is beneficial to connect this space with the support person (resource room or guidance office); the library, computer lab, or other quiet places are also commonly employed. Ideally, this familiar space can serve as the safe haven and crisis prevention alternative, for self or teacher directed time-out. By the middle and high school years, students can be helped to recognize the symptoms that precede a "meltdown." A verbal agreement or written contract, agreed to by student, teachers, and support person, can delineate the steps for instituting this therapeutic time-out, assuaging students' fears of being trapped in situations they cannot cope with or seem to be escalating out of control.

Students with Asperger's Syndrome thrive on predictability and routine. Class schedules and time frames, explained and written on the blackboard or student desk, can reduce the anxiety that can overwhelm these individuals. Whenever possible, explain changes in routine in advance and then again right before the occurrence ("On Friday, there will be a music assembly. That means you will go straight from your second-period class to the auditorium and will miss your third-period class."). Consider the use of social stories or other priming techniques to run the student through scenarios that explain this change. Because many students with Asperger's Syndrome are visual learners, provide a reminder note and suggest that the student refer to it whenever he or she (inevitably) repeats the question. (It is also helpful to have a general discussion indicating that advance notice is not always possible.)

The chaos of school assemblies, strangeness of standardized testing days, or other changes to routine can be disturbing to the point of ruining a whole day. The safe haven can provide an alternative to attending the least compelling events and serve as a testing site.

Special Education Services

These services may be continued or initiated. The range includes special schools, full-time aides, resource room, consultation, 504 plans, related service support, and so on.

Even without specified intellectual difficulties, many students will struggle not only with social, but academic tasks as well. Low frustration tolerance, visual-motor integration and writing problems, inability to understand inference, and general organization difficulties might hamper their understanding or capacity to complete assignments. Reports from the field indicate that services span the continuum, from placement in special schools for developmental disabilities and autism spectrum disorders, to one-to-one aides, to nothing at all. Aides serving as "social interpreters" in classrooms have been used to help students interpret rules of conduct, cue social responses, and manage emotions, as well as organize and address academic tasks. Despite the need for social instruction, this approach might be less beneficial in later school years as it can foster dependency and label the student as incapable of functioning on his or her own.

At the very least, Asperger's Syndrome can be considered as a severe learning disability in socialization; most adolescents will therefore benefit from access to some special support in general or special education classes or through related services, to practice and develop social skills and help learn those unwritten rules. Even generally strong rote learning skills might not be sufficient to meet the more complex demands of high school curriculum, to do more independently, to organize workload, to synthesize, and to infer. Resource room or tutoring support is therefore likely to enhance the secondary student's chances for success. Working directly with the student, the special educator will be able to identify the most relevant adjustments, work on specified skills, and become a valuable resource, sharing what he or she has learned with subject teachers. To promote organization, the IEP might indicate that the student attend a morning or late afternoon session for the purpose of reviewing the day, organizing homework, and planning coping strategies. An IEP or 504 Plan can also legitimize requests for adjustments in classes, including use of word processing, additional visual supports, time limit and place to take tests, and so on. These adjustments can be applied to standardized testing such as SATs and ACTs for the college bound. The special educator can serve as advocate and consultant to general education teachers and might also recruit and train peers as social interpreters and supports.

Promoting Academic Success

Use special interests as bridges to subject areas, carefully choose and educate teachers, specifically teach organization skills, identify and use individualized adjustments, and orchestrate seating and group work.

Rather than considering the student's special interest a liability, look for ways it can serve as a bridge to various subjects. For example, the student with a passion for the Internet could be asked to serve as the group research specialist, with the stipulation that he or she work with others and only search for designated topics. The student could be directed to teach a classmate particular search skills, to prepare for a future switch of group roles. His or her interest in military history could be a springboard for a literature assignment such as a general's biography or a novel related to a particular historic period. In a physics class, teachers might capitalize on a student's fascination with science fiction by having him or her write about, explain, or do a project focusing on the relevant real science. We must, however, move beyond this one area and encourage expansion of interests and activities. Teachers who only work with the student's special interest inadvertently feed the obsession.

As mentioned earlier, the match between teachers and student will be a strong contributor to student success. Historically, we perceive teachers of older students as perhaps more content- than child-centered, but those who maintain a more holistic, student-focused approach are likeliest to work well with this student. Willingness to learn about the condition, make suggested adjustments, and explain social and curricular nuances is mandatory. Given sufficient support, most teachers will find ways to try to meet student needs, but those who are unwilling or unable to bend can cause serious harm. Once we started teaching teachers about Asperger's Syndrome, my son's high school life improved dramatically. He was able to speak openly about his frustrations and misunderstandings, and teachers made efforts to address his concerns, involve other students, and cue him regarding inappropriate behaviors. Although my son—and most with Asperger's Syndrome—generally flourish in structured situations, excessive rigidity in a teacher can backfire. One teacher was uncomfortable abiding by preset arrangements for time-out. Waiting to receive help on a difficult project, my son recognized that his frustration with the assignment was getting beyond his control. In keeping with the plan, he repeatedly asked to be excused to go to his safe haven in the guidance office; the teacher told him he would have to wait. His voice got louder and his nervousness increased; he started pacing, and finally escalated into a full-blown tantrum, complete with head-banging and screams. Only then did she send for support. Given this teacher's style, the lone practical solution was for him to drop this class.

Organizing multiple subjects, getting homework and long-term projects done, and even bringing the right books home each day challenge all transitioning students, but are especially onerous chores to the student with Asperger's Syndrome. A refrain I hear from teachers and parents all the time is, "She has the math assignment but brought her science book home instead!" Handing out an assignment book is no guarantee that it will be used. Automaticity and spontaneous learning are often lacking; the process of planning and organizing does not magically occur but needs to be taught, prompted, and frequently reinforced. If subject teachers can, for example, have the daily homework assignment on the same spot on the blackboard everyday, students can be prompted into a routine of getting into class and writing it down. At the end of the day, students can review their assignments with the resource teacher and make sure to take the appropriate books home. One simple strategy that has saved countless middle and high school parents, teachers and students stress is having a complete second set of books to keep at home. Voila!

Depending on individual student strengths and challenges, a variety of academic adjustments, similar to those we promote for some students with learning disabilities, can ease the way. Explicitness in direction-giving, preteaching or priming (individually introducing) particularly difficult content, reducing the length or scope of some assignments, and providing additional cues for checkpoints on longer independent activities can minimize frustration and misunderstandings. For students with poor visual integration or motor skills, handwriting can be as frustrating to produce as it is for others to read. Cloze-type outlines can help organize notes while minimizing the amount of writing required; notebooks with built-in copies can be used. Keyboarding works well for some students; many with Asperger's Syndrome respond positively to visuals, graphics, models, and especially computers, but we also need to be alert to signs of potential misuse. The Internet offers a venue wherein the effort and anxiety associated with interpersonal connections is greatly reduced; individuals can get to the message, unconstrained by their social limitations, comfortable in their chosen environment, and relieved of the pressure of the public masquerade. One woman with Asperger's Syndrome noted that access to the Web offers individuals with Asperger's Syndrome "the communication they desire (without) the overwhelming sensory overload of human presence" (Singer, 1999, p. 65) Those unhappy with their own persona can simply invent—and operate—a new one. Many parents of teenagers express concern about a child's overuse of the Internet, but given the predisposition toward obsession associated with Asperger's Syndrome, there is heightened danger. We must therefore be careful observers of adolescent Internet use; be alert to the signs of addiction and be willing to intervene.

A safe, comfortable, and predictable classroom environment will soothe students with Asperger's Syndrome. Random seating can be deadly; these students are natural victims and should not be seated next to known bullies or aggressive students. Instead, place them next to the more mature, understanding peers who might potentially serve as buddies or social translators. Proximity matters: Change seats if necessary, unobtrusively or in the context of changing seats for the entire class.

"Form your own groups," were the four words my son dreaded to hear most. He is not alone; group work has been identified by teachers and students with Asperger's Syndrome as one of the most difficult trials of high school. Teachers have commented that they do not know how to handle the student who cannot find a group: "Usually, I just let him work alone." "I'll look around the room and just place her with the smallest group." "No matter what I do, it's a disaster!" In general, we tend to assume that everyone knows how to function in groups. In fact, effective collaboration is a learned behavior and it benefits all students to be taught specific skills and procedures like delineating clear goals, identifying timelines and responsibilities, and setting up group rules. Planning for each group member to have a specified task ensures that no one will be overlooked or permitted to dominate. Tangible indicators of and limits on speaking time (e.g., an egg timer or a group secretary with a stopwatch) will structure the student with Asperger's Syndrome and also help assure more overall balance in participation. It is essential that teachers supervise the makeup and structure of groups. For occasional group work, the socially challenged student should be included with the most empathic and mature classmates. For ongoing cooperative activity, rotating group membership and emphasis on process over personality can facilitate all students' acceptance of differences and improve their ability to work with others.

Extracurricular Activities and Community service

Select carefully, educate the adults involved, and if necessary, build in some external reward to help establish the routine.

One advantage of secondary over elementary schools is the variety of potential activities. Carefully chosen and monitored, they can serve as practice grounds for social skills and even offer opportunities for making friends. Although participation in sports becomes increasingly competitive (we are beyond the state of "everybody plays"), the mathematically inclined enthusiast might find a niche as a manager or keeper of statistics. Starting with the special interest, we can encourage participation in well-structured activities or clubs where abilities might neutralize social deficiencies (e.g., competitive mathematics groups, computer clubs), but ability alone is not enough for success. Look at group membership: Are the other students likely to be kind, supportive, and accepting? What about the organizer or advisor? One individual's interest in history and politics made him a formidable member of a Model United Nations team in fifth and sixth grades. By middle school, adult advisor involvement decreased. In seventh grade, because of his social difficulties, his contributions were marginalized; by eighth grade, he was forced off the team. Activities' personnel require the same information base and support as teachers. Provide straightforward reading material and opportunities to discuss and understand Asperger's Syndrome. In some cases, the student might be comfortable and willing to talk about his or her disability to the group, and openly discuss ways to deal with the problem constructively.

Volunteer service can also provide important benefits, as an outlet for practicing interpersonal skills, and more important, as a potential community for the youngster who believes he or she does not belong. In general, it is well documented that involvement in service can effectively counter feelings of isolation and "outsiderness" and serves as an effective deterrent to suicide. Teens with Asperger's Syndrome, unable to penetrate the mystifying barrier between themselves and peers, assured of acceptance and able to contribute, not only receive, but can thrive in the right service activity, whether helping at the cat shelter or serving meals to the homeless. Again, preparing the director of the activity to effectively address the quirks of those with Asperger's Syndrome, is a crucial step.

Friendships and Social Sills

Model effective interactions, establish or continue direct teaching of social skills, and seek out and encourage connections with empathic peers.

Unlike those with autism, individuals with Asperger's Syndrome are generally aware of their difference and interested in being part of the elusive social world. They just do not know how. Asperger's Syndrome expert Dr. Tony Attwood (1998), discussing adolescent friendships, noted that the individual will be more interested, comfortable, and able to function with one friend, rather than in a group, but that he or she will find intimacy and self-disclosure problematic. He or she will therefore still attempt to interact primarily in the context of a shared activity and struggle when the context shifts to more personal issues, perhaps reacting inappropriately or inexplicably to an unexpected communication.

Should a teacher or other adult then devalue something he or she says, the message to others is clear. Any obvious signs of irritation, impatience, or disdain will be noted and imitated by the student's peers. Alternately, if you model warmth, acceptance, and ways to restate communications that are misunderstood, peers will too. Be creative in connecting the student with those who are most likely to be accepting and open to friendships and help him or her engage in successful conversations. Marks et al. (1999) offered suggestions for teaching conversation skills; Gray's (1995) comic strip conversation and social story strategies lend themselves well to the issues facing teens and can be incorporated into both school and home settings.

Parents and teachers must intervene to diffuse inappropriate behaviors before the student stigmatizes himself or herself even more. Because students with Asperger's Syndrome do not internalize social rules, their behavior is often noticed as irritating, rude, and immature. Observant teachers can matter-of-factly label the experience or comment ("That was a joke; … an accident … a metaphor …") and encourage classmates to do the same. Ongoing research with teachers indicates that the behavior they—and other students—find most annoying is interrupting. We can prevent and discourage this behavior in a number of nonintrusive ways. For the student who must answer every question, or cannot save his or her own, the teacher could lead the class in reviewing the rules prior to a class discussion; could give the student a discussion checklist and remind him or her to review at the beginning of class; have private conversations explaining issues of participation, noting that you appreciate his or her contributions but must give others a turn; instruct him or her to write questions down, perhaps on a special paper and save them for a designated time; or pair classmates to talk about questions together after teacher comments or group discussion. Hand signals or a quiet touch can also be useful reminders about too-loud or inappropriate speech. A simple "stop" hand motion, initiated at the home dinner table, used by several high school teachers, and now in place in college classes, cues one student to lower his or her voice or just stop talking about obscure naval military battles of World War I.

With assistance, older students can be helped to accurately recognize signs of distress in themselves, to take steps to control them, and to take off to the safe haven before an escalating behavior damages their standing in the classroom. Understanding teachers are the connectors between these students and the rest of the class. Through their interpreting, modeling, supporting, educating peers and others in the school, and stating and standing behind the concept that the classroom is a safe community for all students, teachers can make a life-changing difference for these children.

Collaborate With Parents

Share information, avoid judgments, and recognize and respect family exhaustion and sibling issues.

Family members, as well as teachers, often feel isolated in their attempts to remain understanding and supportive of students with Asperger's Syndrome. Although siblings can be an important support, they might worry that they have, or others will assume they, too, have Asperger's Syndrome. Like other invisible disabilities, there are no obvious explanations that might enlist empathy; inappropriate social behaviors then alienate others in the community. Their unimpaired intellect can be especially confusing—it is hard to understand why they repeat the same mistakes time and again. The futility of our attempts to explain, model, or punish yields feelings of frustration, guilt, and helplessness—like all parents, we desperately want to find the answers and the strategies that will lead our child to happiness.

Current attention to and publicizing of issues regarding Asperger's Syndrome has been a tremendous boon to families, enhancing understanding and providing tools to initiate frank discussion with extended family and friends. One college student remarked that his mother's greatest distress regarding his brother's Asperger's Syndrome was the way her own family derided her parental failings. The many parents who have taken advantage of this information explosion to learn all they can about Asperger's Syndrome are an invaluable resource for schools. Sharing information and insights about the ways that behaviors manifest across environments—and the strategies that work to curtail them—will only benefit the child. For those parents who might be in denial or are simply unaware, teachers' documentation of the specific observations that suggest the diagnosis or reflect successful strategies from school might lead to parental acceptance and essential assistance for the student. As children come in all flavors, so do families. Some will offer unlimited support whereas others appear unwilling to even meet. It could be that we are relieved to have professional educators take on the responsibility and savor the welcome break, or we ourselves might be affected by Asperger's Syndrome and lack the social skills or confidence to interact with expert you. As a parent and educator, I can only urge teachers to avoid judging us—we are doing the best we can, 24/7, to address issues that do not go away. In addition to Asperger's-related obstacles, we are struggling to recognize and fight the very real risks of depression and other mental health difficulties that threaten our children, and we end up simply drained. They need all the support they can get, so we welcome you to our corner and appreciate everything you do to help our children and educate the community.

As are their agemates, these teenagers, too, are on the way to the rest of their lives. Understand that in their misspeak, there is never intent to insult or harm; they care about others, although it might not show. Recognize and celebrate their strengths, their honesty, their focus, and their uniqueness, and guide them to shape that narrow interest in a direction where they can contribute something, perhaps of great value, to us all. As you repeatedly teach and cue social behaviors and share your strategies within the classroom, school, family, and neighborhood, know how important you are in these young people's lives. Everyone you influence is a potential support, friend, and advocate in an expanding community. With the research base growing and information about the condition reaching more and more people, if ever, now is a good time to have Asperger's Syndrome.

REFERENCES

Adreon, D., & Stella, J. (2001). Transition to middle and high school: Increasing the success of students with Asperger Syndrome. *Intervention in School and Clinic, 36,* 286–271.

American Psychiatric Association. (2000). *Diagnostic and statistical manual of mental disorders text revision* (4th ed.). Washington, DC: Author.

Attwood, T. (1998). *Asperger's Syndrome: A guide for parents and professionals.* London: Jessica Kingsley.

Barnhill, G. P., Cook, K. T., Tebbenkamp, K., & Myles, B. S. (2002). The effectiveness of social skills intervention targeting nonverbal communication for adolescents with Asperger Syndrome and related pervasive developmental delays. *Focus on Autism and Other Developmental Disabilities, 17,* 112–188.

Barnhill, G., Hagiwara, T., Myles, B. S., & Simpson, R. L. (2000). Asperger Syndrome: A study of the cognitive profiles of 37 children and adolescents. *Focus on Autism and Other Developmental Disabilities, 15,* 146–153.

Carrington, S., & Graham, L. (2001). Perceptions of school by two teenage boys with Asperger Syndrome and their mothers: A qualitative study. *Autism, 5,* 37–48.

Connor, M. (2000). Asperger Syndrome (autistic spectrum disorder) and the self-reports of comprehensive school students. *Educational Psychology in Practice, 16,* 285–296.

Cumine, V., Leach, J., & Stevenson, G. (1998). *Asperger Syndrome: A practical guide for teachers.* London: David Fulton Publishers.

Dellve, L., Cernerud, L., & Hallberg, L. (2000). Harmonizing dilemmas: Siblings of children with DAMP and Asperger Syndrome's experiences of coping with their life situations. *Scandinavian Journal of Caring Science, 14,* 172–178.

Ehlers, S., Nyden, A., Gillberg, C., Sandberg, A. D., Dahlgren, E. H., & Oden, A. (1997). Asperger Syndrome, autism and attention disorders: A comparative study of the cognitive profiles of 120 children. *Journal of Child Psychology and Psychiatry, 38,* 207–217.

Gilchrist, A., Cox, A., Rutter, M., Green, J., Burton, D., & LeCouteur, A. (2001). Development and current functioning in adolescents with Asperger Syndrome: A comparative study. *Journal of Child Psychology and Psychiatry, 42,* 227–240

Gray, C. (1995). *Social stories unlimited: Social stories and comic book conversations.* Jenison, MI: Jenison Public Schools.

Green, J., Gilchrist, A., Burton, D., & Cox, A. (2000). Social and psychiatric functioning in adolescents with Asperger Syndrome compared with conduct disorder. *Journal of Autism and Developmental Disorders, 31,* 279–293.

Gutstein, S. E., & Whitney, T. (2002). Asperger Syndrome and the development of social competence. *Focus on Autism and Other Developmental Disabilities, 17,* 161–171.

Jackson, J. (2003). Families and parenting: The domino effect. In L. H. Willey (Ed.), *Asperger Syndrome in adolescence* (pp. 207–226). Philadelphia: Jessica Kingsley.

Jackson, L. (2002). *Freaks, geeks & Asperger Syndrome.* Philadelphia: Jessica Kingsley.

Koning, C., & Magill-Evans, J. (2001). Social and language skills in adolescent boys with Asperger Syndrome. *Autism, 5*(1), 23–36.

Lamarine, R. (2001). Asperger Syndrome: Advice for school personnel. *Preventing School Failure, 45*(4), 148–153.

Marks, S. U., Schrader, C., Levine, M., Hagie, C., Longaker, T., Morales, M., et al. (1999). Social skills for social ills: Supporting the social skills development of adolescents with Asperger's Syndrome. *Teaching Exceptional Children, 32*(2), 56–61.

Myles, B. S., & Adreon, S. (2001). *Asperger Syndrome and adolescence.* Shawnee Mission, KS: Autism Asperger Publishing.

Myles, B. S., Cook, K. T., Miller, N. E., Rinner, L., & Robbins, L. A. (2000). *Asperger Syndrome and sensory issues: Practical solutions for making sense of the world.* Shawnee Mission, KS: Autism Asperger Publishing.

Rogers, M. F., & Myles, B. S. (2001). Using social stories and comic strip conversations to interpret social situations for an adolescent with Asperger Syndrome. *Intervention in School and Clinic, 36,* 310–313.

Safran, J. S. (2002a). A practitioner's guide to resources on Asperger Syndrome. *Intervention in School and Clinic, 37,* 283–291.

Safran, J. S. (2002b). Supporting students with Asperger Syndrome in general education. *Teaching Exceptional Children, 34*(5), 60–66.

Safran, J. S., & Safran, S. P. (2001). School-based consultation for Asperger Syndrome. *Journal of Educational and Psychological Consultation, 12,* 385–395.

Safran, S. P., Safran, J. S., & Ellis, K. (2003). Intervention ABCs for children with Asperger Syndrome. *Topics in Language Disorders, 23,* 154–165.

Singer, J. (1999). "Why can't you be normal for once in your life?" From a problem with no name to the emergence of a new category of difference. In M. Corker & S. French (Eds.), *Disability discourse* (pp. 59–67). Philadelphia: Open University Press.

Tantam, D. (2000). Psychological disorder in adolescents and adults with Asperger Syndrome. *Autism, 4,* 47–62.

Whitaker, P., Barratt, P., Joy, H., Potter, M., & Thomas, G. (1998). Children with autism and peer group support: Using "Circle of Friends." *British Journal of Special Education, 25,* 60–64.

Willey, L. H. (2001). *Asperger Syndrome in the family.* Philadelphia: Jessica Kingsley.

Willey, L. H. (Ed.). (2003). *Asperger Syndrome in adolescence.* Philadelphia: Jessica Kingsley.

Williams, K. (2001). Understanding the student with Asperger's Syndrome: Guidelines for teachers. *Intervention in School and Clinic, 36,* 287–292.

Wing, L. (1981). Asperger's Syndrome: A clinical account. *Psychological Medicine, 11,* 115–129.

Chapter 9

Supporting College Students With Asperger's Syndrome

Lawrence A. Welkowitz and Linda J. Baker
Keene State College

Little has been written to date about both the nature of Asperger's Syndrome for college-aged individuals and about strategies and therapies for helping at this age level. Yet the challenges for these individuals are great: Thrust into an "adult-like" community with little or no parental-type supervision, the college student with Asperger's Syndrome is like a boat without sails that has been set off to sea. The transition from high school to college is momentous for any student. For many, it means leaving home, sometimes going far away, to embark on his or her most significant transition to adulthood. However nurturing or challenging the home environment has been, it is familiar, family members are accustomed to one another's differences, and have established rituals and routines. Any student going off to college must not only deal with leaving the familiar, often supportive home environment, but learn a new set of skills that affect all aspects of daily living. These include learning how to monitor and make choices about food intake and sleeping patterns, dealing with health problems; creating and following a schedule that changes from day to day and is dictated by classes, assignments, and social pressures; and remembering to show up for meetings and appointments. Of course, for any student, negotiating the social life of college and living full time with one's peers might be the most extraordinary undertaking. Roommates, shared bathrooms and dining facilities, drug and alcohol consumption, sexual norms, and the desire to make new friends initially overwhelm even the most socially competent students.

For students with Asperger's Syndrome, the change is daunting. If they have been successful enough to make it to college, they have almost certainly had intensive support from parents, relatives, teachers, counselors, and special educators, all of whom have put systems in place to maximize their success. Often they have received daily assistance with organization, routine, personal hygiene, and negotiating the social world. One high school student commented that his mother had been his "Week at a Glance." Most important, they have been able to leave their peers and return to the sanctuary of their homes and bedrooms at the end of every school day. This all changes when students go off to college. For those living on campus, negotiating the social scene is primary. For the student with Asperger's Syndrome this means unceasing overstimulation and stress, as well as new opportunities for social development when needed support systems are in place. In this chapter we provide case studies and anecdotal reports of college students with Asperger's Syndrome who are receiving support from our campus-based program.

CASE DESCRIPTION: ARNOLD

Arnold is a 20-year-old college student majoring in geography at Keene State College. He was diagnosed with Asperger's Syndrome at age 14 and spent much of his high school days in the principal's office, typically for explosive or threatening behavior that followed being teased or not being allowed to do as he pleased in class. In addition to his special interests and abilities in geography (he excelled at geography competitions), Arnold became very interested in the college radio station where he worked for a time as an on-air disc jockey. Because of his abilities in solving technical problems at the station, Arnold quickly became an invaluable member of the station's governing board and was generally accepted by his fellow station members, many of whom could be described as "quirky" or "artsy" compared to most students. Because of his work at the station, Arnold was able, for the first time, to establish friendships. He began to feel hopeful about having a more successful social life. Following a relatively minor conflict with the station manager, Arnold lost his temper, made threatening remarks, and was terminated from the station by a board comprised of student peers. Angry at their decision, Arnold most recently decided to seek revenge by initiating a strike of the station. He has been spending more time with his parents in recent months so that they can monitor his activities more closely.

Although college and university-based counseling centers typically offer prepaid psychotherapy services unfettered by managed care restraints, a sympathetic ear of a well-meaning counselor unfamiliar with Asperger's Syndrome might not be sufficient to help the student survive the social and academic pressures of college.

Colleges and universities across the country are just beginning to face the problems of accommodating students with spectrum disorders (Prince-Hughes, 2003). As secondary students of the individual education plan (IEP) generation (i.e., students who received services and accommodations under the Individuals with Disabilities Education Act [IDEA]) grow up and begin to enter college, questions loom about the degree to which higher education will grant these new levels of assistance, especially to students with autism or Asperger's Syndrome. Whether colleges are ready or not, students such as Arnold who have become accustomed to receiving "social" or other supportive services, are beginning to pursue higher education, and their success or failure could be dependent on the degree to which they can be identified and helped by college communities.

Although it is commonly accepted that the transition from high school to college is an extremely stress-producing period (e.g., Baker, McNeil, & Siryk, 1985), and we know that this change can be particularly difficult for those with Asperger's Syndrome or high-functioning autism (Glennon, 2001), we are trying to understand and confront these difficulties. To begin with, college staff and faculty have not been expected to provide the level of social support needed by this population, as opposed to academic support that has been increasingly provided by on-campus disability offices and learning centers. Similar problems might lie with college residential life staff that might be unfamiliar with Asperger's Syndrome or hesitant to work with these individuals. At Keene State College, we (faculty in psychology) have embarked on an "experiment in living" that is designed to mobilize the college community to provide interest in and support for individuals with Asperger's Syndrome. This effort has been funded by a foundation grant and has helped us begin to direct efforts to shifting students with Asperger's Syndrome from outsider social status to insider status. In working hard to help students with Asperger's Syndrome, we hope that we will not only positively impact the experience of the affected student, but that we as a community (professors, staff, neurotypical students) will change as well.

With the help of a grant from the Doug Flutie, Jr. Foundation, we have been experimenting with a multifaceted peer mentor program designed to provide social support and friendship, as well as help develop the interpersonal skills needed to survive in a residential college campus community. In this chapter we focus on the hallmark features and themes of the program and identify pitfalls and areas of success.

CASE DESCRIPTION: GABBY

Gabby is a 20-year-old college student diagnosed with autism in early childhood and currently diagnosed with high-functioning autism. Because of his remarkable abilities in computer science, several faculty have taken an interest in helping him to plan his professional future. Although he also has exceptional abilities in art and graphic design, he has generally had difficulties succeeding in the classroom due to a variety of odd behaviors, including speaking out of turn, asking too many questions, and touching other students' notes or class materials. Although Gabby appears to enjoy campus life, he has been particularly vulnerable to teasing and other forms of social humiliation. Despite his social awkwardness, Gabby's outward friendliness has slowly gained him a number of social contacts and he is now maintaining a fairly high profile on campus.

COLLEGE SUPPORT PROGRAM: OVERVIEW

As faculty members in the psychology department, we are known for our focus on Asperger's Syndrome, and this has led to increasing connections with diagnosed students who are struggling with symptoms that interfere with functioning at college. Students with Asperger's Syndrome or autism who have indicated the need and the interest are assigned one or more peer mentors who are hired on an hourly basis to provide social support and problem-solving assistance. In some cases, the peer mentor is also receiving course credit through the Department of Psychology's practicum (internship) program. Peer mentors have typically been motivated students, often psychology majors, who have approached one of us and expressed an interested in working with individuals with autism or Asperger's Syndrome. They have also agreed to attend regular group supervision meetings and to maintain contact with assigned "mentees." The mentors in turn "contract" with their mentees to meet on a regular (at least weekly) basis. This is especially important for individuals with Asperger's Syndrome who might fail to appear for appointments due to poor organizational abilities or conflicting feelings about regular exposure to social activity. In addition to in-person meetings, peer mentors and mentees eventually correspond by e-mail and telephone as well.

Group supervision meetings for mentors provide an opportunity to review the progress of each mentee, discuss roadblocks to promoting new social behaviors, and plan for the "next step" in their program. They are also an opportunity to discuss a range of issues including confidentiality, maintaining boundaries, and dealing with co-occurring psychiatric problems (e.g., depression, anxiety, conduct problems). Although these meetings were originally viewed as a time for supervising faculty to provide clinical-type supervision, we have discovered that much of our own clinical training does not quite fit these new types of relationships, which clearly are not quite of the therapist–patient or therapist–client sort. As a result, we have shifted more to the role of facilitator in which we raise issues, but try to create an environment that supports "idea flow" in a less hierarchical manner (Peterson & Peterson, 1997). Student mentors often initiate discussion that is enlightening for all of us.

Students with spectrum disorders are referred to the peer mentor program in a variety of ways, including referral from the college's disability office or counseling center or by self-initiated contacts with one of the two supervising faculty. Most recently, parents of incoming students have made the initial contact as a result of hearing about our grant funding on various Internet Web sites. Because of the variability of awareness of one's own condition among college students with Asperger's Syndrome, it is most likely the case that numerous potential participants never make it to our offices. Some might remain unidentified because their symptoms do not include disruptive or explosive behaviors and they might struggle quietly on their own, isolated and lonely. Others might not have been previously identified as having Asperger's Syndrome because this syndrome has only recently been recognized and discussed in the United States. In some cases, potential participants are being newly labeled as having "nonverbal learning disability" (Rourke, 1995), which they probably do not see as being a related spectrum disorder.

PROGRAM ELEMENTS

Social Support

The notion that social networks provide important buffers against stress and depression has become a truism of psychology. Simply put, friends and other helpful individuals such as therapists and caring teachers serve as important sources of validation, empathy, and reflection (Rogers, 1951), as problem solvers (Shure & Spivak, 1978), coaches (Foa, 2001), and models of new behaviors (Bandura, 1997). When individuals with Asperger's Syndrome arrive at college they tend to isolate themselves by staying in their rooms and failing to initiate social contacts with neighbors or other students in class or elsewhere. Or, they might initially make some attempt to talk and socialize with others but might be excluded due to their social awkwardness. In either case, social avoidance becomes a reinforced behavior in that it produces removal of aversive social interactions, and rarely leads to friendships or even friendly acquaintances. As a result, college students with Asperger's Syndrome do not reap the benefits of even small social networks.

Instant social contacts and friendships provided by a peer support program help to create these networks. Because peer mentors are providing services in real-life contexts (i.e., in the dorms, classes, student union, college gym), they usually end up introducing the individuals with Asperger's Syndrome to their friends and roommates, which in turn causes exponential growth in social networks. In our staff meetings we have referred to "insider mentors" (those who receive regular supervision and are paid to do this work) and "outsider mentors" (those who become friends and informal mentors as a result of being introduced to the individual with Asperger's Syndrome by the original mentor). In some cases, outsider mentors have eventually become insider mentors. In one case, an individual with Asperger's Syndrome receiving mentor services simultaneously became a mentor himself to another, more seriously affected student. This insider–outsider distinction has been useful when addressing such issues as confidentiality, in which case insiders are held to a higher level of standard than are outsiders.

It is important to note that there have been unforeseen difficulties that arise from creating social networks as well. Because individuals with Asperger's Syndrome find social interaction stressful (even with supportive, friendly peers) there is often a tendency to retreat into isolation. As Arnold put it, "When I go in to my cave, which is what I call my apartment, I feel more relaxed. I think when I took last semester off and stayed home it actually prevented me from becoming more depressed." Gabby's mother described a recent 2-week vacation for Gabby as being a stress-free respite from the pressures of school: "He was in heaven … he slept until noon each day and would hang out in shopping malls by himself." Because escape will invariably occur, we have found it important to advise mentors to "back off" but also to be available to help the mentee for re-entry into the social world. Mentors are told to become a bit more assertive regarding contact only when the retreat has lasted for a prolonged period (more than a few days).

There are also challenges to maintaining social networks related to the mentee's difficulties with social reciprocation. Put simply, friendships are two-way streets that require mutually reinforcing activities. For example, individuals living in the social world expect that a telephone call will be returned by another call, or that an invitation to one's dormitory room will be reciprocated in kind. Individuals with Asperger's Syndrome do not understand how to maintain such mutually compatible agendas, leading to what Skinner (1969) referred to as *ratio strain,* or too low a rate of reinforcement of other people's behavior. The advantage of regular group peer mentor meetings is that they afford the opportunity to reinforce the reinforcer or at least validate the frustrating feelings of peer mentors who might not feel rewarded by the behavior of their mentees.

Mentors as Coaches

Changes in the U.S. health care system have led to an increased emphasis on shorter term therapies, as insurers and others became concerned about containing the high costs of mental health care. This, combined with increased empirical support for more active types of therapies, including behavioral therapies, lead to the development of new roles for psychotherapists, including the idea of the therapist as coach (e.g., Hallowell & Ratey, 1994) or the therapist as personal consultant or co-active coach (Whitworth, House, Sandahl, & Kimsey-House, 1998). These ideas are increasingly being adopted in educational settings in which children coded with various mental or social disabilities, such as Asperger's Syndrome, are provided with an aide or other staff person who holds brief "check-in" meetings with the affected child to quickly assess any problems, offer quick solutions, and provide emotional support.

In mentoring college students with Asperger's Syndrome or Autism, we have found this model particularly helpful. Both Gabby and Arnold have found it helpful to make brief contacts with a mentor to help interpret a social interaction that occurred that day or to review organizational issues, including blockades to complying with a daily schedule or completion of a homework assignment. Brief meetings serve as buffers against stress and also keep help seeking behaviors under some sort of scheduling (or "stimulus") control. Gabby remarked that he was particularly distressed about a particular problem, but knew that he could talk about it during his brief morning meeting with a mentor, and therefore did not have to call his parents or another dormitory resident very early in the morning or in the middle of the night. A coaching approach also promotes accountability by providing another person who serves as a judge of whether certain social tasks have been carried out. When two of our students with Asperger's Syndrome were recently coached about handling difficult negotiations with professors, our mentors were able to provide immediate follow-up meetings to listen and to provide feedback about their performance.

Social Skills Training

Although it is commonly accepted that individuals with Asperger's Syndrome require some type of social skills training, it is unknown how effective programs designed for children will be for college-age individuals. Goldstein and others (see Goldstein & McGinnis, 1997) have done extensive studies on the effects of behavioral programs on social skill development and their programs are widely utilized in secondary schools in the United States. The basic approach of these programs is to break down social behaviors into clearly identified steps. So, for example, having a conversation might include a greeting, some small talk, making a plan to talk again, and a closing. The trainer helps the student practice these different parts and carries out role plays of simulated social conversations. Therapists and guidance counselors have learned over the years that, although effective in the short run, skills learned in these programs do not generalize to real life-situations. Gray (1995) addressed this issue by replacing such a "scripted" approach with one in which general rules and various perspectives are reviewed and implemented in real-life situations.

Although we utilize elements of all of these types of programs, the advantage of a mentoring program that takes place in the context of where the person with Asperger's Syndrome lives and attends school is the opportunity for repeated social practice in the natural or real-life environment. Peer mentors can analyze the steps or basic approaches to a social behavior, and teach them to mentees, who can then try them out with the mentor's friends. Regular group meetings with mentors also allow for some planning so that one or two social behaviors at a time become the focus, rather than letting both the mentors and college students with Asperger's Syndrome become overwhelmed by trying to fix too much too quickly. Group meetings include some time for analyzing mentees' strengths as well as weaknesses so that new social goals are linked to what behaviorists refer to as current social repertoires (Welkowitz, Bond, & Anderson, 1989).

Another advantage to systematic support for students with Asperger's Syndrome, is that parts of the community that have been unfamiliar with the disability can learn more about the social styles of those with Asperger's Syndrome. This educative process includes presenting workshops to the campus community on the nature of Asperger's Syndrome, showing an educational videotape (*Understanding Asperger's* by Welkowitz & Baker, 2000), speaking about Asperger's Syndrome in the context of multiculturalism, and being available to staff and faculty for consultation whenever problems arise. The goal then is not just to improve the social skill levels of college students with Asperger's Syndrome, but to raise awareness of those around the individual with Asperger's Syndrome so that the community becomes more understanding and appreciative of these people. This educative process was one we began even before receiving financial support for the peer mentorship program. We were aware of the importance of creating a "web of support" on campus for students with Asperger's Syndrome.

Learning Styles

It is difficult to make across-the-board statements about the learning styles of individuals with Asperger's Syndrome compared to those of more "typical" individuals, but there are certain common themes that arise with many of our identified college students. A number of investigators have pointed out difficulties in identifying faces as well as the emotion expressed in faces. We have observed our student with high-functioning autism, Gabby, having difficulty identifying newly introduced friends in situations or places that are very different (e.g., meeting someone for the first time on campus and then seeing that person again in town). In her collection of personal stories of college students with Asperger's Syndrome and autism, Prince-Hughes (2002) presented a student named Darius who refers to similar events as problems in "context-based learning." Arnold, for example, has learned to limit inappropriate remarks in certain social situations, but not in others. Another student, Craig, remembers to use verbal greetings whenever he is with his mentor, but "forgets" to do so when he is on his own. In such cases, the use of social scripts, although useful initially to teach a social behavior, do not ensure transfer to other situations. In addition to use of prompts and other reminders, we have been experimenting with Gray's social stories approach that provides more general rules, descriptions of social scenarios, and various perspectives for addressing this problem (Gray, 1995).

College students with Asperger's Syndrome, just like younger individuals with Asperger's Syndrome, often have problems in nonverbal communication. For college-aged individuals, an inappropriate eye gaze or out-of-sequence comment might be seen as inappropriately sexually aggressive. In our program, several of our adult males have been accused of sexually harassing behaviors, when their intentions might have been otherwise. Our approach has been to encourage a social communication style that emphasizes asking questions. For example, we coach adults with Asperger's Syndrome interested in pursuing romantic interests to ask others such questions as, "Are you going out with anybody?" or "Would it be alright if I asked you out?" In terms of physical contact, we encourage using the questioning approach to obtain consent at every new level of contact (e.g., "Is this alright with you?"). Whereas neurotypicals rely on more subtle cues for obtaining consent, we urge our students with Asperger's Syndrome to be more verbal and overt about this (see Board of Trustees of Antioch College, 1996).

We also encourage our students with Asperger's Syndrome to follow a careful stepwise or hierarchical approach to developing both romantic and nonromantic friendships. Following such a step-by-step program is at the heart of a behavioral approach to building new behaviors (Goldstein & McGinnis, 1997; Watson &

Tharp, 2001). When Craig became interested in developing an intimate relationship with a woman on campus, we talked with his peer mentor about encouraging him to start by asking a fellow student out for coffee after class. The mentor might even need to do some advance coaching that involves modeling, role playing, and providing feedback about his performance. Although this idea of making new social contacts in a graduated fashion might seem obvious, a pervasive focus of our students with Asperger's Syndrome has been on end results rather than process. For example, college students with Asperger's Syndrome often need help understanding that making friends is an integral part of developing a romantic relationship; this is particularly challenging for those who do not yet know how to make friends. Learning how to relate to one's peer mentor can be seen as the opportunity to learn skills and have experiences that enhance any relationship.

Dealing With Stress

Glennon (2001) noted that to help the college student with Asperger's Syndrome manage stress in an optimal manner, it is important to understand how each student experiences stress. She noted that interventions must be tailored to the individual to take into account personal experience. For example, excessive worry about social interactions and their ensuing stress seems to be more relevant to our students with Asperger's Syndrome than to those with high-functioning autism. It seems that individuals with autism do not worry excessively about what others think about them, probably out of a general notion among more individuals with autism that all individuals have access to the same information and therefore think as they do. So, although social interactions might be somewhat exhausting for a person with autism, the person with Asperger's Syndrome experiences a greater amount of social anxiety. As a result, we might utilize more cognitive techniques for reducing social anxiety with individuals with Asperger's Syndrome, focusing more on behavioral skills-based approaches with individuals with high-functioning autism.

Arnold, who receives peer mentoring, also serves as one of several peer mentors for Gabby. Arnold's concerns about what other people think of him are often so extreme as to seem paranoid. After a recent episode that led to his expulsion from a campus organization, he became preoccupied with the idea that everyone in that organization either hated him or was trying to harm him in some way. Several mentors spent a lot of time helping Arnold to challenge these highly irrational ideas (i.e., a form of cognitive therapy). In a similar fashion, Gabby was nearly expelled from the dormitory following an incident in which he reportedly made threatening remarks. Following a disciplinary hearing, he became confident that everyone would rally to his support. Although it was true that several people did come to his defense, it was also true that he misjudged the degree to which people felt supportive. In the latter case, a more behavioral program was devised to help Gabby deal with anger, which included walking away from high-risk situations.

It is commonly accepted that physical exercise is an excellent stress reducer, but it is an equally common observation that individuals with spectrum disorders avoid exercise. Simple instructions to go to the gym or increase walking simply do not work. We have, however, found success in assigning students with Asperger's Syndrome (both at the high school and college level) to mentors who serve as personal trainers. By developing a close relationship with our physical education program, we have recruited several students who supervise students with Asperger's Syndrome in the gym. Because spectrum individuals tend to be visually oriented (Attwood, 1998), we encourage our physical trainer mentors to set weekly and long-term goals and to chart their mentee's progress. We also encourage our trainers to be assertive in insisting that students with Asperger's Syndrome increase the amount of exercise completed each week. Of course, making regular trips to the college gym also serves a social purpose by providing opportunities for increased contacts with students. On the negative side, we have had to monitor teasing of our students with Asperger's Syndrome by other students, as well as inappropriate behaviors by students with Asperger's Syndrome, such as taking naps on the exercise mats or making inappropriate comments to staff.

Internet Addiction and Other Isolating Special Interests

Excessive use of computers, especially time spent on the Internet, is a common concern of parents of both high school and college-aged individuals with Asperger's Syndrome. During high school years parents are better able to monitor and control time spent with electronics, including video games and Internet-based activities, whereas college students living in dormitories or apartments are on their own. For high school students, scheduling of computer time along with parent-delivered consequences for compliance (or noncompliance) is effective, whereas self-directed instructional approaches are rarely helpful. Rather than prodding college students with Asperger's Syndrome to limit computer time, we instead rely on the development of alternative behaviors. Put simply, we see that nonsocial computer time is reduced only when the student with Asperger's Syndrome has more viable agendas to assert for himself or herself. This "nonpathological" approach argues that rather than eliminating or removing nonadaptive behaviors, we instead build or construct more viable alternatives (Goldiamond, 1984; Welkowitz et al., 1989). Thus, meeting a mentor or other friend for coffee at the student center or a movie becomes "habitual" or part of new behavioral repertoires that serve as more attractive alternatives to isolating home activities.

Collaborative Teaming

Although a team-based approach to managing a student's academic and social problems is usually relegated to secondary schools as mandated by IDEA in the United States, we have found it helpful in some cases to have contact with a student's professors. For Gabby, who has high-functioning autism, these meetings helped faculty vent about odd behaviors (taking naps or not paying attention; getting up frequently and walking out of class; asking too many questions), and provide a forum for group problem solving. Although some problems might be difficult to solve, these gatherings are always welcome opportunities to educate faculty about spectrum disorders. Again in Gabby's case, one faculty member was upset that he seemed not to be listening at times, which provided an opportunity to talk about how people with autism might seem not to be listening when in fact they are doing so. When several professors expressed concern about Gabby asking too many questions, the entire group agreed to ask Gabby to limit himself to a certain number of questions and to write down any others so that he could ask them after class. Another professor agreed to use a hand signal to let Gabby know that he should wait until after class to ask any more questions that day.

Although there are two psychology professors (Baker & Welkowitz) who make themselves available for consultation and meetings with faculty, it is important to note that these meetings take up time and professors are not required to attend. As members of our disability office and counseling center become increasingly familiar with Asperger's Syndrome, they have taken increased responsibility in organizing and running these meetings. It is important for these and other student-support-related activities to become a natural part of regular staff activities. Peer mentors, for example, can be supported primarily through internship or independent study credits that are already a part of a psychology department. Glennon (2001) reported using students from a department of occupational therapy.

In a college setting it is important to recognize that professors are not required to attend such meetings and that academic freedom issues must be respected. This differs notably from the IEP requirements mandated by federal law for primary and secondary school students. Colleges do understand, however, that there are unresolved legal issues regarding the provision of services to students with disabilities, and administrators worry both about doing too little (setting themselves up for litigation by students) and doing too much (setting precedents beyond what they can afford to provide). For now, we rely on the good will of faculty and staff who are, in many cases, interested in learning more about how to help students with Asperger's Syndrome in their classes. In our opinion, it is best to spend precious time working with interested faculty, rather than spending time trying to convince disinterested faculty to get involved.

Sophie is a 21-year-old history major with Asperger's Syndrome whose passion is economic analyses of prewar Germany. She had some difficulties doing oral presentations required in a particular class, primarily because she became anxious when the professor would provide feedback about her inappropriate eye contact or odd movements. She became depressed following "debriefing" sessions in the professor's office during which she felt strongly criticized: "He made me feel like all the progress I had made since I was a kid was for nothing ... all that work and I must be just as awkward and odd as ever." Because the professor did not appear to be interested in meeting with us, we simply encouraged Sophie not to take any more courses with him.

Boundary Issues

As clinical psychologists, we are very concerned with the ethical issue of maintaining appropriate boundaries with those with whom we work. We are especially mindful of the pitfalls of dual or multiple relationships. For example, we are concerned about the problems associated with being both a "friend" and a professor to a particular student because it might complicate perceptions of delivery of a fair grade. We certainly work to avoid the dual role of professor and therapist. For peer mentors, however, the lines become blurry by necessity. Student mentors do become friends, albeit hired ones, to our students with Asperger's Syndrome so that their lives become entwined. They eat together, go to ball games together, and generally "hang out" in their dormitory rooms or apartments. Although we continually raise the issue in group supervision meetings, the peer mentors have convinced us that their relationships are different from the ones psychologists have with patients and they insist on utilizing "friendship" as a model.

Problems, of course do arise. Craig makes regular visits to his mentor's dormitory room, but the mentor's girlfriend felt neglected and began to pressure him to make up for lost time. Although such problems clearly mirror those of real life, the ethical issue raised is to what extent should a college support program be responsible for creating these dilemmas. Furthermore, to what extent should group supervision of mentors in an academic setting address such personal issues? As psychologists, our comfort level in dealing with a range of personal issues is great, but we do wonder how other departments, such as sociology or health science, would handle them.

Another boundary issue that has been raised relates to the line between friendships and romantic relationships. We have paired males and females in peer mentor–mentee relationships, but we encourage both to avoid intimate or romantic relationships. We remind all involved that the purpose of the program is to provide support and social skills training, rather than finding a boyfriend or girlfriend. We also consider the psychosexual history of an individual when assigning a mentor, avoiding matches that could lead to unwanted behaviors. For example, in one case an individual with Asperger's Syndrome had repeatedly told us how desperate he was to have an intimate relationship with a woman. As a result, we paired him with a male mentor with the hope that he could provide more objective advice about dating and related activities.

Housing Problems

In some instances our collaborative consultation models have extended to the area of residential life and problems related to living in college dormitories. As a rule of thumb, we recommend that college students with Asperger's Syndrome have their own rooms, unless they indicate a desire for a roommate. Our thinking has been that our participants with Asperger's Syndrome receive sufficient social exposure by simply attending college and living on campus. A single room can provide a much needed refuge in an otherwise stressful life. Problems that arise in the dormitories have included a tendency toward isolation, inappropriate or offensive remarks made at social gatherings, and making excessive requests for assistance from residential advisors. Many of these issues have been resolved through consultation with relevant staff, which is seen as an opportunity to educate more people about the nature of Asperger's Syndrome, as well as provide practical advice for particular problems.

Peer Mentoring as a Cross-Cultural Experience

Largely as a result of Internet-based communication, individuals with Asperger's Syndrome are beginning to share the details of their lives with one another. Prince-Hughes (2002) referred to an emerging "culture of autism" in which this group of individuals is beginning to connect and discuss plans for surviving in a neurotypical world and even thriving in circles dominated by people with autism and Asperger's Syndrome. A common theme is one of feeling like an oppressed minority with frequent reports of being humiliated and put down by others, denied access to jobs, and given limited access to certain social groups. Internet sites such as Oasis (www.oasis.com) have become clearinghouses for their concerns and patient advocacy groups have sprung up in many places in the United States, United Kingdom, and elsewhere. Numerous books have recently been published in which the personal stories of individuals with Asperger's Syndrome or autism are presented (e.g., Prince-Hughes, 2002; Willey, 1999).

Colleges and universities are logical places for incorporating the next phase of this cultural movement. Because these communities hopefully value new ideas and are especially receptive to those related to diversity and multiculturalism, it makes sense that individuals with Asperger's Syndrome might find a safe haven in these places. We have been fortunate to have ideal conditions to support our venture, including psychology faculty with an academic interest in spectrum disorders, collegial relationships with a number of cooperating programs and departments, a college community that emphasizes the importance of diversity, and a larger community that has been supportive of individuals with a range of disabilities. Although there have been individual staff or faculty who have been wary of our efforts, we have found that some have responded with unexpected enthusiasm. We have also dealt with administrative concerns that our efforts might have the "negative effect" of attracting even greater numbers of students with disabilities, resulting in increased liability and costs in terms of disability services. Although these conflicts are far from being resolved, we are confident that we can forge ahead by coming to some reasonable resolution based on the positive effects of our work.

Our strongest argument in favor of continuing support programs for individuals with Asperger's Syndrome is not just that we are able to provide an essential and effective service, but rather the impact it has on us. We have discovered that even when we make limited progress in helping these students with Asperger's Syndrome to change, we find that our own attitudes and behaviors are transformed. Specifically, we have found ourselves to be more understanding and appreciative of both our differences and similarities, and we regard students with Asperger's Syndrome or autism as having a great deal to contribute both to our own learning and personal growth, as well as to our college community as a whole. Spending time with and befriending these students is not just about delivering an essential clinical service, but about what kind of people we want to be and what kind of communities we want to create.

REFERENCES

Attwood, T. (1998). *Asperger's Syndrome: A guide for parents and professionals.* London: Jessica Kingsley.

Baker, R. W., McNeil, O. V., & Siryk, B. (1985). Expectations and reality in freshman adjustment to college. *Journal of Counseling Psychology, 32,* 94–103.

Bandura, A. (1997). *Self-efficacy: The exercise of control.* New York: Freeman.

Board of Trustees of Antioch College. (1996). *Antioch College sexual offense prevention policy.* Yellow Springs.

Foa, E. (2001). *Stop obsessing: How to overcome your obsessions and compulsions.* New York: Bantam Books.

Glennon, T. J. (2001). The stress of the university experience for students with Asperger Syndrome. *Work, 17,* 183–190.

Goldiamond, I. (1984). Training parent trainers and ethicists in nonlinear analysis of behavior. In R. F. Dangel & R. A. Polster (Eds.), *Parent training: Foundations of research and practice* (pp. 504–546). New York: Guilford.

Goldstein, A., & McGinnis, E. (1997). *Skillstreaming the adolescent.* Champaign, IL: Research Press.

Gray, C. (1995). *Social stories unlimited: Social stories and comic book conversations.* Jenison, MI: Jenison Public Schools.

Hallowell, E. M., & Ratey, J. J. (1994). *Driven to distraction.* New York: Pantheon.

Peterson, D. R., & Peterson, R. L. (1997). Ways of knowing in a profession: Toward an epistemology for the education of professional psychologists. In D. R. Peterson (Ed.), *Educating professional psychologists: History and guiding conception* (pp. 191–228). Washington, DC: APA Books.

Prince-Hughes, D. (Ed.). (2002). *Aquamarine blue: Personal stories of college students with autism.* Athens: Ohio University Press.

Prince-Hughes, D. (2003, January 3). Understanding college students with autism. *The Chronicle of Higher Education,* pp. B16–B17.

Rogers, C. (1951). *Client centered therapy, its current practice, implications, and theory.* Boston: Bantam Books.

Rourke, B. (Ed.). (1995). *Syndrome of nonverbal learning disabilities: Neurodevelopmental manifestations.* New York: Guilford.

Shure, M. B., & Spivak, G. (1978). *Problem-solving techniques in childrearing.* San Francisco: Jossey-Bass.

Skinner, B. F. (1969). *Contingencies of reinforcement: A theoretical analysis.* New York: Appleton-Crofts.

Watson, D. L., & Tharp, R. G. (2001). *Self-directed behavior: Self modification for personal adjustment* (8th ed.). Belmont, CA: Wadsworth.

Welkowitz, L. A., & Baker, L. J. (2000). *Understanding Asperger's* [Educational film]. New York: Insight Media.

Welkowitz, L. A., Bond, R., & Anderson, L. (1989). Social skills and initial response to behavioral therapy for obsessive-compulsive disorder. *Phobia Research and Practice Journal, 2,* 67–86.

Whitworth, L., House, H., Sandahl, P., & Kimsey-House, H. (1998). *Co-active coaching.* Palo Alto, CA: Davies-Black.

Willey, L. H. (1999). *Pretending to be normal: Living with Asperger's Syndrome.* London: Jessica Kingsley.

PART IV

Complementary Services

Chapter 10

Sensory Integration

Traci Gilman
Nashua School District

Alex, a 12-year-old middle school student in the top 10% of his class, spends much of his day with his head buried in an ornithology book. He puts on his backpack 3 minutes before the bell rings so that he is able to dart out of the classroom and into the hallway before the majority of his classmates. He carries the entire day's books in his backpack, so that he does not have to go out of his way to go to his locker. Between classes, Alex awkwardly plows through crowded halls, with his eyes facing the ground in front of him and his bird book clutched tightly to his chest, only looking up when approaching stairs. Stairs cause him profound fear despite the number of times he has traversed them. He is almost always the first person to arrive at each class, where he sits down in the back corner of the room and systematically unpacks his backpack. Alex has a routine for how he goes from one class to the next and rarely varies from that set pattern. He has a place for each pencil, paper, and book in his backpack. He lines them up on his desk in a predetermined order. After completing these routines he rests his head on his hands, with his eyes closed and his fingers in his ears, until the teacher begins the class. This same pattern repeats each class, day in and day out. Alex has few friends and spends minimal time talking with them in the hallway or conversing in general with any other students during his school day. Alex has been diagnosed with Asperger's Syndrome and experiences associated sensory processing difficulties.

The features associated with Asperger's Syndrome, as outlined in the *Diagnostic and Statistical Manual of Mental Disorders* (4th ed, [*DSM–IV*]), include "weaknesses in non-verbal areas (e.g., visual-motor and visual spatial skills)" and "motor clumsiness" that "may contribute to peer rejection and social isolation (e.g. inability to participate in group sports)" (American Psychiatric Association, 2000, p. 81). It states "symptoms of over-activity and inattention are frequent in Asperger Disorder" (p. 81). It is a widely held belief that visual-spatial skills, motor coordination, and the ability to focus attention are directly related to the brain's ability to take in and integrate the sensory information received from multiple senses (Ayers, 1979; Henderson, Pehoski, & Murray, 2002; Reeves & Cermak, 2002). Although it is understood that all people diagnosed with Asperger's Syndrome do not have identifiable sensory integrative dysfunction, this chapter addresses those who do have some level of sensory processing difficulties.

THE SEVEN SENSES

The five most recognized senses are the senses of smell, taste, sight, hearing, and touch. However, two additional but less discussed are vestibular (sense of balance) and proprioception (body awareness). These latter two are as important as the other five, especially when discussing sensory processing in people with Asperger's Syndrome.

In the 1950s Ayers, clinician and researcher, began to examine the ways that sensory processing affects learning. Although her original research was with children with learning disabilities, her conclusions and subsequent research findings are relevant for people with Asperger's Syndrome. This section presents basic information about the visual, tactile, vestibular, and proprioceptive sensory systems so that further discussions about sensory processing and praxis (motor planning) will have greater meaning. Credit is due to Ayers, who is responsible for much of this information. Table 10.1 gives a brief outline of the structure and function of each of the sensory systems, as well as behaviors that a person with Asperger's Syndrome and associated sensory processing difficulties might display.

The Visual System

Visual information is received through specialized receptors in the back of the eye that change light energy into electrical impulses, which are sent to the brain. The visual system is extremely complex; for example, there are at least three pathways that carry visual information that must be integrated with the rest of the nervous system. The primary function of human vision is the ability to visually identify objects in our environment and to visually guide motor actions (Lane, 2002). Different parts of the brain process different pieces of visual information. Object vision is related to processing in the temporal lobe, and vision regarding spatial issues tends to be processed in the parietal lobe (Lane, 2002). The visual system is the sense on which most people primarily depend. It often overrides other senses when there is disparity in the sensory information. An example of this is the tendency to press on the brake of your car when observing movement of an adjacent

TABLE 10.1

Sensory Systems	Receptor Location	Function	Qualities for Alerting	Qualities or Calming	How Processing Difficulties Might Impact Someone With Asperger's Syndrome
Olfactory (smell)	Nose	Provides information about types of smell; closely associated with the gustatory system	Cinnamon, noxious smells	Vanilla, sweet fragrances	• May not understand how their own body odor could be offensive • May have extreme reaction to perfumes, shampoos, cleaning products, air fresheners, environmental smells
Gustatory (taste)	Tongue, tastebuds	Provides information about different types of taste (salty, sweet, bitter, and sour)	Sour, spicy, tart, mint	Sweet, warm, smooth	• May have very restricted or odd diets, although may understand basic nutrition • May be very ritualistic regarding eating establishments and menu options
Visual (sight)	Eyes Rods and cones	Gives us information about light, distance, dimensionality, and movement as well as guides our motor actions	Bright, high contrast	Low or natural lighting	• May have difficulty with depth perception affecting driving abilities • May shy away from many sports requiring eye–hand coordination • May have rigid preferences regarding the positioning of desks, etc.
Auditory (hearing)	Middle and inner ear	Translates sound waves into electrical impulses that give information about sound quality	Loud, high pitch, irregular beat	Soft, rhythmical, lower tones	• May be able to hear sounds or voices that are far away • May appear to not hear as difficulties processing multiple sensory input often allow only one sense to work at a time

(continued on next page)

TABLE 10.1 (continued)

Sensory Systems	Receptor Location	Function	Qualities for Alerting	Qualities or Calming	How Processing Difficulties Might Impact Someone With Asperger's Syndrome
Tactile (touch)	Skin; each area has different density of receptors	Protective functions such as the F/F/F response; provides information about the quality of the touch (soft, firm, sharp, cold)	Vary—usually light touch or scratching	Vary—usually more firm pressure	• May appear to overreact to casual touch • May have difficulty with relationships due to touch sensitivity • May have delayed or underresponsiveness to pain • May have very rigid clothing requirements, not based on style • May seek out opportunities for touch
Vestibular sense of balance	Inner ear; semicircular canals and the otolith organs	Provides information about the position of the head in relation to gravity; also gives information about acceleration; works closely with visual system	Rotary, angular, arrhythmic	Linear, rhythmic	• May shy away from sports or be obsessed with activities such as running • May suffer motion sickness • May become easily disoriented by common activities such as sitting in rocking or swivel chairs, getting in and out of a car, walking on uneven surfaces, water beds • May display risk-taking behavior, or seek movement often or intensely • Often rituals are derived from accommodations inaccurate vestibular processing

The qualities are general principals that vary with each individual.

car, even though you are parked and actually not moving. The vestibular system is not being activated because there is no movement, but the visual input of observing the car moving next to you creates a disparity of information to the brain. The reason that you press on the brake immediately is because the brain relies heavily on visual information and will assume that it is more accurate than other forms of input, such as vestibular. Persons with Asperger's Syndrome often use the visual system to compensate for other less efficiently functioning sensory systems, such as touch and proprioception.

The visual and vestibular systems work in unison to maintain a stable visual field through the vestibulo-ocular reflex. This allows the eyes to focus on a single visual target despite head movement, such as looking at a person while shaking your head "no." Difficulty processing this information might make a student like Alex, in our clinical vignette, avoid sports and other activities that require eye–hand coordination. The visual system is also able to accommodate moving visual information with the optokinetic reflex which combines with the vestibulo-ocular reflex to maintain a stable, constant image on the retina of the eye (Bundy, Lane, & Murray, 2002). This combination allows us to focus visually on the scenery while riding in a car, or approach and negotiate a set of stairs with moving people on them. Alex has difficulties processing this kind of visual information and combining it with his own movements, which makes moving through the hallways with other students very difficult. Other people with Asperger's Syndrome might have rigid rules about furniture or desk placement; this, too, might be rooted in visual processing differences.

Touch or Tactile System

The tactile system gives the brain information regarding the location, pressure, temperature, and quality of the touch. It also relays information regarding pain and vibration. Tactile receptors in the skin are essential to stereognosis. *Stereognosis*, or touch memory, is the ability to identify a common item with touch only. Because of stereognosis, we are able to locate our car keys at the bottom of our pocket or purse without needing to look for them with our eyes. If the tactile system is not functioning effectively, all hand movement might have to be paired with visual contact. This varied tactile input is relayed via two main nerve pathways to the brain that integrate it with other sensory information.

The tactile system, the most mature sensory system at birth, is critical to the nervous and motor development of infants. It develops from the same part of the embryo as the central nervous system. Many primitive reflexes are tactually based (e.g., grasping, rooting, and sucking). Tactile information is decoded in the brain spatially and temporally, and organized in the cortex spatially and temporally. For example, when a shirt is removed, the body can perceive the tactile movement of the shirt moving up the back (lower back, then fractions of seconds later midback, then upper back). The brain can then plan when it would be most efficient to reach behind the neck to grab it. Most people with developed sensory and motor systems can remove their shirts without thinking about it. This motor pattern, based on the spatial and temporal information from the tactile system, has allowed the brain to free up cognitive energy for other tasks (e.g., getting ready to swim). This system of decoding and organizing helps develop the internal map of the body from which motor plans are made and interaction with the world is interpreted and organized (Bundy et al., 2002).

A dysfunctional tactile system can cause a variety of difficulties in perceiving and interpreting the world. Usually the difficulty is in being overresponsive or underresponsive to the input. Many people with Asperger's Syndrome, such as Alex, are overresponsive to tactile input (tactile defensive). Being stroked, hugged, or inadvertently bumped by another person in a crowd might be experienced as noxious by a person with tactile defensiveness. This sensation has been described as itching, feeling like there is a hole in one's skin, or feeling like one has been attacked. An infant with tactile defensiveness or tactile processing difficulties will not use touch to explore his or her own body, and will avoid pushing against gravity. Antigravity movement is crucial to adequate vestibular development and the development of abdominal muscles needed for the future postural support necessary for sitting, crawling, and walking. The inability to accurately process and tolerate tactile information can have a global effect on an individual's motor performance. As illustrated in the opening vignette, Alex did not process tactile information accurately. Being bumped in the hallway was torture that he simply endured. He could not understand how anyone would want to stand in the hallway to talk.

An individual who is underresponsive to tactile input might make extraordinary efforts and use a great deal of time seeking out tactile input or simply withdrawing from the world. People with sensory processing difficulties might need additional, stronger, or more frequent tactile input as a way of regulating their arousal level. For a person with Asperger's Syndrome, the associated lack of social awareness could be a recipe for disaster. For example, some people need to feel soft smooth, things such as nylons, a smooth rock, or hair as a regulatory mechanism. Imagine the social condemnation when a person with Asperger's Syndrome, in particular a large teenage boy, walks up to a woman and begins to feel her legs or touch her hair. Irregularities in tactile processing differences can have a huge impact on a variety of life activities.

Some of the behaviors and rituals in persons with Asperger's Syndrome might have originated in poor tactile processing (or other sensory issues). Some of these behaviors or traits can include:

- Preoccupations with certain types of touch.
- Rigid avoidance of certain situations or items such as crowds, polyester, glue, water, and so on.
- Inability to determine how firm to touch, move, or handle things, often grasping fragile items too hard or breaking them.

- Poor tactile processing has a significant impact on the body's ability to develop an internal map on which motor plans are based.

Vestibular System

The vestibular system provides information to the brain about the position of the head in relation to the rest of the body. It is the body's sense of balance. Without using visual cues, one can perceive that one's head is off center or tilting. The vestibular receptors are in the inner ear, specifically the semicircular canals and the utricle and saccule. These receptors also relay information regarding acceleration and intensity of movement. For example, an intact vestibular system can handle an average car ride. However, if the driver uses the brake and gas alternately, causing rapid acceleration and deceleration with increased frequency, it does not take long for the vestibular system to become overaroused and possibly create other autonomic signs such as nausea. Vestibular input directly influences muscle tone and arousal or alertness level. There are many integral functions for the vestibular system; however, as stated, one of the more important functions is the coordination with other systems to maintain a stable visual field and image.

A properly functioning vestibular system is critical to developing coordinated motor skills, as well as managing alertness and activity focus. Someone whose system is hypersensitive to movement is often said to have *gravitational insecurity*. This condition makes small movements appear to the brain like intense, drastic movement. For example, moving the head to look down before approaching the stairs might feel like moving upside down and cause a sense of imbalance and fear, to the person with gravitational insecurity. People like Alex simply accommodate to this fear by grasping the railing with a death grip, avoiding the stairs when possible, and not engaging in extracurricular sports activities. Clinicians and parents have observed that young children with gravitational insecurity often avoid activities like running, bike riding, climbing, or even walking along the edge of the curb. As the child matures, if there is little engagement with these types of experiences, abnormal spatial perception as well as poor motor coordination and decreased muscle tone and strength can occur. Irregularities in vestibular processing such as gravitational insecurity can have a domino effect and influence many different parts of a person's daily routine.

If the system is underresponsive to vestibular input, an equally difficult scenario is likely. For the vestibular system to reach a threshold that the brain can register, the person needs to engage in intense movements. We can all relate to the need to get up and move around during study periods as a way to wake up or increase alertness. However, if the body needs extra or more intense movement to increase alertness, it might be driven toward activities such as jumping on a trampoline, hanging upside down, or spinning. Imagine the social exclusion a student experiences when needing to engage in one of these activities to regulate his or her arousal level to make it through a classroom lesson or lecture. Imagine the frustration of the person with Asperger's Syndrome when needing to move but being told to sit down, be quiet, and pay attention to the speaker. Often attention to the speaker cannot happen when sitting down. It can only occur when moving. A dysfunction in this system can not only create performance difficulties, but it could lead to social isolation.

Proprioceptive System

The proprioceptive system provides information to the brain regarding the position of one body part in relation to other body parts. Proprioceptive input is received through receptors in the muscles and joints that constantly send information to the brain. The proprioceptive system allows the brain to identify the position of the body without having to rely on visual or tactile cues.

Accurate proprioceptive input is integral to establishing a mental map of one's own body. Ayers (1979) referred to this as a *body percept.* Once a mental map, or percept, of the body is made, the brain can start organizing the movement of the different parts, thus carrying out coordinated motor movements, for example, scratching one's head. Motor clumsiness, an associated feature of Asperger's Syndrome, appears to be more directly related to difficulties with the proprioceptive system.

Proprioceptive information is coordinated with other sensory information to allow a person to engage in advanced coordinated sequences, such as hitting a baseball or kicking a soccer ball. The mental map of the body coordinates with the visual perceptual information of the playing field and ball, and the vestibular input of the correct stance or weight shifting that is necessary to make contact with the ball. Simultaneously, the brain is blocking out or modulating the tactile input from the scratchy uniform, the auditory input from the loud fans, the olfactory input of the field grasses, and so on. When viewed from this perspective, coordinated motor movement is most certainly a sensory integration issue.

In people with Asperger's Syndrome, poor proprioceptive processing is often combined with poor tactile and vestibular processing. Thus the internal map, as well as perception of movement and space, is altered or malformed. This constellation of symptoms often leads to difficulties with spatial concepts such as geometry, left–right orientation, and negotiating space, such as locating a room within a building or on a campus.

The proprioceptive system also serves to modulate and organize other sensory input. Because proprioceptive and tactile input are transmitted to the brain via the same central nervous system pathways, the two systems are often discussed together and referred to as the *somatosensory system.* Interaction of tactile and proprioceptive input in the thalamus of the brain might help to explain why proprioception and deep touch pressure seem to reduce the sensation of pain and tactile defensiveness (Fisher & Dunn, 1983). This might be why we rub an area of the body when we get hurt, or why persons with sensory defensiveness benefit from structured brushing programs or weighted vests and blankets.

Regulation of arousal is another major function of the proprioceptive system. There are organizing and calming chemicals released in the brain as a result of movement (Ayers, 1979; Bundy et al., 2002). Proprioceptive information stimulates reticular formation, which regulates arousal and consciousness (Bundy et al., 2002). Following this theoretical framework, occupational therapists try to include "heavy work" activities (resistive large muscle activity) into people's daily routines to assist the system in modulating other sensory challenges such as loud noise or prolonged inactivity.

THE INTEGRATION OF SENSORY INFORMATION

It is not enough to understand how each separate sensory system works. It is critical to understand how all of the sensory systems work together to allow an individual to make sense of the world and plan motor engagement within it. Sensory integration involves the ability to:

- Accurately take in the sensory information and orient to the stimulus as new or necessary information; this is often referred to as *registration* (Ayers, 1979).
- Rely on the brain to increase or decrease the intensity of the information; this is referred to as *modulation* (Ayers, 1979).
- Interpret the information and compare it with other simultaneous sensory information and motor memories of past experiences.
- Use the combination of new information and motor memories to plan a motor action or adaptive response.
- Complete the final step, the initiation of or carrying out of a coordinated motor plan.

This concept is best illustrated by the simple task of writing a heading at the top of a paper. The individual must take in or register the visual input of the blank paper and pencil, while tuning out the other noises in the room such as whispering, foot tapping, and pencil scratching of other students; the pencil sharpener of the adjacent classroom, and so on. The individual must make a decision to block out the tactile experiences of clothing and the inadvertent touches of the other students in the group. Modulation of extraneous sensory input is often very difficult for persons with Asperger's Syndrome. Next, the individual's brain must compare the visual input with previous experiences, and then decide to write. This must be organized into a motor plan of picking up and manipulating the pencil correctly; holding the paper correctly; and stabilizing the feet, head, neck, eyes, arms, and trunk to move the pencil on the paper. This adaptive response also involves the ability to understand a visual stimulus (e.g., the letters of the alphabet) and figure out how to replicate it with pencil and paper. This involves an understanding of space and an accurate internal map of one's body in relation to the objects involved, such as paper, desk, and pencil.

The last two steps of this sequence are referred to as *praxis* or *motor planning*. Ayers (1979) suggested that praxis is the ability to plan and carry out novel motor actions for purposeful engagement with the environment. For the purposes of this example, writing a heading on the top of a paper was a novel action. Ayers believed that poor motor planning, or motor clumsiness, occurred as a result of a poor body percept. A poor body percept occurred as a result of inaccurate sensory processing and integration (Bundy et al., 2002).

SENSORY INTEGRATION AND LEARNING

Figure 10.1 (Williams & Shellenberger, 1996) indicates the importance of a properly functioning sensory system on the development of higher level skills such as academic learning. Ayers (1979) suggested that the early years of movement and play provide a sensory foundation for the development of intellectual, social, and personal development. She repeatedly emphasized the need for a properly developed body percept or internal map. She stated that most engagement with the world requires movement, and all movement involves additional sensory input. This combination of action on the environment and resulting sensory feedback is key to developing a solid internal map, which is the foundation for planning motor actions. If people with Asperger's Syndrome have difficulty processing sen-

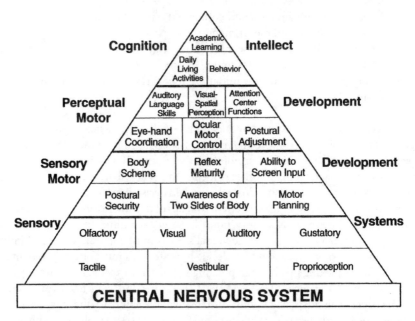

FIG. 10.1   Central nervous system effects on cognitive development. Figure created by M. Taylor/Maryann Trott. From *How does your engin run?* (pp. 1–4), by M. S. Williams and S. Shellenberger, 1996, Albuquerque, NM: TherapyWorks. Copyright © 1996 by Maryann C. Trott. Reprinted with permission.

sory information, then they will have difficulty establishing a solid body percept. An inaccurate internal map makes planning a novel motor action difficult, resulting in motor clumsiness.

SENSORY INTEGRATION THERAPY

As a result of the theory of sensory integration, a form of therapy called sensory integration (SI) therapy was developed. SI therapy was aimed at addressing the underlying neurological deficits of sensory processing difficulties, by providing and controlling sensory input that will allow the person to integrate the sensory information. Dr. Ayers (1979) described SI therapy as a holistic approach that requires the entire body, senses, and the brain to work together in an internally motivating manner. Therapy begins with an internal desire to interact with the environment, then with the guidance from a trained therapist, the client moves from a level of security to just beyond the comfort zone, where new skills are developed. This is often referred to by therapists as offering the just-right challenge. Clinicians offering SI therapy are often occupational therapists. However, other professionals with solid training in neurology, psychology, and physics are trained to deliver this type of therapy as well. Occupational therapy however, focuses on purposeful activity that is intrinsically motivating and interactive with the environment. These basic tenets are used to assist the individual in overcoming or preventing dysfunction toward the ultimate goal of independence. Therefore, it stands to reason that occupational therapy would be the profession most often involved with SI therapy.

Persons with Asperger's Syndrome and sensory processing difficulties often do not have the social understanding to compensate for poor or inaccurate sensation, or the motor planning skills necessary to engage in novel tasks. It takes a trained professional to understand the intricacies of this type of deficit, and to craft therapeutic intervention around the deficit while still addressing the whole person. For example, many people with Asperger's Syndrome are hypersensitive to olfactory (smell) input, and might not be able to modulate noxious input such as bad breath, body odor, perfume, or other smells. They might have difficulty moving to a different position or location to avoid the smell and they might have difficulty socially addressing the issue. A person with Asperger's Syndrome might make frank factual comments such as "Your breath stinks" or "What smells?" or act out or withdraw as a response to overarousal. This is often when they are seen as bullies, troublemakers, or just odd. Thus, an understanding of how sensory processing effects the "whole" person is essential to adequate treatment of people with Asperger's Syndrome.

DETERMINING THE NEED FOR INTERVENTION

Besides the diagnostic criteria already discussed, issues that often lead parents, teachers, and students to question the need for evaluation or intervention include pickiness with eating, dressing and grooming, and major meltdown behaviors around these issues. The dislike of social or crowded activities; vehement avoidance of certain foods, activities, and situations; and preoccupations with other activities or objects are also indicators of the need for further assessment. Often students with sensory processing difficulties need so much structure that they prefer to play by themselves or with adults only. As with any disability, one must look at the whole person and how the characteristics of Asperger's Syndrome are affecting the roles or occupations, daily routines, and engagement with the environment. Certainly the manner in which Alex traversed the hallways and plugged his ears is odd, and might indicate poor sensory processing. However, only when these behaviors interfere with daily role functioning do they need to be evaluated. Alex was unable to socialize with peers and had difficulty with friendships. This is an example of how sensory processing differences can have an impact on occupational roles, for example, the role of friend. Generally, some simple questions to ask are:

- What tasks can the person carry out independently?
- In what areas of performance is the person having difficulty?
- How might these difficulties be related to sensory processing differences?

There are many tools available to assist an evaluator in answering some of these questions. Some are simple questionnaires. One of them, the Sensory Profile (Dunn, 1999) is an example of a useful tool for beginning to assess how sensory processing issues might be affecting a person's ability to function within life roles. It is one of many questionnaires available for examining sensory processing. The questionnaire designed for younger children is meant to be completed by a family member, teacher, or close care provider. The adolescent/adult questionnaire is a self-report style questionnaire. The Sensory Profile is a norm-referenced tool and has three versions that span birth through adulthood. It also identifies issues of individual sensory processing, oral motor issues, sensory modulation issues, and emotional components of sensory difficulties. This questionnaire can be administered by any professional. However, it is best interpreted by a professional with more advanced clinical knowledge of sensory integration. There are many other questionnaire-type evaluation tools available.

The Sensory Integration and Praxis Test (SIPT; Ayers, 1991) is an intensive, standardized test for children 4 years of age through 8 years, 11 months of age. Ideally the child should have moderate verbal processing ability and at least intermittent ability to engage in structured tabletop tasks. Administration and scoring requires a specially trained professional. This is an excellent test for identifying precise praxis and motor planning issues. The results will suggest profiles that research has identified repeatedly. There is a certification process that professionals must undertake to become qualified to administer this evaluation tool. An SIPT-certified therapist has succeeded in completing the training necessary to administer this specific evaluation tool. There is no general certification for treating SI dysfunction and there has been considerable misunderstanding about SI certification. The certification is only to administer the SIPT. Currently, Western Psychological Services in connection with the University of Southern California, as well as Sensory Integration International (SII), offer training and SIPT certification.

Structured clinical observations by a trained examiner often make other objective data meaningful. There are many forms of structured clinical observations; most are developed by a given center or school, based on the client's age, environment, and presenting skills and challenges. All good clinical observations will address function, reflex integration, and skill performance.

Any of these evaluation tools, or the many others available, can indicate the need for intervention. Sensory integration disorder or dysfunction of sensory integration is not currently a stand-alone diagnosis according to the *DSM–IV TR*. Once the determination that intervention is needed has been made, the task of developing an appropriate course of intervention follows. Intervention can be in the form of (a) teaching a specific skill, (b) modifying the environment, (c) clinically treating the underlying cause of the disability, (d) teaching coping strategies using tools such as the Alert Program developed by Williams and Shellenberger (1996), or (e) combining all of these.

SENSORY INTEGRATION AND THERAPEUTIC INTERVENTION

It is important to understand that not all therapies can be conducted in all settings. By definition, SI therapy requires active involvement by the client. Thus, the treatment space must be adequate to allow clients to choose freely the types of activities with which they wish to engage. A clinician can provide this type of environment and effective therapy within that clinic environment. However, modifying an educational setting effectively or carrying over the therapy from the clinic to the educational setting requires consultation with the school-based therapist and teachers. Except in rare cases, it is difficult for an occupational therapist in an educational setting to provide SI therapy, due to the set-up and space limitations of school systems, as well as the Individuals with Disabilities Education Act (IDEA) regulations requiring service delivery within the least restrictive setting. The law mandates that when ever possible, the services should occur in the natural setting (*Occupational Therapy Services for Children and Youth,* 1999). It is often necessary for a person with SI difficulties to have two different therapists who address complementary issues: one in a school and one in a well-equipped clinical setting.

Ayers (1979) began her research after working in a clinic environment with children with learning disabilities. She understood that her theories were relevant to clients on the autistic spectrum. Currently there are many case studies (Case-Smith & Bryan, 1999; Linderman & Stewart, 1999) and a few larger studies (Ottenbacher, 1982) that have demonstrated the benefits of SI therapy and theory. There is still little solid clinical research that validates the benefits of SI therapy, but there are many parents and caregivers who will testify to the positive impact of SI therapy on a child's functioning in school, family life, and everyday functioning. Over time, the theory has been applied to a variety of contexts and used in schools and other settings with an array of clients and diagnoses. The application of Ayers's theory has proven extremely useful with students and adults with Asperger's Syndrome across a variety of settings. As science learns more about the brain and the sensory systems as they relate to behavior, the value of clinic-based SI therapy continues to be recognized.

SI is a theory that can be considered a way of thinking about an individual. When viewing it as a theory rather than a technique, it can be applied to a variety of situations and contexts and easily combined with many other theories and therapies. As stated earlier, intervention can be in the form of:

1. Teaching a specific skill.
2. Modifying the environment.
3. Teaching coping strategies.
4. Clinically treating the underlying cause of the disability.
5. Combining of all of these.

Not all of these types of therapeutic intervention are considered SI therapy.

Teaching a Specific Skill

Teaching specific skills such as writing, keyboarding skills, bike riding, and so on. are viable treatment options when the individual demonstrates specific areas of performance difficulty, but not global deficiencies in overall functioning. This type of therapy is also useful when assisting a client to develop particular skills necessary for functioning within a given environment, such as an educational environment. Occupational therapists are specifically trained in task analysis, or breaking tasks and skills down into task components to create manageable, learnable units. They are also trained in adapting and grading activities so that the individual can maximize independence. Most occupational therapists are qualified to provide this type of therapy. The SI frame of reference might be useful to analyze tasks for teaching.

Table 10.2 illustrates how considering the sensory components of the task and the environment can influence the effectiveness of the teaching. Using SI as a theoretical frame of reference assists the therapist in deciding on the most appropriate way to teach the skill, even if not doing standard SI therapy. For example, if a child is overly sensitive to tactile input, visual demonstration, rather than the use of hand-over-hand assistance, would be more effective. The preferred teaching method should correlate with the person's relative strength. For example if easily overwhelmed by visual input, verbal instruction would be more effective. If someone is tactually defensive and visually strong, computer programs with engaging visual graphics would be the most effective. For a task such as keyboarding, factors such as the tactile input of the home row indicator keys might need to be altered. The level of vestibular, proprio-

TABLE 10.2
Sensory System Suggestion for Task Teaching

Sensory System	Considerations for Teaching a Task
Olfactory	• Consider the environment, what kinds of smells are there (air fresheners, fresh flowers, bathroom odors, perfume, deodorant or hairspray of the instructor), as well as breath (mint, cough drop, garlic, etc.) of the instructor. Casual odors might be overwhelming for the person with sensory processing difficulties and make it difficult to maintain a regulated state. • Consider using scented markers for those students that might be underaroused and need additional input.
Gustatory	• Usually not important in teaching a skill, but instructor must be cognizant of the fact that lunch or snack tastes might still be in the client's mouth and influencing attention to task.
Visual	• Consider the type of lighting in the environment. Fluorescent tends to be overalerting, natural tends to be clearer, and often no lights will create the most productive learning environment. • Consider the amount of visual information being presented. A clear workspace is less confusing. Often half a worksheet is easier to understand than the entire worksheet at once. • Consider using highlighters to clarify the most important pieces of information when presenting written information.
Auditory	• Consider what is environmentally making noise: fans, other people talking, auto traffic, wind chimes, humming of a computer, bathroom noise, intercom noise, music, chairs moving on the floor. • Consider what types of noises are constant and what kinds are unpredictable. Unpredictable noises are more likely to overarouse or disturb a person with hypersensitive hearing. • Consider what kinds of noises the client makes. These might be regulatory and an attempt to block out sound (e.g., humming or vocalizing will reduce the amount of auditory input that registers in the auditory system). • Consider using alternate means of instruction besides verbal that might overwhelm the client's nervous system.
Tactile	• Consider what kinds of clothing the student has on and behaviors that he or she might use to regulate his or her own arousal level. • Reduce the amount that the instructor touches the student as well as the amount of incidental touch that could be given such as hair falling on the student's arm or back or long, baggy sleeves that could touch the student accidentally. • Consider verbal or visual instructions rather than hand-over-hand demonstration. • Firm touch is often more easily tolerated than light touch.

(continued on next page)

TABLE 10.2 (continued)

Sensory System	Considerations for Teaching a Task
Vestibular	• Find out if they tend to seek this input or are overwhelmed by this input. Find out if they use this input to regulate their arousal state. • To reduce the input, have the student sit down or lean against something solid, or present visual information on a slant board so that the student's head does not have to tilt in a downward direction. Avoid long rides on a bus. • To increase vestibular input, have the student sit on a movable surface, such as a blow-up cushion, therapy ball, T-stool, or partially inflated beach ball; stand to do work; and participate in regular periods of exercise.
Proprioceptive	• Consider increasing the weight or resistance of the activity by using weights or beanbags, or increase the weight of tools such as pencils or forks. These types of modifications often work with students with praxis or motor planning issues. • Consider using sensory diet tools such as lap beanbags, therapy bands around the feet of the chair, chewy or resistive foods, or structured brushing and joint compression programs. • Consider having student lean on table or use fidget tools such as stress balls or racquetballs.

ceptive, and visual processing would influence decisions such as timing of keyboard training, placement of the screen, position of the chair, design of the keyboard, and seating options such as cushions and arm rests. There is no presumption of general neurological change. Carryover of the taught skill into contexts other than the one in which it was taught does not usually happen naturally or automatically for people with Asperger's Syndrome. They must practice each skill in various contexts. Teaching a specific skill using the theory of SI cannot be considered SI therapy. Table 10.2 might help to clarify the ways in which the theory of SI can be used to determine how a student learns skills best.

If a child has poor proprioceptive and vestibular processing, teaching a direct task such as bike riding might be very frustrating. It might be more appropriate to encourage scooter riding until underlying vestibular and proprioceptive issues improve. For a student like Alex, this might not be the best treatment option. Direct treatment of the vestibular or proprioceptive system would need to occur before direct instruction of a task.

Modifying the Environment

The second form of intervention, modifying the environment, is a method of managing sensory processing difficulties. Modifications can have one or any combination of four different elements:

1. Altering the activity.
2. Changing the location or set-up of the environment in which the activity occurs.
3. Reorganizing the sequence or timing of the activity.
4. Following a specific sensory diet.

Altering the Activity.   Altering the activity can be as simple as using a pen rather than a pencil if the sound or vibration of writing with a pencil is more than the individual can tolerate. Techniques for altering an activity can also be as complicated as taking a spelling test orally while moving rather than writing on paper, or using a computer for academic tasks. It is important to ask the question, "What is the objective of this task?" If the outcome is a correctly spelled word, then is it really necessary that the words be handwritten in two parallel columns with a space between each row? Alterations to accommodate spatial deficits need to be made for the student to be successful. In the case of Alex, it might be more appropriate that he take the elevator to get to class rather than taxing his system with the challenge of negotiating the stairs. He might then have the energy to engage in social interactions within the classroom before class starts.

Another common way of altering an activity to accommodate a sensory processing challenge comes in the choice of clothing. Often, cotton that is well washed, with elastic waists and no tags, is more easily tolerated by people with sensory processing differences. A diagnosis of Asperger's Syndrome, in addition to a sensory processing difficulty, requires that rules around this sensory processing difference be established. There are certain dressing protocols for different situations. For example, sweatpants might be the preferred item of clothing, but they are not appropriate for some settings, such as church, a wedding, or a job interview. A person with Asperger's Syndrome might not pick up on this independently. However, elastic-waist cotton pants that have been washed several times might be acceptable to the individual for a limited period of time. Working within the family values and context will help clarify acceptable choices. Myles (2002), a 12-year-old author, in her book *Practical Solutions to Everyday Challenges for Children With Asperger Syndrome*, offered advice in a child-friendly format about a variety of everyday social issues that tend to confuse students with Asperger's Syndrome. She suggested that asking a parent or close friend what they are wearing for a special occasion might help establish guidelines in these situations.

Changing the Location or Set-Up.   Changing the location or set-up of the room or activity is another way of modifying the environment. It can involve the position of the student's desk (near natural light if visually sensitive to artificial light, away from high-traffic areas if tactile defensive, facing the wall if visually distractible) or adding or taking away sensory input such as sound. It might be easier for some people to study with the radio or TV on loud, whereas others need the quiet of the library. Some people need to hold a fidget tool (a small item manipulated with the hand that might add tactile or proprioceptive input, or serve as an outlet for extra energy) while public speaking or listening to a lecture, whereas others need to have something in their mouths, adding oral tactile input. By simply discussing a given situation, it is often possible for a person with Asperger's Syndrome to articulate what changes in the environment need to be made. Alex knows that he needs to be in the back of the room, away from much of the noise and possibility of being touched. His teacher allowed him to choose his seat, instead of using the traditional assigned seat.

Sequencing and Timing.   Sequencing or timing of events such as shopping at 11:00 at night in an uncrowded grocery store, rather than on a crowded Saturday morning where one will likely be bumped unexpectedly is another way of manipulating or modifying the environment. One adult man reported that he could only brush his teeth in the shower with the radio on because the sound and vibration of the act of brushing his teeth was too much for his auditory and vestibular system. Although this worked for his morning brushing, it was problematic in the evening when he did not need to take a shower. Without guidance, a person with Asperger's Syndrome would stop there and not look for alternate solutions. The social consequences of poor dental hygiene would not be a consideration in the problem-solving equation. After learning about SI, this man restructured his routine to brush his teeth in the early evening after he worked out and had gotten lots of proprioceptive input, rather than in the evening when he had not had much proprioceptive input. He was able to accomplish the task with only the water running for sound. There was not an acceptable alternative to tooth brushing, and taking two showers a day was not something that he wanted to do, so a simple altering of his routine with particular attention to sensory processing revealed a routine within which he could function. In this case, intensive therapy was not necessary; a thoughtful modification provided the solution. For Alex, a change in timing, such as the ability to move from one class to another 1 to 3 minutes before the bell rang, would reduce the number of times that he was inadvertently touched, and might allow him to engage in social conversation with his peers after arriving in class.

Sensory Diet.   Establishing or altering a sensory diet is yet another method of altering or modifying the environment. A *sensory diet* is nothing more than a thoughtful, preplanned, daily routine of activities, structured to regulate arousal level and modulate sensory input (Wilbarger & Wilbarger, 1991). One common misconception is that a sensory diet and a structured brushing program are the same thing, which they are not. Structured brushing programs, such as the Wilbarger protocol (Wilbarger & Wilbarger, 1991), can be utilized as part of a person's sensory diet or daily routine, but should never be the only method used to regulate arousal level.

Another common misconception is that sensory diets are food related. Sensory diet is a term used to demonstrate the need for small sensory events throughout the day. This is similar to a food diet. We all eat throughout the day—breakfast, lunch, dinner, and snacks. We do not eat our entire daily allotment in one sitting and then fast for the rest of the day because it would not be healthy. The same is true for sensory input; it should not be assumed that engaging in a sensory regulation activity in the morning would be adequate and that no other input would be necessary for the rest of the day. To further complicate this issue, food can be used as part of a person's sensory diet. One junior high student with Asperger's Syndrome and associated sensory issues takes her peanut butter and jelly sandwich (because she will only eat peanut butter and jelly for lunch on school days) on a bagel or pita bread instead of soft, white bread, to offer her more intense proprioceptive input. This allows her to modulate all of the smells and sounds of the cafeteria. Drinking water through her water bottle or milk through a straw creates an opportunity for sucking, which has a calming effect. She also uses the water bottle throughout the day as part of her sensory diet. Wall pushups, a lap beanbag that looks like a stuffed dog, and tart candies are also part of her sensory diet, as is a Walkman for the bus ride home.

Teaching Coping Strategies

Education regarding coping strategies is another form of therapeutic intervention. The Alert Program developed by Williams and Shellenberger (1996), is a remarkable resource to assist individuals of any age in developing a cognitive understanding of how to communicate what is happening inside their bodies. Cognitive understanding increases the likelihood of success and independence. Identifying internal states tends to be very difficult for people with Asperger's Syndrome. The Alert Program offers a concrete way of understanding internal feelings and, in particular, arousal levels. Once people with Asperger's Syndrome understand that: (a) there is a reason they feel the way they do, (b) there is a way to explain the way they are feeling, (c) others might feel that way, and (d) they are not going crazy, they are more likely to make changes and choices independently. Isn't independence ultimately the goal of anyone that is seeking help?

Clinically Treating the Underlying Cause of the Disability

One of the most common methods of treating SI disorders, but least well understood by the general public, is direct clinical treatment. The basic tenets of SI therapy are that it is facilitated by a specifically trained therapist, it is child or client directed, it is specific to one person and varies with the client, it addresses underlying vestibular and somatosensory processing, and it is an active and purposeful process (Cermak & Henderson, 1990).

Classic clinical environments with suspended equipment, balls, crash pads, and specially trained therapists are extremely beneficial, although there is not yet substantial clinical research to support this type of therapy. With emerging requirements for evidence-based practice models for treatment, it will be important to see if clinical research can validate this type of direct therapy. This form of therapy looks for the root causes of an individual's constellation of difficulties. Figure 10.1 illustrates how therapy that addresses the underlying neuromotor issues can influence skill performance. SI therapy, in this type of setting, addresses issues using this pyramid as a foundational model. It requires adequate space that is set up properly, as well as specially trained therapists to carry it out. This method might be more intense or prolonged, and is sometimes covered by insurance.

MISCONCEPTIONS ABOUT SI THERAPY

When discussing SI treatment, there are a number of misconceptions. Here are the four most common.

Misconception 1: Sensory Integration Is a Specific Technique That Only Qualified Professionals Can Do

SI therapy is a specific therapeutic technique that is usually conducted by specially trained professionals. However, not all people with Asperger's Syndrome and sensory issues will have access to this type of therapy, due to financial or geographic limitations. Nevertheless, anyone with additional training is capable of using parts of this theory to increase meaningful, purposeful adaptive behavior and independence. It is most useful to think of SI as a theory or way of thinking. SI is a way of understanding or describing the sensory demands of an environment, an activity, or an action, and comparing it to a person's sensory processing abilities and challenges. It is a way of looking at a behavior and seeing its possible functions and causes. It is a way of looking at an environment and noticing the "feel" (e.g., the scents or lighting). It is a way of looking at our own actions and seeing how they might be perceived sensorially by another person. Although specific intervention strategies can and should be carried out by a qualified professional, most people are capable of, and indeed do, manage their own behavior with the use of SI strategies.

Misconception 2: The Brain Is Only Plastic Until the Age of 8, So If the Child Has Not Received Services Before That Time, It Is Useless

Ayers' (1979) original research indicated that the critical period for sensory motor integration was before the age of 10. She believed that older children and adults had more difficulty establishing new sensory interconnections (Ayers, 1979). Over the years, this has been misinterpreted to mean that the brain is incapable of learning or adapting at later ages. This misconception has been proven false repeatedly. Research indicates that the brain is capable of changing throughout the life span (Lenn, 1991; Lund, 1978).

Misconception 3: Direct Therapist Intervention Is Preferable to Consultation

There is a time and a place for direct therapy and consultation, as well as modification and sensory diets. Although direct treatment in a clinical setting might facilitate some underlying neuronal changes that will support future changes and improvements, these changes are often slow to occur. Educating and consulting with the people with Asperger's Syndrome and their care providers about SI theory; self-regulation; and ways to adapt and alter environments, activities, and interactions is often extremely productive. It can facilitate independent change in the person with Asperger's Syndrome and their care providers. These adaptations can then occur in natural contexts to improve function and ultimately increase the person's sense of self-confidence and self-control. A good therapist will see the benefit of implementing many different service delivery models to address the unique needs of each client.

Misconception 4: Sensory Integration Therapy Can Be Provided in Any Environment

By definition, SI therapy is child directed; the therapy is crafted by the therapist for the client to provide a just-right challenge. Many of the theoretical assumptions of SI therapy are based on the work of Piaget. He was one of the first to understand that active engagement and interaction with the environment is critical to child development. Ayers (1979) applied Piaget's work and neurological research to create SI therapy. She recognized that clients must have an inner drive to engage in activities that might be challenging for them and that were previously associated with failure to develop successful adaptive responses. This is where environment is critical; it must be enticing, safe, and client directed. How many occupational therapy rooms in schools or hospitals can allow for child direction and access to all aspects of the room? It stands to reason that true SI therapy can occur only in a specialized clinical environment. These specialized environments might be found within schools, hospitals, or private clinics.

FINDING A TRAINED THERAPIST

A good way to find a professional that has had advanced training in SI is to make use of the Internet. Currently there are two primary agencies offering training and testing certification in SI. One is SII and the other is a collaborative effort by the University of Southern California and Western Psychological Services. The Web sites of each of these agencies list therapists that have been certified to administer the SIPT, but usually do not list the therapists who have advanced training in the treatment of SI.

Another method for finding a therapist is by contacting the state occupational therapy association. One can request a list of practicing therapists and many times this list will also indicate the therapist's area of practice. Most therapists trained in SI work in pediatrics, so it can help to look for that specialty area. It is important to note that although they might be listed as pediatric therapists, they might also work with adolescents and adults with sensory issues.

As stated in *Occupational Therapy Services for Children and Youth Under the Individuals With Disabilities Education Act* (1999), the IDEA mandates that occupational therapy be available for students within the school system. Even if one does not have children that attend the public school, a conversation with the occupational therapist working in that setting might be a good starting point. The occupational therapist might be able to suggest people that are otherwise difficult to find. If one is affiliated with the local school district, the occupational therapist might be willing to sit down with parents or caregivers and brainstorm about how to make a successful sensory diet developed at school work at home. Occupational therapists are concerned about the whole child.

A registered occupational therapist can provide all aspects of therapy, including evaluations. Certified occupational therapy assistants (OTAs) with clinical supervision can carry out many activities suggested by the registered occupational therapist, including treatment, sensory diet set-up, and maintenance. They might be able to offer suggestions for home. OTAs do not perform evaluations including the SIPT, nor are they usually traditionally trained to do SI therapy.

Most hospitals have occupational therapy departments, usually called OT/PT, or rehabilitative services. Occupational therapists and physical therapists at these facilities (especially those specializing in pediatrics) might provide a contact or a lead. Some physical therapists are trained in SI therapy and can actually provide the services you require.

If the "client" is a child, one must understand federal legislation to figure out where to get services, in particular the IDEA. This legislation determines who "the client" is and whether the occupational therapy services are delivered as a primary or secondary service. These rules are complicated and decisions about eligibility of services and the nature of the provider are contained within the IDEA. Table 10.3 summarizes the information. Copies of this law can be accessed through the Internet at www.ed.gov/office/OSERS/IDEA, or by writing to the U.S. Government Printing Office.

TABLE 10.3
Eligibility for Services Under IDEA

Age	Client	Idea	Service
Birth to age 3	Child and family	Part C	Occupational therapy can be a primary service and delivered in isolation.
School age, 3–21 years	Student	Part B	Occupational therapy is a related service and cannot be delivered in isolation.

WHAT'S NEXT?

There are currently two major stumbling blocks to getting effective and affordable treatment to people with Asperger's Syndrome and SI disorders. The first is the difficulty of educating and providing information for consumers about occupational therapy, what it is, and how it can benefit people with Asperger's Syndrome and other disabilities. There has been a great deal of work done by state organizations as well as the national organization, but the need for additional public awareness persists.

The second issue is inconsistent coverage of SI therapy by insurance companies. There is a movement to include dysfunction of sensory integration in the *DSM–V* as a separate and viable diagnostic category. Inclusion in the *DSM* would identify it as a medical diagnosis, thus allowing school systems to identify students that are having difficulties within the educational environment, but have scored within the average range on academic testing, as "other health impaired." This would allow students to receive much needed, educationally related occupational therapy services. Insurance reimbursement would be much easier to obtain in clinical settings and by community-based therapists as well, if a separate and viable diagnosis existed.

The second reason there is not more effective and affordable SI treatment for clients with Asperger's Syndrome and SI difficulties is that there is not enough solid clinical research that demonstrates a correlation between SI therapy and sensory processing and neuronal changes. The assumption of SI therapy is that intervention will facilitate underlying nervous system change. On the other hand, there is research to support the idea of neuroplasticity (Lenn, 1991; Lund, 1978). Neuro- plasticity refers to neuronal change, in particular increase in speed and efficiency of nerve function, that can occur through out the life span. At this time we can observe changes in behavior and performance and attribute these changes to therapeutic intervention. However, there is not yet technology available to measure the correlation between SI therapy and neuronal changes. There are therapists conducting correlational studies to support the relationship between lower cortical functions (SI) and higher cortical functions such as motor and academic skills (Mulligan, 2002). The results of current research on the efficacy of SI intervention are mixed. Because of the design of SI therapy, researchers are having difficulty controlling all of the variables in human behavior, both of the test participants and the therapists. However, extensive clinical research is not necessary to convince many people with Asperger's Syndrome and sensory processing differences, and their families, that SI intervention is directly correlated to improved daily performance. There are also many professionals, not only in the field of occupational therapy, whose clinical impressions would attest to the fact that improved sensory processing is directly correlated to improvement in behavior and engagement with the environment. There is a need for more clinical data and research that clearly delineates the causal relationship between SI intervention and improved behavior and daily living skills.

Case-Smith (2001) summarized it nicely in her chapter on occupational therapy research, in a book edited by Miller-Kuhaneck titled *Autism: A Comprehensive Occupational Therapy Approach.* Occupational therapists have helped families and other professionals understand how sensory processing can affect behavior and function, and have developed important intervention approaches based on this understanding. She pointed out that "although occupational therapists have gathered evidence of the effectiveness of sensory-integration approaches, they have not engaged in experimental research of its efficacy" (p. 328).

REFERENCES

American Psychiatric Association. (2000). *Diagnostic and statistical manual of mental disorders* (4th ed., text revision). Washington, DC: Author

Ayers, A. J. (1979). *Sensory integration and the child.* Los Angeles: Western Psychological Services.

Ayers, A. J. (1991). *Sensory Integration and Praxis Tests manual.* Los Angeles: Western Psychological Services.

Bundy, A. C., Lane, S. J., & Murray, E. A. (2002). *Sensory integration: Theory and practice* (2nd ed.). Philadelphia: Davis.

Case-Smith, J. (2001). Occupational therapy research on children with autism. In H. Miller-Kuhaneck (Ed.), *Autism: A comprehensive occupational therapy approach* (pp. 317–328). Bethesda, MD. American Occupational Therapy Association.

Case-Smith, J., & Bryan, T. (1999). The effects of occupational therapy with sensory integration emphasis on preschool children with autism. *American Journal of Occupational Therapy, 53,* 489–497.

Cermak, S. A., & Henderson, A. (1990, March). The efficacy of sensory integration procedures. *Sensory Integration Quarterly, 1,* 23.

Dunn, W. (1999). *Sensory profile.* San Antonio, TX: Psychological Corporation.

Fisher, A. F., & Dunn, W. (1983). Tactile defensiveness: Historical perspectives, new research: A theory grows. *Sensory Integration Special Interest Section Newsletter, 6,* 3–20.

Henderson, A., Pehoski, C., & Murray, E. (2002). Visual-spatial abilities. In A. C. Bundy, S. J. Lane, & E. A. Murray (Eds.), *Sensory integration: Theory and practice* (pp. 123–140). Philadelphia: Davis.

Lane, S. J. (2002). Structure and function of the sensory systems. In A. C. Bundy, S. J. Lane, & E. A. Murray (Eds.), *Sensory integration: Theory and practice* (pp. 35–70). Philadelphia: Davis.

Lenn, N. J. (1991). Neuroplasticity: The basis for brain development, learning, and recovery from injury. *Infants and Young Children, 3,* 39–48.

Linderman, T., & Stewart, K. (1999). Sensory integrative-based occupational therapy and functional outcomes in young children with pervasive developmental disorders: A single subject study. *American Journal of Occupational Therapy, 53,* 207–213.

Lund, R. D. (1978). *Development and plasticity of the brain.* New York: Oxford University Press.

Mulligan, S. (2002, November). *Advances in sensory integration research.* Paper presented at the New Hampshire Occupational Therapy Association Conference, Manchester, NH.

Myles, H. M. (2002). *Practical solutions to everyday challenges for children with Asperger Syndrome.* Shawnee Mission, KS: Autism Asperger Publishing.

Occupational therapy services for children and youth under the Individuals With Disabilities Education Act. (1999). Bethesda, MD: American Occupational Therapy Association.

Ottenbacher, K. (1982). Sensory integration therapy: Affect or effect? *American Journal of Occupational Therapy, 36,* 571–578.

Reeves, G. D., & Cermak, S. A. (2002). Disorders of praxis. In A. C. Bundy, S. J. Lane, & E. A. Murray (Eds.), *Sensory integration: Theory and practice* (pp. 71–100). Philadelphia: Davis

Trott, M. C., Laurel, M. K., & Windeck, S. L. (1993). *SenseAbilities: Understanding sensory integration.* Tucson, AZ: Therapy Skill Builders.

Wilbarger, P., & Wilbarger, J. (1991). *Sensory defensiveness in children aged 2–12: An intervention guide for parents and other caretakers.* Denver, CO: Avanti Educational Programs.

Williams, M. S., & Shellenberger, S. (1996). *"How does your engine run?": A leader's guide to the Alert Program for self-regulation.* Albuquerque, NM: TherapyWorks.

Chapter 11

The Language of Social Communication: Running Pragmatics Groups in Schools and Clinical Settings

Elsa Abele
Sargent College, Boston University

Denise Grenier
Lexington, Massachusetts

In a world that values social competence so highly, most people are continually evaluating each other's social competence to make decisions about forming friendships or working relationships or simply sustaining conversations. For individuals with Asperger's Syndrome this spells trouble, because they do not learn the language of social interaction intuitively or readily. Instead, they learn language social skills only if taught in an explicit, step-by-step manner, thereby enabling them to taste the benefits of the social world.

The use of language is much more complex than learning the correct script. For example, a first-grader named Danny learned to close a conversation with, "Bye bye, see you tomorrow." After he said it not only to his conversational partner at their school lockers, but also repeated it to another child, and another, and another, all the children were laughing while he was left bewildered by their reactions. Danny subsequently learned in his social skills group about using the context to decide what is appropriate to say at particular times. In this chapter we discuss how to form and run social groups for those persons who need explicit teaching to master the social skills involved.

217

We look at social skills and the development of social competence from a language perspective. Pragmatic language is the appropriate use and interpretation of language in relation to the context in which it occurs. Pragmatic competence is, therefore, dependent on the specific situation in which it is assessed (Bishop & Baird, 2001). Another way to look at pragmatics is to look at the parts of a communicative event. According to Twachtman-Cullen (2000), about 7% are the words; 23% are the prosodic features such as intonation, inflection, pitch, rate, fluency and loudness; and 70% are the non-verbal or body language aspects.

A person might have mastery of the foundation language skills but when putting the parts together to produce conversation or narratives, his or her communication might break down. This chapter demonstrates some of the ways that the language of social communication can be explicitly taught. If we review some of the specific elements of social skills deficits, we can begin to readily identify those children or adults who need our intervention. These individuals often and unintentionally behave in what others experience as an irritating manner. They consistently invade others' personal space, carry on about arcane topics, interrupt conversations, talk more loudly or softly than a situation dictates, or speak with an incorrect emphasis on words or word syllables in a sentence. Such a person might change the topic of conversation abruptly, or gaze in a different direction from the person to whom he or she is speaking, exhibiting poor eye contact. These are the children who have few or no friends or the adults we might tire of at a cocktail party.

We are in the early stages of learning that with early intervention and remediation, this population can learn how to communicate effectively and create strategies to counteract the blind spots that their set of neurological problems can cause. Based on the social interaction theory of language development (Bloom & Lahey, 1978; Owens, 1988), we know that mastery of form and content are typical developmental tasks that we are 'wired' to master along with the opportunity for social interaction. Form includes what are commonly thought of as grammar and the sounds of language. Children learn that "I went" rather than "I goed" is the correct form to use at an early age. Content refers to meaning communicated by vocabulary and word relationships. Form, content, and the integration of the two will support children's developing understanding of how to use language. Use, or pragmatics, the actual purpose of communicating to get needs and desires met, also begins to develop as form and content emerge. Pragmatics includes appropriate discourse, decisions about how and when to tell a narrative, correct prosody and appropriate body language to communicate and therefore connect with another person. For people with neurointegrative difficulties, the challenge lies in pragmatics.

We began offering pragmatic language groups in the Academic Speech, Language and Hearing Clinic at Sargent College of Boston University in 1992. At that time, the social skills groups that were offered in the Boston area were mainly designed around motivational issues for children whose primary problems were emotional and behavioral and whose strategies for social interaction were dysfunctional. There were some children on the spectrum who had been in these kinds of social skills groups year after year and enjoyed them because they were safe, small, structured opportunities to interact with peers, but their skills did not improve. Children with deficits in neurointegration, like those with Asperger's Syndrome, need explicit step-by-step skill development that includes a great deal of practice. They have a void that needs to be filled by strategies to guide them in social interactions. They do not respond to the motivational methodologies used in the treatment of children with primarily emotional problems. Unfortunately, the pattern of mixing the two groups is still prevalent in both schools and clinical settings. Consequently, children with Asperger's Syndrome are not learning those strategies that will enable them to grow in their ability to have successful social interactions.

THE DIAGNOSTIC PROCESS: IDENTIFYING THE NEED FOR PRAGMATICS SKILLS TRAINING

Consider the following situations:

- Brad is sitting alone at a table lost in a book when one of us observes him in the high school cafeteria.
- Mark is knocking over the carefully built block fire engine that several other boys are pretending to ride to reach and extinguish a fire when one of us sees him in his preschool classroom.
- Emily is arguing her point endlessly, not letting go, during a social studies class discussion, when one of us visits her middle school classroom.

These are some of the red flags that call attention to possible neurointegration difficulties in the social communication milieu of a child's world. Brad might be so anxious and unsuccessful at conversation with classmates during lunch that he copes by isolating himself from the noise, rejection, and confusion of the "script" called cafeteria. Mark, a preschooler, wants to join in playing but has no skills at entering an activity, let alone a pattern or schema for playing fireman. His peers get angry at his wrecking entry. Emily is anxious in her social studies class. When her anxiety escalates, she often becomes argumentative.

CLINICAL OBSERVATION

School or Workplace Visit

The purpose for such visits is to identify the signs and symptoms that indicate that pragmatic skills intervention is needed. The most effective way to evaluate social communication skills is through observation of a person's behaviors within his or her natural environment, behaviors that penalize him or her by causing peers to distance themselves. When we are doing a school evaluation, we want to observe in academic classes, as well as in differently structured classes such as art, music, or physical education; in unstructured settings such as getting off the bus and going to homeroom in the morning; and in transitions between classes, recess, lunch, and assembly. These observations provide data on the child's adjustment to the behavioral requirements and social communication dynamics of both "free" settings that are controlled by peers and structured settings that are controlled by teachers (Walker, Schwarz, Nippold, Irvin, & Noell, 1994). For persons with Asperger's Syndrome who do not comprehend, attend to, or act on social strategies, these settings present occasions for stumbling blocks to effective social communication.

Recording and Analysis

We use a protocol to synthesize and record our observations. The Prutting Kirchner Pragmatic Protocol (Prutting & Kirchner, 1987) provides a checklist of pragmatic language factors to be rated for appropriateness, and spaces for specific comments. The protocol includes the speech acts or the usage of conversational intentions, purposes, and variety; topic management factors such as selection, introduction, maintenance, and change; turn taking, marked, for example, by initiation of a turn, response to a topic, pause time between responses, repair and revision of a thought or sentence, and interruption or overlap; lexical selection, including factors of cohesion; paralinguistic aspects such as intelligibility; vocal intensity, intonation and stress patterns, pitch, and fluency; and nonverbal aspects like physical proximity, body posture, foot or leg and arm or hand movements, gestures, facial expression, and eye gaze.

The taxonomy of conversational intentions that follows is an adaptation of several lists of speech acts or conversational intentions that are widely used. Because most persons with Asperger's Syndrome have good language foundation skills, they are usually capable of producing them within structured settings. In natural settings, people with Asperger's Syndrome restrict the number of intentions that they use in social interactions, thereby limiting the breadth of their communication possibilities. The following list of intentions is compiled from several sources, as noted here.

1. Requesting information—Gestures and utterances that direct the listener to provide information about an object, action, or location.
2. Requesting action—Utterances that solicit action or the cessation of action.
3. Rejection/denial—Gestures and utterances that indicate unwillingness to accept or consider information.
4. Naming/labeling—Gestures and utterances that serve to name or label objects, events, or location.
5. Answering/responding—Gestures and utterances that acknowledge the speaker's statements, questions, or requests.
6. Informing—Utterances that state facts; express beliefs, attitudes, and emotions; or describe an event.

7. Reasoning—Utterances that justify fact or action; statement of causes or motives.
8. Summoning/calling—Gestures and utterances that secure the listener's attention, usually in the form of names, exclamations, or physical contact.
9. Greeting—Gestures and utterances that express recognition following an introduction or entrance of a speaker into a conversation.
10. Closing conversation—Gestures and utterances used to terminate conversation. (Bates, 1976; Coggins & Carpenter, 1981; Roth & Speckman, 1984).

Observations From Parents, Teachers, and Other Professionals

Although professional observation is essential to the evaluative process, it does have the limitation of being a slice of time that might not be reflective of typical communicative behavior. In behavioral parlance, we say that any observation might be a "sample" but not a "sign" of behavior. It is important to get reports of communication in school, at home, and out in the community from parents, teachers, and other professionals to round out the picture. Many checklists are available for this purpose, but one by Bishop and Baird (2001) from the United Kingdom, is particularly useful because it is speech and language based. These scales address the need for a systematic assessment of the pragmatic aspects of communication. Sample items include: Would have difficulty in explaining to a younger child how to play a simple game; Uses terms like "he" or "it" without making it clear what she is talking about; Keeps telling people things that they know already; Talks to everyone and anyone; Will suddenly change the topic of conversation; Takes in just one or two words in a sentence, and therefore often misinterprets what has been said; and May say things that are tactless or socially inappropriate.

Both parents and professional raters are asked to rate each statement as "definitely applies," "applies somewhat," or "does not apply." The five scales assessing inappropriate initiation, coherence, stereotyped language, use of context, and rapport form a pragmatic composite. There is a set of items assessing aspects of speech production and another assessing syntactic complexity. Two additional sets of items, which assess social relationships and interests, are included to give an indication of how far nonlanguage autistic features cluster with pragmatic impairments (Bishop & Baird, 2001).

CLINICAL EVALUATION

Personal Interview

In the clinical evaluation, we begin with an interview of the person with Asperger's Syndrome. Answering direct questions is not always an easy task for them, so we start with a rating scale about school or work. We explain the scale, which ranges from 1 to 10, with 10 being the best and 1 the worst. Then we ask the person to tell us, for example, "What is the worst thing about school?" We explain that it can be a class, a teacher, some part of the school day, or a more general thing about school. We get answers such as homework, lunch break, or math. Eventually, we guide the conversation to the subject areas and to people in school. We never ask for a list of friends because there is often no one for that list. We might ask; "Who is the nicest person in your school?," "Whom do you like to talk to most?," or "Who is the best kid you know in school?" Responses to these questions help to identify potential conversational partners as well as providing a picture of the person's social world.

We then ask what the person likes to do when he or she is not in school: with family; with persons in the neighborhood; with people his or her age; and in clubs, lessons, or activities. More often than not, persons with Asperger's Syndrome are engaged sufficiently by this task. Occasionally someone will say that they cannot make these choices or that they "don't know" the answers. An effective follow-up strategy is to ask for a choice between options (e.g., "Do you like math better or reading"), which increases the probability of responding.

The rating chart taps into a phenomenon that we have noted in persons with Asperger's Syndrome and yields responses that we use frequently in treatment. Many persons with Asperger's Syndrome like to collect data, organize it, and synthesize it in graphs, percentages, or charts. Their natural tendency to be analytic and to look for trends and meaning is a good tool for a therapist to use both in evaluation and in the explicit teaching of social communication skills. In treatment, for example, we might show a video and ask the student to tally all the instances of eye contact they see. Further into treatment we might ask them to take a survey and ask people their favorite flavor of ice cream. The skills being worked on are initiating conversation, politely asking and recording the results, and saying "Thank you."

Narrative Skills Assessment

After we have information about the person's pragmatic language in various dialogue or interactive contexts, we examine the child's narrative skills. These skills require the ability to formulate and articulate ideas in a connected and organized discourse that structures the information so that the listener can follow it. In personal event narratives, like "Guess what I did over the weekend?" the expected answer gives enough, but not too much information in a sequential manner. It is a mini-monologue segment of a conversation. The ability to adjust to the informational needs of the listener is critical here.

According to Owens (1991), *narratives* are extended units of expressive language containing one or more series of events that are temporally and causally linked. They must be organized in a cohesive and rule-governed manner and contain information regarding the progression of the overall plot, also providing all of the information needed by the listener to follow this unique style of discourse (Owens, 1991). How much and what background are needed to bring the conversational partner along in the telling is key. Some people with Asperger's Syndrome do not say enough, leaving the burden of gaining more information with the conversational partner. The important idea here is known as *scaffolding*, which is the assistance we provide to another in discourse by asking questions, filling in blanks in the information provided, and providing organization that makes the narrative cohesive. The adult might scaffold for a child, but a peer is likely to decide that it is just too much work and walk away. Others who do not have a schema or pattern for 'telling' will say entirely too much and include too many details, figuratively dumping it all at the conversational partner's feet as if to say, "Here it is. I don't know how to organize it. You do it." The problem is the same; the person does not have strategies to use as a framework for these mini-monologues that are frequently inserted into conversation. Either style puts too much of the burden on the conversational partner and results in that person wanting to exit the situation.

A sample of overly brief responses in a narrative might look like this:

"Did you have a nice weekend?"	"Yeah, New Hampshire."
"Do you have a camp up there?"	"Yeah."
"Where is it?"	"Lake Winooski."
"Whom did you go with?"	"Parents. And Bob and Carol were there."
"Oh, nice. Who are Bob and Carol?"	"My aunt and uncle."

A sample of a narrative with excessive detail might look like this:

"Did you have a nice weekend?"

"Yeah, our family went to New Hampshire. We left on Friday night and it took us 27 minutes to get through the tolls on Route 3 because there was so much traffic, and then we stopped at the liquor store for beer for my dad and that took another 18 minutes, and finally, we got a good stretch of road where we could make some time. And, Bob and Carol were up there too because they were getting their boat out of the water. They come from New York and it's even longer for them. Oh, and we go to Lake Winooski to the camp that my Grandma and Grandpa own, well they owned it until Grandpa died and then it was just too much work for them ... that was in 1990 and now we go there and so do other people in the family a, you know, my Uncle Dick and his family always go the first week in July, uh, let's see, and we couldn't swim any more because it is too cold."

Elicit a Personal Event Narrative.   As the first part of the narrative skills assessment, we begin by offering a choice of three pictures. The person chooses the one that triggers a personal event narrative or story and we then ask them to tell it to us.

We hope that during the interview we have elicited some spontaneous personal event narratives to analyze along with the one or two generated from these pictures. If the person needs more structure to formulate and produce a narrative than is afforded by individual pictures, we ask them to tell a story using a wordless picture book. Mayer's (1969) series is particularly good for this purpose because even older children, teens, and young adults enjoy telling *Frog Goes to Dinner*.

Elicit a Procedural Narrative to Tap Sequencing Skills and Strategies. Ask what happens from the time that a person wakes up in the morning until he or she leaves for school or work. The response offers a good picture of sequential and logical organization skill. Sometimes a sports buff will do better relaying how to play soccer or baseball, or a swimmer will talk about a swim meet. An artistic person might relate the step-by-step process for doing needlework, painting a picture, or producing a collage. We often ask a client to explain to an alien how to use a pay phone.

Elicit an Expository Narrative to Check Organizational Skill and Content. We ask for an expository narrative in which the person organizes and communicates information that is more like that learned in school. Often a special interest will suggest the content for this narrative. If the person tends to provide excessive detail, use a 3-minute sand timer to set limits. The fact that a sand timer is silent might be important because people with Asperger's Syndrome are often hypersensitive to noises and have become immune to verbal prompts and other attempts to limit how long they talk. It is important to have enough choices for narrative production so that the client can choose a topic interesting to him or her. Poor narratives might be the result of lack of engagement or a lack of interest in the subject as well as poor skill conversational skills.

Problem-Solving Skills. The first of two problem-solving tasks from Simon (1994) that we find helpful are whether or not the father in the family should help with the housework. One surprise answer we got was, "I wouldn't know, because to tell you the truth, we hire someone to do the housework so none of us do it." We pursued it as a gender issue and a good discussion ensued with that particular high school student. The other is introduced by showing a picture of an ad with a man in a shirt and tie. The person pretends that he or she is buying a shirt for his or her father for Father's Day. He or she calls home to ask the mother's opinion of the shirt that the client has to describe, and whether the mother thinks he or she should get it. We listen carefully for the way the person solves the selection problem and the way he or she organizes the phone call to the mother.

At about this point, we usually test theory of mind by showing a box of bandages with the items pictured on the sides. We ask what is in the box. When told bandages, we say, "No, I took out the bandages and put in crayons." The client opens the box and confirms there are crayons in it. We then ask the client what their parents in the waiting room would say is in the box if we showed it to them. If theory of mind is not yet developed, the client will say "Crayons."

Standardized testing might be necessary to document language foundation skills in some evaluations. Often people with Asperger's Syndrome get scores on these tests that are exceptionally high. If this is the only kind of testing done in a school setting, the results will indicate no language difficulty and no need for special education services. The examining professional will report results that do not begin to match classroom performance for two reasons: First, in standardized testing, many of the sensory distractions that deter good classroom performance in Asperger's Syndrome persons are eliminated. Second, foundation skills are usually intact and often quite exceptional. It is only in the multilayered use of language in social communication that the deficit appears. Standardized tests will never tap those deficits because they are context dependent and they require a consistent context that is not natural communication. Even some of the new attempts at simulation testing that project a person into a computerized situation or setting lack the complexity of real-life situations.

There are several tests of higher language functioning and general skills that include some of the pragmatic uses of language that are useful to administer: The Oral and Written Language Scales (Carrow-Woolfolk, 1996) tests the integration of language skills, including some items of pragmatic significance. For example, "There is a new student in your school. Tell me two things you could say to make him/her feel welcome." The Comprehensive Assessment of Spoken Language (Carrow-Woolfolk, 1999) has a good section on supralinguistic skills and identifies such skills as language in context, drawing inferences, and pragmatic judgment. The Test of Language Competence (Wiig & Secord, 1993) also taps higher language skills such as ambiguous sentences and figurative language. Some evaluators find the Test of Problem Solving (Zachman, Jorgensen, Huisingh, & Barrett, 1984) useful in seeing how the person uses both visual and verbal cues to solve social problems.

Many parents and professionals say that you only need to be in a room with a person with pragmatic language deficits for 5 minutes to know that he or she has this difficulty. Although this might be true, it is nonetheless important to identify precisely the deficits that will ultimately be targeted for change.

CONSIDERATION AND APPLICATION OF CURRENT THEORIES

Before considering the topic of group treatment, it is important to discuss the three psychological deficits that affect the explicit needs of people with Asperger's Syndrome. They are observed in all diagnostic work and treatment.

Theory of Mind

Baron-Cohen referred to theory of mind impairment as "mind blindness" (Baron-Cohen, 1995, p. 4). Cumine, Leach, Stevenson, and Stevenson (1998) described it as the "ability to think about other people's thinking—and further, to think about what they think about our thinking—and even further, to think about what they think we think about their thinking and so on" or stated psychologically it is "the ability to appreciate that other people have mental states: intentions, needs, desires and beliefs which may be different to our own" (p., 19). Often, people with Asperger's Syndrome might be fearful and avoid other people because they cannot appreciate their perspective or predict their behavior. Nathan, for example, likes to read and play games that guarantee the exclusion of others. Because it is difficult to read the intentions of others and discern their motives, persons with Asperger's Syndrome are frequent targets of teasing and humiliation. For example, Jake wrote a diary about his school experiences and when he shared it with various classmates they laughed because he had been explicit in his complaints about teachers. Jake was pleased to have all that attention and thought he was making new friends, when in fact he was being laughed at for his lack of discretion and judgment. His peers knew that he might get into trouble and he was actually suspended from school.

Central Coherence Deficit

Frith described this lack as an inability "to draw together diverse information to construct higher-level meaning in context" (Cumine et al., 1998, p. 25). It is the failure to see the whole picture in the first place and consequently to miss seeing the gestalt of a situation. People who have great difficulties or are simply unable to pull the pieces of a whole together or to understand the main idea or the overall schema are considered lacking in central coherence. The impact on learning in a traditional class environment for someone with challenges in this area is significant. These students need the teacher to clarify the purpose of an activity: "The point of this lesson is _____." In group treatment we close the session with asking that the group tell what they have learned that day in 10 words or less. It gives a closing gestalt and helps the verbose learn to synthesize and present in a concise manner.

Executive Function Deficit

Ozonoff pointed out that "rigid, inflexible and perseverative behavior interferes with the flexible suspension of judgment that goes along with considering many pieces of information before settling on a specific solution or course of action" (p. 27). She further maintained that impulsive behavior that occurs despite a large store of knowledge that the person is unable to draw on in that moment, and not seeing the "whole social picture" typifies this group with difficulty in social cognition (Cumine et al., 1998, p. 27). Language specialists use a helpful acronym for the executive functions—initiate–sustain–inhibit–shift (ISIS)—needed to overcome these problems. Each person has his or her own set of challenges and strengths in attention and executive function and therefore showing what you know depends on one's own profile and the nature of the task at hand. We are reminded of the lament of many a teacher who works with a child with Asperger's Syndrome: "He could do this yesterday, why can't he do it today?"

Cumine et al. (1998) wrote about the shift from focusing on the importance of "content" to the true underlying cause of social difficulties, namely the way in which people communicate. As stated earlier, Twachtman-Cullen (2000) reported that only 7% of a communicative event is relayed through the use of words. The Prutting–Kirchner Protocol considers this in the evaluation. We need to consider both the overarching psychological constructs and observe and analyze the different parts of a communicative event to design effective treatments.

TIPS FOR TEACHING THE CHILD WITH THESE CHALLENGES

1. The frame of an overhead helps to clarify what is important to attend to rather than whiteboards with many other messages written on them. We use a slightly different term, *template*, for frame, and suggest that children use them and then learn to make them for themselves as focus points and sequences for production; for example, "Clear your space before you begin to work," or "Think as you count to 10 to yourself before you respond." Templates can be used for "how-to" processing or for content information in step-by-step format, or recipes for specific processes, such as how to contribute to class discussion. The steps in a process can also be illustrated via a flowchart because this type of a graphic display represents information sequentially from left to right. Examples of these processes could be compiled in a "strategy notebook" that the student uses as a reference. Sticky notes are good to have on the desk and then store in a binder or notebook for subsequent use. Separate sticky notes for each step of a task can provide the satisfaction of crossing out work done or actually throwing away the note as each step is accomplished. Using the metaphor of the camera to zoom in on detail and zoom out to the main idea is another useful tool.

2. Set goals with a special focus on accuracy and time limits for completion.

3. Utilize mnemonic devices that focus on working memory; that is, the memory that helps you to hold the information in mind while you act on it.

4. Provide previews of the day: the pragmatic group session, the errands in the car, and so on. Agendas for group sessions are particularly effective for students who do not have a good temporal sense and keep asking how much time is left. It is essential to include a way in the plan to let the student know that you cannot predict what the day will bring.

5. Task cards are very useful for some. Have categories like (a) I need (my pencil), (b) things to do (open book to the right page), and (c) things I should not do (talk out of turn, sing to myself). A task card can remove the repetitive instruction typically heard as nagging, because the teacher can point to the card rather than speaking.

6. Persons with Asperger's Syndrome often say that a short paragraph of instruction is acceptable if it is necessary, but one sentence would be better, and just "showing me" or demonstrating without words is best.

Intervention

Intervention in social communication requires a group process. The dynamic between one adult and one client in individual treatment is different from peer interaction in a natural context. Some people do need to begin the process in individual treatment to prepare for participation in a group. Others need a group of two, then three, and then four to be able to work effectively. Our experience supports four as the ideal group size. A larger number limits the time each person gets. Even with young adults, who sometimes prefer a larger group, it is easy for more than six to feel like a chaotic crowd rather than a working group.

Not every person with Asperger's Syndrome has the same set of problems in the use of verbal and nonverbal language. It is therefore imperative that "canned" curricula not be used as is to teach this group. These skills are hard to learn and take a lot of time. It is important to prioritize the list of penalizing behaviors for each group member, and design the curriculum around their needs. Penalizing behaviors are those parts of a communicative event that are executed poorly and that interfere with peer interaction. The curricula that are on the market have many fine activities and tasks for explicitly teaching the skills of pragmatic language and by all means should be used. It is nonetheless important to select tasks that fit a particular group's priority list and to be flexible according to group needs. As you get to know each person, adjust the priorities and add or delete items that seemed on target only in the evaluation process. Each session has to be designed taking into account what happened in the preceding session. The learning process will often take longer than anticipated. The point is not to spend 6 weeks on initiating conversation with a group of four who already obtained that skill if turn taking is a more widespread deficit.

Talking about it is not learning until it is practiced and the person can "do" it in a timely fashion or apply the intellectual knowledge that was gained. Recent functional MRI research indicates that these learned skills will not become automatic, but that more efficient step-by-step processing can result in improved performance. The application of a principle followed by generalization to similar situations is the goal, but there are steps in that sequence.

The Four Steps

When teaching any pragmatic skill to a person with Asperger's Syndrome, it is useful to follow a stepwise model that includes developing self-awareness, which allows one to self-monitor and then to maintain self-control. Following this sequence is critical to the increased mastery of these skills.

1. Self -awareness: Social competence and social language will not change unless there is awareness of the skill in others and in oneself. Watch selected videos with and without sound to systematically gather data about how others use eye contact, take turns, gesture, and so on. Also, videotape and play back video of the group working together, or of particular role plays that you have assigned. For example, you can have each group member present advertisements of an object made of clay or of food or a particular brand of soda. After each person has taken a turn, play back the video and identify what all group members did that was effective in their communication, avoiding critical comments.

2. Self-monitoring: Move from the activities and hierarchies of self-awareness to self-monitoring. An upper elementary or middle school student can chart the times that he or she spoke out inappropriately in class. On the chart, the student can make a tally of times that he or she almost spoke out and caught himself or herself. The learning hierarchy here seems to be just talking out, then simultaneously raising one's hand and talking out, then raising one's hand and waiting to be called on. A first grader can put a piece in a puzzle for every time he or she initiates a conversation with a peer. At home the student can chart all the times that he or she gave a compliment to someone in the household.

3. Self-control: Can the student generalize a skill to a variety of situations in which he or she systematically looks for cues to identify an appropriate response, self-selects appropriate words, and then responds in a timely fashion? For those who have particular difficulty with impulsivity, this might mean learning to use self-instructional techniques or "self-talk" (examples include "Just a second while I think" or "I can take my time"). By implementing strategies that compensate for what is not easy or appropriate behavior in social interaction, one can develop the self-control that will enhance communication (Winner, 2000).

4. Mastering the sequence: Self-awareness emerges when a person sees or is aware of his or her behavior and interprets or foresees its results or potential consequences. This ability leads to self-monitoring, sustained awareness of one's behavior, allowing decisions to be made about initiating communication and responding to others. Self-control or the ability to make good decisions and act on them is the ultimate goal.

Thirteen-year-old Joshua came to a group meeting for the first time. He was angry, sullen, and silent. His mother was "making" him come. Peter and Matt had been in the group for a year and enjoyed it. They decided to take Joshua on. Systematically, they demonstrated their development of self-awareness, self-monitoring, and self-control by trying one strategy after another to bring Joshua "out of himself," get acquainted with him, and help him to settle into the group. The following is a snippet of their conversation:

"Just tell me how old you are?"

"Shut up."

"Well at least tell us what grade you're in."

[Silence]

"We know how you feel, we hated the group when we first started too, but it's just an hour a week and its really pretty good. We do lots of role plays and that's fun."

"Shut up, I said."

"Look, here's a dollar. I'll give you this dollar if you'll tell us what grade you're in."

[Silence]

"Come on, you don't have to just make us all miserable."

The next week Matt brought a deck of cards and suggested to me before group that he could teach everyone to play a cool new card game he had learned. He said he thought it might make Joshua more comfortable to play cards. It worked. Joshua played. He began to talk a little, and then as the weeks passed, to fit into the process. Joshua's mother, who was watching behind the one-way mirror, was embarrassed by her son's behavior. Matt's mother said that he had started out angry and unco-operative, too. Peter's father chimed in to say that Matt and Peter began group just as lost and bewildered about what they needed to learn as Joshua. Matt had been an-noyed and irritated, and Peter had been scattered and rigid in his responses. Neither boy was that way now that they had acquired some skills.

The Group Leader's Role

Overall, the job of the group leader is to create a "matter-of-fact" atmosphere. The more specific and concrete the learning can be, the better. Talking with a group of young adults about body proximity and keeping enough distance be-tween yourself and the others with whom you are speaking seems concrete in words. However, one better approach is to hand out yardsticks to the group mem-bers. Have these group members mill about the room snacking and talking as if at a reception until you call a "freeze" and everyone measures their distance from the person with whom they are speaking at the moment. It was powerful for Dennis to realize over three or four trials that he was always farther away from his conversa-tional partner than anyone else in the group and that it created psychological dis-tance. It was equally important for Susan to realize that she was "in the face" of people she talked with and that they continually felt like "backing up." Younger learners are helped by using their own appendages to measure distance that is ap-propriate. An arm's length is good for conversation; elbows on hips are good dis-tance meters for sitting in a group on the floor. Be sure to talk about the point of the activity in the context of body language, nonverbal communication, prosody, or conversation and listening skills. Build a repertoire of skills that will produce insight over time. It is our clinical experience that as a child's skills strengthen, generalization begins to take place. It is not fruitful to have a generalization activity for each separate skill, but rather to develop a cluster of strengths that can be implemented naturally. A good example is in using eye gaze or eye contact effectively. Pair it with initiating, turn taking, and closing a conversation, or as Attwood (1998) suggested, view eye contact as the punctuation of spoken language. If the person cannot bear to make eye contact, or makes it at inappropriate times by staring in too intimate a fashion, fall back and practice facing the whole body toward the partner to signal joint attention. Later, move up the hierarchy. Have that person look at the upper body rather than at the legs and feet, then move to looking at the head, perhaps starting with the chin, then nose, bridge of the nose, and finally eyes. Remember that the way to learn these skills is to talk about them very little while practicing them profusely.

Being matter-of-fact about social conventions is hard for those of us socialized by our families and communities not to be more explicit than absolutely necessary when making social comments, especially critical ones. Instruct or share information in a calm, well-modulated voice. Think of how simple you try to make instructions or directions to a hotel for someone who is visiting from another country and does not share your culture or language. The more simple and straightforward the communication, the clearer the message. This is the key for treatment as well as living with people with Asperger's Syndrome. Be matter-of-fact before you get irritated. People with Asperger's Syndrome have been on the receiving end of much impatience, scolding, and irritation.

To be effective as a teacher in this way is counterintuitive. We are taught that to be subtle and say things indirectly is the kinder, gentler way. As the teacher or parent we need to learn to be calm, direct, and explicit. We often need to say in response to swearing or bathroom talk in our pragmatic groups, "Swearing is not allowed in the group. We are learning to describe how we feel in other words here." If there is minimal emotion expressed in your voice in the statement, it is usually taken at face value. This is not to say that it will not have to be repeated, but it will work to establish a rule for the group.

Overall Group Goals

Having talked about individual treatment designs that address penalizing behaviors and ways to design sessions according to these priorities, I want to suggest three overall group goals that will provide a language and framework within which to design an intervention plan for each group member.

What do I say? What did you say? Learn the conversational hierarchy and the listening hierarchy. Foster a safe and predictable environment in the group and design tasks for peer interaction. Observe how much of the group time students talk and how much of the time the leader talks. The goal is for group members to have most of the time.

The Conversational Hierarchy.

1. Get joint attention: Eye gaze is the typical way to establish joint attention. Facing the body toward the person, then looking at the upper body if not the eyes, then at the face (chin, mouth, or nose) are steps for those who have difficulty with eye contact. Gestures, like tapping someone on the shoulder, are another technique.
2. Initiate: One person starts saying something or initiates the conversation. A greeting and small talk are usually viewed as initiating talk. Calling a person's name is helpful.
3. Respond: The conversational partner replies to what the other initiated.
4. Turn-taking: There are usually four to six turns in informal conversation by American cultural standards. The rules are not to interrupt or talk over the other and know when to relinquish your turn or how to expand it to an appropriate length.
5. Topic introduction: Bring up the main idea for talking to that person.
6. Topic maintenance: The partner says something on the same topic and adds new information to the conversation about that topic.
7. Topic change: One partner changes the topic when it is appropriate to move on to something else. It is important to use bridging phrases and linking sentences like "that reminds me ..." to bring the conversational partner along to your new topic.
8. Topic repair: Rephrase what you say so it is clearer to the other person. Find different words to use and avoid using the same words.
9. Topic closing or ending: Bring the conversation to an end without being rude or abrupt. Use a closing statement like, "I have to go now, nice talking to you," or "Bye, see you tomorrow."

The Listening Hierarchy.

1. Hearing: Listen to the words and their prosodic features.
2. Behavioral and social factors: Do not interrupt or talk over someone else. Keep body and hands still. Follow directions.
3. Comprehension: Stop and think. What is the other person saying? Identify the topic. Read nonverbal cues. Seek clarification by asking questions.
4. Paying attention: Keep your eyes on the speaker. Keep your face and body toward the speaker. Nod your head. Verbally indicate that you are paying attention. Focus on the speaker's topic (Abele & Elias, 2001). Give speaker your full attention; try not to do two things at once.

Narrative

Tell me about it. Learn the narrative skills needed for effective mini-monologues within conversation and other discourse genres such as group discussion. Comprehension of narratives requires knowledge of story grammar and the ability to infer implicit information. Both of these skills might be lacking in the person with Asperger's Syndrome who is not able to comprehend or get the gist of a narrative.

There are several types of narratives, including personal event, procedural, and expository types. To produce a narrative, the person can recount a salient personal experience in a personal event narrative, or relate a routine series of events (e.g., how to play soccer) in a script or procedural narrative, or relate factual information in a clear logical manner in an expository narrative. In the explicit teaching, it helps to give the student a reason for producing the script, such as explaining to a new student how to manage a visit to the cafeteria, or explaining to an alien how to ride a bicycle.

Every narrative needs the following:

- Story macrostructure or overall maturity is reflected by the degree of organization and the number and type of story grammar elements included in the narrative, such as the setting, different characters, problems to be overcome, and solutions to be implemented.
- Cohesion or clear and appropriate use of linguistic markers such as pronouns, prepositions, and articles to provide cohesive ties throughout the story.
- Use of precise and diverse vocabulary, a literate language style, advanced structure of the episodes presented, and highlighting of the high point or crux of the story so that it is clear and interesting. Peterson and McCabe (1983) referred to this aspect as *sparkle* (adapted from Paul & Paul, 2001, p. 435).

Because we use so many mini-monologue narratives in conversation in this culture it is essential that the person with Asperger's Syndrome learn these skills. Use of a symbol system to concretize the elements in a narrative, like a grammar marker, is often helpful. We use the *wh*-questions and in a group sometimes have people stand under signs for each question as they tell an event narrative, moving from who to what to where as their story unfolds. As they gain more skill we add problem and solution signs to include greater complexity. Having each person in the group tell one event from his or her week each session provides ample opportunities for practice and development of this skill. We also recommend use of a sand timer to aid in limiting the narrative from 1.5 to 2 minutes to structure the narrative as part of a conversation or "chat."

Verbally Mediated Problem Solving

Many people with Asperger's Syndrome have not developed "self-talk" or "self-instructional" skills. Young adults in our group were astounded to learn that neurotypicals talk to themselves, rehearsing what and how to say things in upcoming interactions. A typical homework assignment for group members is to watch people in cars at traffic lights to see how many of them are talking to themselves. This does not refer to the stream-of-consciousness talk that relates verbally all that is going on with a person and is actually penalizing behavior. It is, alternately, the planning and revising process of internal verbal mediation in which one decides what to say and how to say it. Many of us can relate to this process if we think of deciding what and how to present to a boss a proposal we are making, or the careful word choices we make when encountering a person for the first time after fighting with him or her. It is considering options and choosing the best one.

This process, then, is expanded to include situations and contexts to determine what to do or say. Some examples of this might include how to enter a group conversation, how to consider what is going on when you enter a room, how to word a criticism, how to persuade, or how to invite a friend to go to a movie.

ORGANIZATION OF THE SESSION

- Groups typically meet once a week for an hour.
- The maximum group size is four for school-aged children or five or six for older high school students.
- Remember that some children need to start out with just one or two other group members so that they are not overwhelmed.
- All group members share the purpose of working at the language of social communication.
- Each person in the group needs to have enough time to practice.
- Normally developing peer models do not belong in a skill-based treatment group. For group members to take the considerable risks required to learn and shape new skills, they need to feel that those in the group also have risks to take as they learn new skills. If normally developing peers are in the group, they present those with deficits in social cognition with constant reminders of how easy social interaction is for most people, and this can be a demoralizing influence for those who must work hard at it.
- Small group settings within the school or in outside activities with normally developing peers are good generalization opportunities for children who are gaining applied skills in the treatment group.
- Some school systems are beginning to do groups as extracurricular activities so that they can get the right combinations of children together from different schools in a given district.

Sequential Session Design

Chat Time.   Begin working as the children arrive for the group. At first, all conversation is likely to be generated by one student and directed to the group leader. From the beginning, coach individuals to include others in the conversation. Over time, there will be a shifting away from directing all conversation to the adult and more will be directed to the group of peers or to one other child. By the end of 3 months, group members will easily chat amongst themselves (it might even become difficult for the adult to get a word in edgewise). The chat time can be deferred until the end of the session. If group members obsess on their areas of special interest (e.g., Pokemon, Magic cards, or Dungeons and Dragons), it is sometimes wise to restrict conversation to the last 5 minutes of the session and then let them choose those topics to chat about.

Specific Instruction.   Students with Asperger's Syndrome tell us that they deal best with processing only short paragraphs of instruction. They prefer to be shown what to do or say. Engage students in discussing practical, concrete issues like, "What is the first thing you say when answering the phone?" or "What would you like to have someone talk to you about on the telephone?" This breaks up the didactic instruction and involves them in the learning.

Structured Activity.   Move into a structured activity, for example, a one-page script of Sue and Betty talking on the phone and Betty not holding up her end of the conversation. Have two students take the parts and read the script. Talk about what goes wrong. Have them reread it. The other two students can use stopwatches to time the talking time of each person to demonstrate how Betty is not holding up her end of the conversation. Then, while they are still playing the roles of the people in the script, coach them to continue the conversation and try to make it better. In one session, the Betty figure asked the group leader about every statement she made before she said it to Sue in the phone. Another structured activity would be to use a television clip of 3 to 5 minutes with everyone timing the turns taken to become aware of turn-taking and to monitor any interruptions. Barrier game activities, where one student gives verbal pencil-and-paper instructions that the others follow, are good for structured listening practice. When you are eliciting possible things to say, such as closing statements for a conversation, be sure to fill a whiteboard with possibilities to systematically increase rigid thinkers' flexibility in developing a repertoire of options to use in different contexts. Furthermore, it is imperative that the leader help them to consider the context and the tone they should be using to create conversational options. Danny volunteered, "Bye, bye, see you tomorrow," as a good closing statement for a conversation. We put it on the board, he used it in his role play, and then he chose it to use a second time. The group leader was running short of time and let him repeat his closing choice. The next day Danny and his mother called after school and he said with great distress, "It doesn't work!" As the tale unraveled, it became clear that Danny had used the closing very successfully to end a conversation with the boy at the school cubby next to his. It even worked moderately well when he said it to another boy at another cubby, but when he got out of the context and said it in turn to five or six other students at their cubbies, all of the children were laughing. Because the rules for conversation are complex, a simple script with only one option does not work.

Group Activity.   Move into a group activity that is designed to get the children to talk among themselves. The leader's role is to coach and to listen for any generalization of skills worked on previously that might be occurring in this more naturalistic context. Mixer activities are good, like providing a bag of gumdrops and a box of toothpicks and asking the group to construct a building of some sort together—one building. Younger children can use blocks or a similar type of building toy. At first when they have little skill in interaction and negotiation they are likely to each build a part of the structure and then at the last minute stick them together to make one structure. Decorating a sheet cake together, making a scarecrow, designing a town on poster board, making instant pudding, or turning a sheet into a monster can all be group activity tasks. Making feeling books and sharing them, or keeping "Me Posters" while adding items over many weeks and talking about them are also good interactive activities.

The Coach Role.   This role can include using a strategy called "freeze" like the childhood game, or conversational autopsy (from Lavoie's [1994] social autopsy idea). All conversation stops midstream and everyone looks at what is going on, evaluates what needs fixing or celebrating, and then reproduces the discourse in a more effective way before proceeding. Saying it the revised way is the key to learning. The coach can also simply comment on the conversation or help someone to relinquish a turn so that others can speak.

Here are some tips for interacting with students collectively and individually:

- It is worth repeating: Be matter-of-fact!
- Be concise: A short, clear statement is best if you cannot show the person what to do or say.
- Engaging students in difficult group tasks requires a sense of humor and a willingness to wait, not push. Offer strategies that might simplify an organizational task or a processing task like presenting two options rather than waiting for a formulated response. For example, "Did you feel more angry or scared?" or "Would you like to use the markers or colored pencils to draw on the poster?"
- When a student is struggling to communicate a thought or idea, the coach should not try to be helpful by asking questions along the way. Many people with Asperger's Syndrome will have to begin all over again to process and formulate what to say when their train of thought has been interrupted, even if the intention was to be helpful.
- Pick battles carefully, if rules need to be laid down. Often, if the rule is stated and then the coach backs off and gives the student a few minutes, or is lenient in how precisely the rule is followed, the group member will tend to comply with the task at hand. Another option is to ask the person to do something physical. In the classroom a student stated that 1,784 people were killed in the battle of Gettysburg when the teacher said approxi-

mately 2,000. The student could not let go of the exact figure and was becoming increasingly argumentative. The teacher remembered her
Asperger's Syndrome training and asked the student to get up from his
desk and write the exact number on the board so that she could refer to it.
The act of getting up, walking to the board, writing the number, and re-
turning to his seat, as well as being valued as a source of information,
helped this student to calm his rising anxiety and desire to argue and move
on in the discussion.

- Choosing a few rules that focus on limiting criticism and increasing positive comments helps maintain a positive group tone. "No put-downs" is a
great rule and it seems easier to call another on breaking that rule than to
say that one personally hates being put down.

- Do not spend much time in a group session on behavior management or
nothing else will be accomplished. It is not really so important in a group
treatment setting that members are always seated and have their feet on
the floor. Focus instead on what needs to be taught.

- Competition is not comfortable for people in areas in which they feel in-
competent. Earning group points to reach a magic number that only the
leader knows is much more effective if you want to reward group members. Awards can be administered based on the total number of points
earned by the group, rather than any individual. Group points can be
earned by watching a video of a group role play and pointing out things
that other group members did well.

- When giving group instructions, name the child who probably does not see
himself or herself as part of the group. An eighth-grade science teacher was
frustrated with Patti, who rarely responded to group instructions to turn in
her lab notebook. Although the teacher initially viewed this as willful disobedience, the teacher felt differently after following advice to include an additional instruction ("Patti, don't forget to put your lab book in the basket").
The teacher came to understand that Patti did not view herself as part of a
group of people and therefore did not respond to such "general" instructions.

- Tell the students what to do, not what not to do. The double-negative processing might be too difficult for the person with Asperger's Syndrome.

- Do not ask open-ended questions. They are the hardest to answer. They require an organizational schema that your students might not be able to de-
vise. Examples are, "Why did you say that?" "What do you think about ... ?"
Although it has been mentioned before, write an agenda for the session that
will help to structure tasks for the student with Asperger's Syndrome.

- Script the process on paper, posters, or sticky notes. Verbal communication is so time limited, said and then gone, that any concrete visual or verbal prompts are useful.

- Be sure to design activities for the group that are as realistic and natural as
possible. When practicing greetings, for example, have two people go

down the hall one way and two the other way so that they meet as people
might do naturally and greet one another.

REFERENCES

Abele, E., & Elias, K. (2001, March). *Pragmatic language disorders and social skill development.*
Paper presented at the meeting of Educational Resources Inc., Marlborough, MA.

Attwood, T. (1998). *Asperger's Syndrome: A guide for parents and professionals.* London:
Jessica Kingsley.

Baron-Cohen, S. (1995). *Mindblindness: An essay on autism and theory of mind.* Cambridge,
MA: MIT Press.

Bates, E. (1976). *Language in context: Studies in the acquisition of pragmatics.* New York: Academic.

Bishop, D. V. M., & Baird, G. (2001). Parent and teacher report of pragmatic aspects of communication: Use of the Children's Communication Checklist in a clinical setting. *Developmental Medicine & Child Neurology, 43,* 809–818.

Bloom, L., & Lahey, M. (1978). *Language development and language disorders.* New York: Wiley.

Carrow-Woolfolk, E. (1996). *Oral and Written Language Scales (OWLS).* Circle Pines, MN:
American Guidance Service.

Carrow-Woolfolk, E. (1999). *Comprehensive Assessment of Spoken Language (CASL).* Circle
Pines, MN: American Guidance Service.

Coggins, T., & Carpenter, R. (1981). The communicative intention inventory. *Journal of Applied Psycholinguistics, 2,* 213–234.

Cumine, V., Leach, J., Stevenson, B., & Stevenson, G. (1998). *Asperger Syndrome: A practical
guide for teachers.* London: David Fulton.

Lavoie, R. (Producer). (1994). *Learning disabilities and social skills—Last one picked ... first
one picked on* [Videotape]. (Available from PBS Video, 1320 Braddock Place, Alexandria,
VA 22314)

Mayer, M. (1969). *Frog goes to dinner.* New York: Dial.

Owens, R. (1988). *Language development, an introduction,* (2d ed.). New York: Macmillan.

Owens, R. (1991). *Language disorders: A functional approach to assessment and intervention.*
New York: Macmillan.

Ozonoff, S., Rogers, & Pennington, B. (1991). In "Asperger's Syndrome: Evidence of an empirical distinction from high-functioning autism." *Journal of Child Psychology and Psychiatry and Allied Disciplines, 32,* 1107–1122.

Paul, R., & Paul, V. I. (2001). *Language disorders from infancy through adolescence: Assessment
and intervention.* Philadelphia: Mosby.

Peterson, C., & McCabe, A. (1983). *Developmental psycholinguistics: Three ways of looking at
a child's narrative.* New York: Plenum.

Prutting, C. A., & Kirchner, D. M. (1987). A clinical appraisal of the pragmatic aspects of language. *Journal of Speech and Hearing Disorders, 52,* 105–119.

Roth, F., & Speckman, N. (1984). Assessing the pragmatic abilities of children: Part 1. Organizational framework and assessment parameters. *Journal of Speech and Hearing Disorders, 49,* 2–11.

Simon, C.. (1994). *Evaluating communicative competence.* Tucson, AZ: Communication
Skill Builders.

Twachtman-Cullen, D. (1998). Language and communication in high-functioning autism and Asperger Syndrome (pp. 199–233). In E. Schopler, G. B. Mesibov, L. J. Kunce (Eds.), New York & London: Plenum.

Walker, H., Schwarz, I., Nippold, M., Irvin, L., & Noell, J. (1994). Social skills in school-age children and youth: Issues and best practices in assessment and intervention. *Topics in Language Disorders, 14*(3), 70–82.

Wiig, E., & Secord, W. (1993). *Test of Language Competence-Expanded Edition (TLC)*. San Antonio, TX: Psychological Corporation.

Winner, M. G. (2000). *Inside out: What makes a person with social cognitive deficits tick?* San Jose, CA: Author.

Zachman, L., Jorgensen, C., Huisingh, R., & Barrett, M. (1984). *Test of Problem Solving (TOPS)*. East Moline, IL: Lingui Systems.

PART V

Special Concerns

Chapter 12

Sexual Relationships

Isabelle Hénault
Montréal, Quebec, Canada

Among recent theories and treatment models related to Asperger's Syndrome, themes that target interpersonal relationships are among those that attract the attention of families, therapists, and people who themselves manifest the syndrome. Behavior is only one aspect of sexuality, a word that also implies love, intimacy, communication, emotions, experiences, and social skills. It is critical to address sexuality in all its complexity to adequately understand and intervene with the population of people who have Asperger's Syndrome. This chapter presents current information on the sociosexual profile of individuals with Asperger's Syndrome and issues related to teaching social and sexual skills.

SEXUAL DEVELOPMENT

Several authors (Aston, 2001; Gray, Ruble, & Dalrymple, 1996; Haracopos & Pedersen, 1999; Hellemans & Deboutte, 2002; Hénault & Attwood, 2002) have suggested that individuals with Asperger's Syndrome have a distinct sexual profile: Their sexual interest and needs are comparable to those of the general population, but they show them in different ways.

Reviewing the factors that influence the sexual development of individuals with Asperger's Syndrome, Griffiths, Quinsey, and Hingsburger (1989) wrote that the lack of sociosexual knowledge of those with Asperger's Syndrome is due to discomfort associated with the topic. They observed that a tendency by caretakers to overprotect their children with Asperger's Syndrome leads to a lack of communication about sexuality or a denial of its existence (asexualization). Put simply, parents often avoid talking with their children about topics that they believe will be too difficult for them to understand or too upsetting to discuss.

It is likely that children with Asperger's Syndrome are sexually abused at a higher rate than other children. The American Academy of Pediatrics (1996) and the National Center on Child Abuse and Neglect (National Information Center for Children and Youth With Disabilities, 1992) found an average of 36 cases of sexual abuse per 1,000 children with a disorder of development, a rate 1.7 times as high as that found in the general population. For those with Asperger's Syndrome, their lack of sexual knowledge and social skills might interfere with notions of consent. By failing to understand the social world, they might misperceive the intentions of others, thereby setting themselves up to be victims as well as perpetrators of sexual misconduct.

Gender segregation, social isolation, and other restrictions in their environment prevent individuals with Asperger's Syndrome from developing sexual awareness in the same way as their neurotypical peers. Policies and rules related to sexuality are more strict—and enforced more severely—for individuals with autism than for those with intellectual deficiencies (Roy, 1996). According to Griffiths (1999), teams that work with people with Asperger's Syndrome should create an environment that is open to the issue of sexuality by preventing abuse, offering appropriate education, and recognizing the sexual needs and rights of the individuals they work with. Recognizing the sexual rights of these individuals also implies respecting their privacy and intimacy. Given appropriate opportunities, they can learn about intimacy and can therefore explore a range of emotions, establish communication, and expand their social networks.

Several studies have examined the sexual repertoire of individuals with autism and Asperger's Syndrome (Haracopos & Pedersen, 1999; Hellemans & Deboutte, 2002; Konstantareas & Lunsky, 1997; Van Bourgondien, Reichle, & Palmer, 1997), confirming the presence of an active sexual life that includes masturbatory practices comparable to those of the general population (Masters & Johnson, 1988, cited in Haracopos & Pedersen, 1999). Other sexual activities, such as kissing, caressing, and sexual intercourse, are also reported.

The Sexual Profile

The sexual profile of individuals with Asperger's Syndrome or high-functioning autism was elaborated from a sample of 25 adults from Canada, Australia, and the United States (Hénault & Attwood, 2002) and studied using the Derogatis Sexual Functioning Inventory (DSFI; Derogatis & Melisaratos, 1982), which measures 11 aspects of sexual understanding and behavior. This study provided valuable information on developmental issues, behavior, emotions, and sexual roles. When compared to preestablished general population norms, the results obtained from the sample revealed a lack of sexual experience in the study participants. Sexual interest was found to develop at an average of 14 years of age, but first sexual experiences took place only at 22 years. Of the 25 participants, 9 were virgins. Their lack of sexual experience was accompanied by psychological and physiological symptoms such as nervousness, loneliness, and anxiety. Despite curiosity about sexuality, general information scores for the participants were lower than those for the general population.

On the other hand, the sexual needs of the participants seem to have been fulfilled by a rich and diversified fantasy life, contradicting the notion that people with Asperger's Syndrome have a limited imagination. Participants reported a fantasy life filled with sexual diversity and free of social constraints and taboos. They were open-minded and appeared to act according to their desires, whether directed to a person of the same sex or the opposite sex.

Clinical observations and Internet discussions with members of a group of transgendered individuals with pervasive developmental disorders revealed a possible link between Asperger's Syndrome and gender identity disorder. Gender dysphoria, as described by Israel and Tarver (1997) is "a discomfort characterized by a feeling of incongruity with the physical gender assigned to one at birth" (p. 7). Certain people with Asperger's Syndrome do not view their transgendered nature as a disorder, but rather as sexual flexibility and diversity. One woman (male to female transsexual) told me, "When I experience sexual desire, I am attracted to the person, regardless of his or her biological sex."

In a study conducted with a sample of 34 individuals with autism, Haracopos and Pedersen (1992, cited in Hellemans & Deboutte, 2002) reported that 35% experienced sexual desire for both genders and 9% for their own gender; 15% described their gender preference as undetermined. It is therefore possible that people with Asperger's Syndrome will exhibit more homosexual and bisexual behaviors than the general population. This hypothesis merits further empirical attention.

Those with Asperger's Syndrome sometimes provide reasoned explanations for their sexual diversity. One adolescent boy explained it as follows: "When I'm a girl, I don't have Asperger's." By giving himself another role he became another person. Some individuals even adopt a new name to denote the gender change. Others wish for a sex change to become accepted by their peers. One 13-year-old boy with Asperger's Syndrome dressed as a girl and wore makeup to resemble his mother, two sisters, and their friends. He felt more comfortable playing and interacting with them by temporarily becoming a girl, when, as he said, "I no longer feel different or deficient."

In certain adolescents with Asperger's Syndrome, gender dysphoria, or the desire to change gender, can become an overriding interest or even an obsession. In such situations, all activities, conversations, gestures, and motivation are aimed at ensuring that the "transformation" is a success. Lack of judgment and the individuals determination can become a significant problem. One mother told me that one morning her adolescent boy wore makeup and her bra—over his shirt—to go to school; he wanted to show his "gender change" to his friends. From that moment on, he insisted he be called Lucie instead of Luc. When obsessions peak, parents and partners often feel helpless and unsure as to what attitude they should adopt. Professional assistance is then recommended.

The sexual profile of individuals with Asperger's Syndrome indicates that they have sexual needs and drives comparable to those of the general population. Their attitude toward sexuality is positive. They have fantasies but lack experience, generally because interpersonal difficulties prevent easy progression into sexual relationships. One study participant summarized the problem by saying, "Situations with lovers are very awkward. It seems as though my loneliness and lack of sexual experience show on my face. Several people look at me and laugh ... one can't help but feel inferior and unhappy."

The difficulties faced by people with Asperger's Syndrome—with typical sexual needs but whose social awkwardness prevents the development of sexual relationships—underscores the need for sex education and social skills training. Intervention can be helpful from as early as preadolescence so that individuals with Asperger's Syndrome can have satisfying interpersonal and sexual relationships in adulthood.

Behavioral Problems

Individuals with Asperger's Syndrome can express their frustration by inappropriate and aggressive sexual behaviors, such as unwanted touching, exhibitionism, fetishism, and sexual compulsions. Some people with Asperger's Syndrome describe themselves as asexual, having no sexual desires or behaviors, but the majority fall within general population norms along the continuum to the point of compulsive sexuality. This state is accompanied by an excessive interest in everything sexual and the constant seeking of sexual stimulation, sometimes by inappropriate sexual behaviors. Some behaviors are directed toward establishing a perfect sexual repertoire or routine, at the expense of diversity and, often, intimacy (Aston, 2001).

Sexual obsessions naturally interfere with work, relationships with partners, and other areas of life. Consider, for example, the case of a man in his 20s with Asperger's Syndrome who spends 4 hours a day looking at pornography on the Internet, masturbates during his breaks at work, constantly seeks sexual contact with women, and fantasizes and talks about different sexual scenarios he would like to enact. Because it is obviously not possible to experience sexuality at a rate matching his obsession, he will experience anxiety to a degree that can, without professional intervention, lead to loss of control. Several treatment models for sexual compulsions can be adapted to the Asperger's Syndrome profile (Carnes, 1989, 1993; Coleman, 1991).

As one would expect, masturbation is the most common sexual behavior manifested by adolescents with Asperger's Syndrome. Self-stimulation, per se, is not generally a problem until its frequency interferes with other activities or it is performed in public or otherwise inappropriately. (Hellemans & Deboutte [2002], citing the work of Wing, DeMyer, & Gillberg, reported masturbating in public to be the most frequently encountered inappropriate behavior of individuals with autism.) The intense pleasure of masturbation can become a source of distraction or even a sexual compulsion. Some people with Asperger's Syndrome will resort to excessive masturbation if they are insufficiently stimulated at school or work or during free moments.

Some individuals with Asperger's Syndrome experience sensory auditory and tactile hypersensitivity that is linked to a neurological disorder (Autisme France, 2003). Neon lights, ambient noise, or a perfume's scent can be very disturbing and might even cause attention difficulties. In these cases, the environment should be set up to limit sensory overload. With respect to sexuality, oversensitivity can hinder the development of an intimate relationship because various sensations are experienced as uncomfortable or even painful (Smith-Myles, Tapscott-Cook, Miller, Rinner, & Robbins, 2000).

In contrast, hyposensitivity is defined as a weak response to mild stimulation. In these cases, overexposure to stimuli is required for the individual to experience sensations. In masturbation, stimulation must be sufficient for orgasm to be reached. When they masturbate, hyposensitive people with Asperger's Syndrome might need to stimulate themselves more vigorously than most people to experience sexual satisfaction, increasing the risk of genital injury. The use of lubricants such as KY Jelly can increase pleasurable sensations and reduce these harmful effects. Shyness, shame, or accompanying guilt can also be complicating factors in the inability of males to ejaculate. The use of specialized educational materials can help adolescents resolve these difficulties. Two educational videos with their accompanying books are recommended for such situations: *Hand Made Love* (Hingsburger, 1995) for men and *Fingertips* (Hingsburger & Haar, 2000) for women.

The difference between chronological (actual) age and developmental age (usually lower by a couple of years) found in certain individuals with Asperger's Syndrome can affect their judgment and lead to problems. Consider the case of a 20-year-old adult with Asperger's Syndrome who regularly has sexual relations with a 16-year-old girl. Such a compromising situation could lead to a court case if the girl or her parents pressed charges. Subsequent to a psychosexual assessment, the 20-year-old could be found to have a developmental age of 15 to 16 years, which would render him equal to the girl in terms of sociosexual development, maturity, and judgment. However, according to the law, he could be charged with sexually exploiting a minor. In certain cases such as this, individuals with Asperger's Syndrome have been found guilty, despite the fact that the developmental age of the sexual partners is equal (Griffiths, Richards, Fedoroff, & Watson, 2002).

Interpersonal Relationships

Communication, appropriate expression of emotions, and intimacy are essential to successful interpersonal relationships for any person, but people with Asperger's Syndrome often have difficulty with these aspects of any relationship. Many have difficulty interpreting and managing their emotions (Attwood & Caswell, 2002), in addition to decoding the emotions that others can read easily on human faces (Baron-Cohen et al., 2002).

The development of social skills and of the theory of mind is an important part of sexuality. The goal is for those with Asperger's Syndrome to recognize what constitutes social relations, behave appropriately in a variety of contexts (school, recreation centers, family, etc.), and finally expand their circle of friends. Social skills training refines and increases their repertoire of appropriate behaviors. On a basic level, certain skills must also be acquired, such as establishing contact with another person, participating in a conversation, expressing emotion, decoding nonverbal cues, and so on. This training should, ideally, be offered in a group.

If individuals with Asperger's Syndrome feel overwhelmed by their emotions, they are more likely than others to become illogical and experience cognitive fixation. Rather than think through their actions, they will react impulsively, which can lead to problem behaviors. Given their difficulties in managing situations that involve emotions, individuals would greatly benefit from interventions aimed at managing responses to emotional situations.

Emotional rigidity limits experience and self-expression (Attwood, 1999). The aim of interventions is initially to help individuals create relationships based on their special interests in the hope that trust and significant relationships will develop. The main objective is to teach those with Asperger's Syndrome a variety of emotions to help them express exactly what they feel. They can discover emotions, ranging from joy to anger, that can then become part of the shared experience of relationships. The concept of emotional intelligence summarizes essential elements for forming and maintaining relationships, including recognizing one's emotions, managing them to be context appropriate, and recognizing a range of emotions in others (Hess, 1998).

Some people with Asperger's Syndrome might have acquired technical knowledge about recognizing and responding to the cues of others but lack the dexterity and know-how to accomplish the task. Their tendency to linger on facial details makes the task even more difficult. Interventions should be aimed in part on reducing and decoding the flood of information that accompanies human faces and emotions. Recent discoveries (e.g., Channon, Charman, Heap, Crawford, & Rios, 2001; Young, 2001) suggest that individuals with Asperger's Syndrome suffer from dysfunction of the amygdala, the region in the brain responsible for general intelligence when recognizing social cues. Therefore, technical knowledge alone might not be enough to recognize faces and emotions.

Several activities are useful to address these difficulties. Baron-Cohen's (Baron-Cohen et al., 2002) *Mind Reading* Software, Attwood and Caswell's (2002) *Emotion Project*, Attwood's (1999) *Cognitive Behaviour Therapy* techniques, and the Biofeedback Biotouch Interactive Mood Light from Sharper Image Design (1999) can all be used to improve the expression of emotion. These tools and programs offer specific strategies such as reading emotions in someone's gaze, exploring and managing one's own emotions, and recognizing bodily signs of emotional change.

The *Making Waves: What Is a Good Relationship Anyways?* program of activities (available for free on the Internet at www.mwaves.org) is an additional resource. Using a simple and effective format, the program guides users about the different types of relationships that can exist between two people. An initial questionnaire assesses knowledge of a variety of themes, such as time and space, affection, sexuality, and friendship. Based on the results, the educational program explores interpersonal relationships to assess limit setting and the presence of abuse. Individuals are constantly required to participate in concrete examples and role-playing scenarios. This program package contains a wealth of valuable examples, advice, and resources. The interventions are constructed in a manner that enhances the special capabilities of those with Asperger's Syndrome and use their strengths (Attwood & Gray, 1999a) so as to maintain their interest and motivation.

The debate has been put to rest about whether individuals with autism or Asperger's Syndrome have the desire for relationships. In the 1970s and 1980s, certain authors (Wing, DeMyer, Elgar, Melone, & Lettick, cited in Hellemans & Deboutte, 2002) contended that these individuals had no such interest. Haracopos and Pedersen (1999), Hellemans and Deboutte (2002), and Hénault and Attwood (2002) argued that people with autism or Asperger's Syndrome express sexual desire and interest in having partners, and have the right to a rewarding sexual life. The main difficulty lies in the discrepancy between their needs and their social skills. Individuals with Asperger's Syndrome should benefit from teaching programs that are adapted to their level of functioning and to their sociosexual profile (Hellemans & Deboutte, 2002; Hénault & Attwood, 2002).

The sociosexual skills training program (Hénault, in press) proposes group activities that focus on effective relationships and sexuality. As it explores issues of love and friendship, respect, insecurities, compromise, and specific interests, the program offers practical activities such as concrete examples and role playing.

SEXUAL EDUCATION

Here are a few elements behind the philosophy of sexual education:

- There is no positive correlation between knowledge and interest in sexuality. Curiosity and exploration mark adolescence as a developmental period. It is normal, during this period, to observe an increase in desire and in the frequency of sexual behaviors. Participation in an education program or in workshops will not cause new sexual behaviors to emerge.
- Ignorance breeds fear (in parents, counselors, and the individuals themselves). The more information that individuals with Asperger's Syndrome have, the greater their capacity to develop judgment and to react more effectively in abusive situations.

- There is less risk that a behavior becomes excessive if it is accepted and well directed than if it is forbidden and ignored.
- Sexual desire should not be repressed. Rather, it should be directed in such a way that its expression is appropriate.
- Sex education must include learning social skills, understanding emotions, and improving communication.

INTERVENTIONS

According to the National Information Center for Children and Youth With Disabilities (1992), sexual education programs must promote information, develop values, encourage interpersonal skills, and increase individuals' sense of personal responsibility. According to Haracopos and Pedersen (1999), sexuality must be considered in its entirety, including intimacy, desire, communication, love, deviance, and self-satisfaction. Intervention programs must address issues of sexual identity, behavior, needs, and sexual development (Chipouras, Cornelius, Daniels, & Makas, 1979; Griffiths et al., 1989; Hellemans, 1996).

Structured education programs, adapted to the needs of individuals with Asperger's Syndrome, must be an integral part of services for that population. Several authors (Griffiths et al., 2002; Kempton, 1993) report that the more informed individuals are with respect to sexuality, the greater their ability to make enlightened and autonomous choices. In addition to decreasing the risk of sexual abuse, such programs provide access to a rewarding social and sexual life.

The sexual education program (Hénault, in press) consists of workshops based on 10 themes:

1. Love and friendship.
2. Physiological changes.
3. Sexual relations.
4. Emotions.
5. Contraception and prevention of HIV and sexually transmitted diseases.
6. Sexual orientation.
7. Alcohol, drugs, and sexuality.
8. Sexism and sexual roles.
9. Sexual abuse and inappropriate behaviors.
10. Theory of mind, communication, and intimacy. (Activities adapted from Durocher & Fortier, 1999.)

The group activities take place over 10 to 15 consecutive weeks; each session takes 90 minutes. The group format allows participants to develop friendships. Each group should include both genders to allow for a more comprehensive discussion. Informal socializing fosters the development of friendships and increases the quality of interpersonal relationships within the group. The use of stimulating visual materials (videos, computer software, photos) maintains attention and teaches learners how to approach someone and express interest in a respectful way.

SEX EDUCATION

Those who work in the area of sexuality (sexologists, psychologists, social workers, therapists) are usually familiar with various approaches to sex education. However, it is important that they have some understanding of Asperger's Syndrome if they want to adapt their programs to the specific needs of this population.

Figures 12.1 and 12.2 show a few activities taken from the socio-sexual education program. The complete program will be available in a future publication.

The exercise in Fig. 12.1 is aimed at exploring values and the manner in which these affect the establishment of interpersonal relationships. Participants have 10 minutes to complete the activity. They are then invited to name the five values

Theme 1: Love and Friendship, COMPLEMENTARY ACTIVITY

MY VALUES IN INTERPERSONAL RELATIONSHIPS

By establishing what is important in your life you can become aware that values, according to how you rate their importance and how you use them in interpersonal relationships, vary from one person to the next. Do this exercise on your own and compare your response with the other participants. This may enable you to understand one another better. Write the numbers 1 to 18 in the corresponding boxes (1 being most important and 18 being least important).

☐   Self-respect   ☐   Respect of Others

☐   Beauty   ☐   Fun

☐   Friendship   ☐   Freedom

☐   Love   ☐   Admiration of Others

☐   Happiness   ☐   Honesty

☐   Fidelity   ☐   Giving of One's Self

☐   Intelligence   ☐   Sexuality

☐   Self-confidence   ☐   Sense of Humor

☐   Tenderness   ☐   Equality

FIG. 12.1   Sample activity on love and friendship relationships (adapted from Durocher & Fortier, 1999).

Theme 5: Contraception and Prevention of STD and AIDS, COMPLEMENTARY ACTIVITY

QUIZ ON CONTRACEPTION AND PREVENTION

Youth often have unplanned and irregular sexual relations. Several studies on the subject have shown that adolescents make little use of contraceptive means and methods to prevent STDs. What you know about this topic is very important in that it allows you to make appropriate choices in your sexual life. Pick up your pencil and complete this quiz! Maybe you'll learn something new.

1.	"Natural" methods, such as the "calendar method" are not recommended for adolescents.	□	True
		□	False
2.	There is a risk of pregnancy when ejaculation occurs near the vulva.	□	True
		□	False
3.	Condoms are an effective method of contraception for preventing STDs.	□	True
		□	False
4.	The morning after pill can be taken up to three days after unprotected sexual relations.	□	True
		□	False
5.	The pre-ejaculate contains a sufficient amount of sperm for the possibility of fertilization.	□	True
		□	False
6.	The pill is very effective at preventing pregnancy when taken correctly.	□	True
		□	False
7.	The pill does not protect against STDs.	□	True
		□	False
8.	Condoms cannot be re-used.	□	True
		□	False
9.	Adolescents are fertile from the beginning of adolescence.	□	True
		□	False
10.	The morning-after pill and abortions are emergency measures and not methods of contraception.	□	True
		□	False

FIG. 12.2 Sample activity on contraception and prevention of HIV and sexually transmitted diseases (adapted from Durocher & Fortier, 1999).

that seem most important and the two that seem least important to them. This discussion allows them to situate sexuality within the context of interpersonal relationships. For some, sexuality is a high priority. For others, it is found at the bottom of their list. During the exercise, participants gain awareness of the priorities of others. The workshop continues with two other activities that address the themes of love and friendship.

Learning about contraception is the first step toward safer sexual behavior. The activity shown in Fig. 12.2 continues with a demonstration of proper condom use on a model and a handout of the different steps. The workshop aims to sensitize those with Asperger's Syndrome to the reality of sexually transmitted diseases and HIV and to develop a positive attitude toward the use of contraceptives.

The program yields considerable results with respect to enhanced social and sexual skills, as shown by Attwood and Gray's friendship skills grid. Introduction skills, conversation, and helping behaviors were among those that showed the greatest improvement. At the end of the program, participants had a greater fund of general knowledge in sexuality and were more nuanced in their judgment. Inappropriate behaviors also decreased. These results were derived from observations on the Aberrant Behavior Checklist (Aman & Singh, 1986) and on the DSFI (Derogatis & Melisaratos, 1982). Isolating behaviors decreased and friendships within the group increased. In all, changes were observed in both domains of sexuality and interpersonal relationships.

Research into sexual education intervention programs must continue to offer maximum support and learning opportunities to those with Asperger's Syndrome. These are the objectives of the sexual education program discussed here. Social and interpersonal skills training is of great benefit to the Asperger's Syndrome population. In addition to increasing the quality of social interactions, intervention programs allow new behaviors to be generalized to participants' personal or "out of school" lives. Despite the fact that several authors underline the importance of such programs (Gray et al., 1996; Haracopos & Pedersen, 1999; Hellemans & Deboutte, 2002), very few initiatives now exist. School and community-based clinicians can be of great help by inserting elements of these programs into existing social curricula.

REFERENCES

Aman, M. G., & Singh, N. N. (1986). *Aberrant Behavior Checklist: Manual.* East Aurora, NY: Slosson Educational.

American Academy of Pediatrics. (1996). Sexuality education of children and adolescents with developmental disabilities. *Pediatrics, 97,* 275–278.

Aston, M. C. (2001). *The other half of Asperger Syndrome.* London: National Autistic Society.

Attwood, T. (1999). *Modifications to cognitive behaviour therapy to accommodate the cognitive profile of people with Asperger's Syndrome.* Retrieved January 30, 2004, from www.tonyattwood.com

Attwood, T., & Caswell, D. (2002). *Project on emotions.* Unpublished manuscript.

Attwood, T., & Gray, C. (1999a). *The discovery of "aspie" criteria.* Retrieved January 30, 2004, from http://www.tonyattwood.com

Attwood, T., & Gray, C. (1999b). *Understanding and teaching friendship skills*. Retrieved January 30, 2004, from http://www.tonyattwood.com

Autisme France (Autism France). (2004). Retrieved January 30, 2004, from http://autisme.france.free.fr/

Baron-Cohen, S., et al. (2002). *Mind reading: The interactive guide to emotions*. Cambridge, England: Human Emotions.

Carnes, P. (1989). *Contrary to love: Helping the sexual addict*. Minneapolis, MN: CompCare.

Carnes, P. (1993). *S'affranchir du secret: Sexualité compulsive [Free from secrets: Compulsive Sexuality]*. Minneapolis, MN: CompCare.

Channon, S., Charman, T., Heap, J., Crawford, S., & Rios, P. (2001). Real-life problem-solving in Asperger's Syndrome. *Journal of Autism and Development Disorders, 31,* 461–469.

Chipouras, S., Cornelius, D., Daniels, F., & Makas, E. (1979). *Who cares? A handbook on sex education and counseling services for disabled people*. Baltimore: University Park Press.

Coleman, E. (1991). Compulsive sexual behavior: New concepts and treatments. *Journal of Psychology and Human Sexuality, 4,* 37–52.

Derogatis, L. R. (1982). *Derogatis Sexual Functioning Inventory*.

Durocher, L., & Fortier, M. (1999). *Programme d'education sexuelle [Sex education program]*. Montreal, Canada: Jes Centres Jeunesse de Montréal et la Régie Régionale de la Santé et des Services Sociaux, Direction de la Santé Publique.

Gray, S., Ruble, L., & Dalrymple, N. (1996). *Autism and sexuality: A guide for instruction*. Bloomington, IN: Autism Society of Indiana.

Griffiths, D. (1999, April 7). *La sexualité des presonnes présentant un trouble envahissant du developpement [Developing positive sexuality and dealing with inappropriate sexual behavior]*. Consortium de Service, Montréal, Canada.

Griffiths, D., Quinsey, V., & Hingsburger, D. (1989). *Changing inappropriate sexual behavior: A community-based approach for persons with developmental disabilities*. Baltimore: Brookes.

Griffiths, D., Richards, D., Fedoroff, P., & Watson, S. L. (2002). *Ethical dilemmas: Sexuality and developmental disability*. New York: NADD.

Haracopos, D., & Pedersen, L. (1999). *The Danish report*. Society for the Autistically Handicapped. Kettering, Northants, UK.

Hellemans, H. (1996, January). *L'education sexuelle des adolescents autistes [Sex education for adolescents with autism]*. Conference Project Caroline, Antwerp, Belgium.

Hellemans, H., & Deboutte, D. (2002). *Autism spectrum disorders and sexuality*. Melbourne, Australia: Melbourne World Autism Congress.

Hénault, I. (in press). *Asperger's Syndrome and sexuality: From puberty to adulthood. Sexual education and intervention*. London: Jessica Kingsley Publishers

Hénault, I. (in press). *Sociosexual skills training program*. London: Jessica Kingsley Publishers.

Hénault, I., & Attwood, T. (2002). *Sexual profile of individuals with Asperger's Syndrome: The need for understanding, support and sex education*. Melbourne, Australia: Melbourne World Autism Congress.

Hess, U. (1998). *L'intelligence emotionnelle* (Notes de cours [Emotional intelligence] [PSY 4080]), Montreal, Canada: Université du Quebec à Montreal.

Hingsburger, D. (1995). *Hand made love: A guide for teaching about male masturbation through understanding and video*. Newmarket, Canada: Diverse City Press.

Hingsburger, D., & Haar, S. (2000). *Finger tips: Teaching women with disability about masturbation through understanding and video.* Newmarket, Canada: Diverse City Press. www.diverse-city.com

Israel, G. E., & Tarver, D. E. (1997). *Transgender care.* Philadelphia: Temple University Press.

Kempton, W. (1998). *Socialization and sexuality: A comprehensive training guide.* Syracuse, NY: Author.

Konstantareas, M. M., & Lunsky, Y. J. (1997). Sociosexual knowledge, experience, attitudes, and interests of individuals with autistic disorder and developmental delay. *Journal of Autism and Developmental Disorders, 27,* 113–125.

Making Waves. (2003). Making waves: What is a good relationship anyways? [Internet program]. Retrieved January 31, 2004, from http://www.mwaves.org/.

National Information Center for Children and Youth With Disabilities. (1992). Sexuality education for children and youth with disabilities. *NICHCY News Digest, 17,* 1–37.

Roy, J. (1996). *Comparaison entre les attitudes des intervenants travaillant aupres d'adolescents autistes et ceux travaillant auprès d'adolescents deficients intellectuellement à l'egard des comportements sexuels de ces jeunes: Rapport d'activites de maîtrise en sexologie [Comparisons between the attitudes of interveners working with autistic adolescents and those working with adolescents with intellectual deficits with regard to sexual behaviors].* Montreal, Canada: Universite du Québec a Montréal, Department of Sexology.

Sharper Image Design. (1999). *Biotouch interactive mood light.* Retrieved October 28, 2002, from http://www.sharperimage.com

Smith-Myles, B., Tapscott-Cook, K., Miller, N. E., Rinner, L., & Robbins, L. A. (2000). *Asperger Syndrome and sensory issues.* Shawnee Mission, KS: Autism Asperger Publishing.

Van Bourgondien, M., Reichle, N. C., & Palmer, A. (1997). Sexual behavior in adults with autism. *Journal of Autism and Developmental Disorders, 27*(2), 113–125.

Young, E. (2001). A look at theory of mind. *The New Scientist, 29,* March.

AUTHOR'S NOTE REGARDING CHAPTER 13 ADDED IN PROOFS

Note re sources: In writing this chapter the author relied solely on the law—as enacted, and as interpreted by those charged with enforcing it. This metanote explains the various acronyms relating to those sources and how readers may, if they wish, go straight to the horse's mouth.

Starting with the law as written: U.S.C. means United States Code and C.F.R. means the Code of Federal Regulations; the former codifies statutes (laws enacted by Congress) and the latter, implementing regulations propounded by the Department of Education. Thanks to the Internet, both are freely and easily available. One can access a searchable version of the U.S.C. at *<http://www4.law.cornell.edu/ uscode/C.F.R. at and the C.F.R>* and a searchable C.F.R. at *<http://www.access. gpo.gov/nara/cfr/index.html>*. The Office of Special Education Programs, or OSEP, is the branch of the Department of Education most directly involved with interpreting the federal laws relating to educating children and youth (persons from birth through age 21) with disabilities. Its home page, from which the all-important *Letter to Williams* can be accessed, is *http://www.ed.gov/about/offices/list/osers/osep/ index.html?src=mr>*.

As to enforcing the law, enforcement necessarily involves interpretation, that is, applying general directives to the specific circumstances of one disabled child's (or youth's) entitlement to special education or accommodations. With regard to specific interventions for children with Asperger's syndrome, the most illuminating decisions are made under the radar of the courts, by state-level administrative decision-makers, typically referred to as administrative law judges or administrative appeal officers. Each state has a state education agency, or SEA. Each SEA, in turn, has a website. But the on-line availability of the SEA-level decisions discussed in this chapter is spotty. The author instead relied on the Individuals with Disabilities Education Law Reporter (IDELR) database of educational decisions produced by LRP Publications. Readers may obtain additional information about the IDELR and LRP's other education law products by accessing its web site at *http://www.lrp.com>*.

Judicial decisions that provide more generalized guidance are also discussed in the chapter, with the author providing the standard citation (based on volume and page number in the print publication of the West publishing company). Decisions made by all three levels of federal courts—the trial level (identified by district in the "F. Supp" citations), the appeal level (identified by circuit in the "F." citations) and the Supreme Court—are discussed here. Many of the courts publish opinions electronically. Readers who access <http://www.uscourts.gov/links.html can link from there to each federal court's web site.

Chapter 13

Legal Issues

Susan Gorn
Hatboro, Pennsylvania

The most salient legal issues relating to understanding interventions for children with Asperger's Syndrome were resolved in 1975, when the United States Congress enacted the Individuals with Disabilities Education Act (IDEA).[1] That legislation made the moral imperative to assist disabled individuals a legal one by ordering schools to provide therapeutic or remedial services to children with disabilities, and directing states to pay for them, no matter what the cost. Like all complex pieces of legislation, the IDEA statute sometimes seems to create more questions than answers. Thus this chapter addresses the legal issues related to providing interventions for children with Asperger's Syndrome in connection with eligibility, identification, provision of interventions, educational setting or placement, and transition services.

ELIGIBILITY

If the threshold question is whether Asperger's Syndrome is considered a disability under the IDEA, then the answer is a firm "probably."

A medical diagnosis of Asperger's Syndrome does not per se afford a basis for eligibility as a child with a disability under the IDEA. "Whether a child with Asperger's Syndrome or any other identified impairment would be eligible for services under the IDEA is a determination that must be made on an individual basis in light of the

---

[1]The legislation, codified at 20 U.S.C. §§ 1400-1485, was originally entitled the Education for the Handicapped Act, with the name changed some years later.

child's unique educational needs." That is the mantra of the IDEA, recited by the Department of Education's Office of Special Education Programs (OSEP) at the outset of its *Letter to Williams*, 33 IDELR 249 (OSEP 2000).[2]

However, like all generalizations about the law, it does not tell the whole story. A student's entitlement to interventions under the IDEA depends on meeting two criteria: One is, indeed, determined on an individual basis, but the other is categorical. An eligible student's impairment must meet the definition of at least one of 14 specifically identified disabilities. If the student cannot be categorized—or, in plain language, labeled—as having at least one of these, then that student is not eligible.[3]

The IDEA statute at 20 U.S.C. § 1401(3)(A)(i) defines an eligible "child with a disability" as a "child with mental retardation, hearing impairments (including deafness), speech or language impairments, visual impairments (including blindness), *serious emotional disturbance* (hereinafter referred to as 'emotional disturbance'), orthopedic impairments, *autism*, traumatic brain injury, *other health impairments*, or specific learning disabilities" (italics added).

What might strike you first about this exclusive list is not so much what is on it, but what is not, namely, Asperger's Syndrome. However, its omission is not the end of the story. Although some of these terms look like medical diagnoses, each is actually a legal term with a precise meaning set out in implementing IDEA regulations adopted by the Department of Education. Some are congruent with medical usage, but others are not. None depend on, or incorporate by reference, *Diagnostic and Statistical Manual of Mental Disorders* (4th ed.; *DSM–IV*) classification. Autism, for example, is defined at 34 C.F.R. § 300.7(c)(1) as:

> (i) a developmental disability significantly affecting verbal and nonverbal communication and social interaction, generally evident before age 3, that adversely affects a child's educational performance. Other characteristics often associated with autism are engagement in repetitive activities and stereotyped movements, resistance to environmental change or change in daily routines, and unusual responses to sensory experiences. The term does not apply if a child's educational performance is adversely affected primarily because the child has an emotional disturbance, as defined in paragraph (c)(4) of this section. (ii) A child who manifests the characteristics of

---

[2]OSEP is charged with responding to correspondents' questions about departmental interpretations of the IDEA statute or its implementing regulations. In its response to noted educational consultant and parent advocate Michelle Williams, OSEP comprehensively addressed her questions about the rights of students with Asperger's Syndrome and school districts' responsibilities to serve these children under the IDEA.

[3]The IDEA statute also gives states and school districts the option to create the additional eligibility category of "children aged 3 through 9 experiencing developmental delays." This category is defined at 34 C.F.R. § 300.7(b) as a child "(1) Who is experiencing developmental delays, as defined by the State and as measured by appropriate diagnostic instruments and procedures, in one or more of the following areas: physical development, cognitive development, communication development, social or emotional development, or adaptive development; and (2) Who, by reason thereof, needs special education and related services."

'autism' after age 3 could be diagnosed as having 'autism' if the criteria in paragraph (c)(1)(i) of this section are satisfied.

In one sense, advocates for children with Asperger's Syndrome might take heart: Autism is not limited to autism. Having jumped that hurdle, however, other definitional barriers remain. A child with Asperger's Syndrome, might, for instance, be considered a stellar verbal communicator, if that term is considered to be the verbal intelligence measured by the verbal scale of the Wechsler Intelligence Scale for Children (3rd ed.; WISC–III). Aside from autism, though, eligibility for a student with Asperger's Syndrome might be established under two other classifications: "serious emotional disturbance," defined at 34 C.F.R. § 300.7(c)(4),[4] or "other health impairment, " at 34 C.F.R. § 300.7(c)(9).[5] Both are clearly legal "terms of art," made out of whole cloth from the point of view of *DSM-IV* congruence. Both are also only arguably applicable to students with Asperger's Syndrome. The bottom line, then, as OSEP acknowledged in *Letter to Williams, supra.,* is that Asperger's Syndrome has no assured designation as a disability triggering a school district's obligation to provide interventions.

That said, most states have adopted a pragmatic position. A student with Asperger's Syndrome might be a "child with autism" or whatever else works well enough for classification purposes, so long as the actual diagnosis is recognized for purposes of appropriate programming. See, for example, *Sch Dist of Wisconsin Dells v. Z.S.,* 184 F. Supp. 2d 860 (W.D. Wis. 2001) and *Quaker Valley Sch. Dist.,* 31 IDELR 255 (SEA PA 1999). But, as stated earlier, this is not a guaranteed result. For example, in 1998 a due process hearing officer affirmed an Oregon school district's position that a *DSM–IV* diagnosis of Asperger's Syndrome did not entitle the student to IDEA services under the categories of "autism," "learning disability," "communication disorder," "serious emotional disturbance," or "other health impairment." It is hard to find fault with the technical aspects of the legal analysis in the opinion, published as *Corvallis Sch. Dist.* 509J, 28 IDELR 1026 (SEA OR 1998),

---

[4]A serious emotional disturbance, also referred to as an emotional disturbance, is defined at 34 C.F.R. § 300.7(c)(4) as follows: "(i) The term means a condition exhibiting one or more of the following characteristics over a long period of time and to a marked degree that adversely affects a child's educational performance: (A) An inability to learn that cannot be explained by intellectual, sensory, or health factors. (B) An inability to build or maintain satisfactory interpersonal relationships with peers and teachers. (C) Inappropriate types of behavior or feelings under normal circumstances. (D) A general pervasive mood of unhappiness or depression. (E) A tendency to develop physical symptoms or fears associated with personal or school problems.

(ii) The term includes schizophrenia. The term does not apply to children who are socially maladjusted, unless it is determined that they have an emotional disturbance."

[5]Other health impairment is defined at 34 C.F.R. § 300.7(c)(4) as meaning: "having limited strength, vitality or alertness, including a heightened alertness to environmental stimuli, that results in limited alertness with respect to the educational environment, that—(i) Is due to chronic or acute health problems such as asthma, attention deficit disorder or attention deficit hyperactivity disorder, diabetes, epilepsy, a heart condition, hemophilia, lead poisoning, leukemia, nephritis, rheumatic fever, and sickle cell anemia; and (ii) Adversely affects a child's educational performance."

although the author submits that the result defies both common sense and the underlying intent of the law.

Once the barrier of disability classification is surmounted, the second prong of the statutory definition of eligibility—that the student needs "special education and related services" as a result of the disability—is not generally a barrier.[6] 20 U.S.C. § 1401(3)(A)(ii). Special education is yet another legal term of art, defined at 34 C.F.R. §300.26.[7] The gist of the definition is that modifications in how a student is instructed, as opposed to how students are typically instructed, to take into account the student's disability-related learning needs qualify as special education.

In addition, interventions that might otherwise meet the definition of "related services" under 34 C.F.R. § 300.24 of the IDEA, such as speech pathology, occupational therapy, or—most pertinently—social skills training, might also qualify as special education.[8] As OSEP explained in *Letter to Williams, supra*.:

> If the only service that a child needs is a related service, such as speech pathology, occupational therapy or physical therapy, that service could be considered special education, if the service consists of specially designed instruction, at no cost to the parents, to meet the unique needs of a child with a disability, and "is considered special education rather than a related service under State standards."

Thus, recognize that, in the absence of such a reclassifying, a student with Asperger's Syndrome who needs social skills training, but no other special education, is not eligible under the IDEA. Perhaps aided by the sense that the overall purpose of the IDEA supports a finding of eligibility in arguable cases, most school districts consider social skills training to be special education for students with Asperger's Syndrome. See, for example, *Dublin Unified Sch. Dist.*, 37 IDELR 22 (SEA CA 2002) and *West Des Moines Community Sch. Dist.*, 36 IDELR 222 (SEA IA 2002).

Assuming, then, that interventions to address social deficits are deemed to be special education, only the last piece of the puzzle—whether a particular student with Asperger's Syndrome needs them—has to be filled in to complete the picture. *Needs*, as it turns out, is also a legal term of art. Not every student with Asperger's Syndrome who would benefit from receiving, for example, social skills training, "needs" it, as a matter of law. The author explains when a disabled stu-

---

[6]Surprisingly, no one (now, with the exception of me) seems to comment on the tautology of the definition of a child with a disability who needs special education as a child with a disability who needs special education.

[7]Special education is defined at 34 C.F.R. § 300.26(a)(1) as follows: "As used in this part, the term special education means specially designed instruction, at no cost to the parents, to meet the unique needs of a child with a disability, including—(i) Instruction conducted in the classroom, in the home, in hospitals and institutions, and in other settings; and (ii) Instruction in physical education."

[8]The second part of the definition of special education, the one that allows students with Asperger's Syndrome to slip, like the proverbial camel's nose, under the tent of IDEA eligibility, is set out at 34 C.F.R. § 300.26(a)(2): "The term [special education] includes each of the following, if it meets the requirements of paragraph (a)(1) of this section: (i) Speech-language pathology services, or any other related service, if the service is considered special education rather than a related service under State standards."

dent with Asperger's Syndrome does not "need" this intervention—or, put another way, when a school district is not obligated to provide it—later in connection with Provision of Services.[9]

IDENTIFICATION

A school district must provide interventions to students with Asperger's Syndrome whose disabling condition and need for special education has been confirmed by an evaluation conducted in accordance with all the protocols and requirements set out in the IDEA regulations at 34 C.F.R. §§ 300.532-300.533. Those requirements are discussed later in connection with evaluation, but the point to be made here is that a medical (psychiatric) or psychological diagnosis of Asperger's Syndrome alone is not sufficient to establish IDEA eligibility. What it does establish is the need to conduct an evaluation to determine eligibility. Thus, a parent might trigger the evaluation process by presenting a privately obtained diagnosis, or a privately obtained complete psychoeducational evaluation, to the school district.

Nonetheless, the IDEA does not place the burden of identification on parents, who are not required to identify a child as disabled or ask school officials to evaluate a child they suspect might be disabled. See, for example, *Venus Indep. Sch. Dist. v. Daniel S. by Ron and Patricia S.*, 36 IDELR 185 (N.D. Tex. 2002), *State of Hawaii v. Cari Rae S.*, 158 F.Supp. 1190 (D. Hi. 2001). To the contrary, the IDEA expressly imposes on school districts an affirmative legal duty, commonly referred to as "child find," "to identify and evaluate *every* [italics added] child who has or is suspected of having a disability, and who may be in need of special education" (34 C.F.R. § 300.125).

Despite its breadth, the child find duty is triggered only when a school district has reason to suspect a student might have a disability and require special education as a result. No uniform screenings for all possibly disabling conditions are required.[10] Willful ignorance, however, will not relieve a school district of its child

---

[9]Sally Fields might have been thrilled that we really, really liked her, but students with disabilities do not have to really, really need special education, just needing them is enough. See, for example, *West Chester Area School District v. Bruce C.,("Chad C.")* 194 F. Supp. 2d 417; 2002 U.S. Dist. LEXIS 5880 (E.D. Pa. 2002). "Truly necessary" is an overly restrictive interpretation of the eligibility requirement.

[10]The extent of the child find obligation—and its limitations—was described accurately, if not curmudgeonly, by the administrative due process hearing officer in *Hillsboro Sch. Dist.*, 29 IDELR 429 (SEA OR 1998):

Even if District staff were to pull a handcart full of parental consent-for-evaluation forms through the streets of the villages and Portland suburbs comprising the District, ringing a bell, and crying, "Bring out your disabled children!," it would not likely find each and every disabled child residing in the District. There would likely be at least one disabled child locked away in a closet somewhere by abominable parents residing within the district, one disabled child in a private school for the disabled supported by parents residing within the district who did not need or want any public school assistance, one or two disabled children running around the streets with parents who didn't care, two or twenty—depending on the season—disabled children laboring in the fields while residing within the District for a week, and two or three children like P.R. whose parents were out when the handcart came by. *(continued on next page)*

find obligation. The legal standard for exoneration is not actual lack of reason to suspect, but rather lack of a reasonable basis for suspicion. See, for example, *Wiesenberg v. Board of Educ. of Salt Lake City Sch. Dist.*, 181 F. Supp. 2d 1307 (D. Ut. 2002), *State of Hawaii v. Cari Rae S.*, supra.

Asperger's Syndrome, like a learning disability or attention deficit disorder, is neither visible nor patent. Nonetheless, where child find is concerned, "every" means "every." No one has said it better than the administrative review panel in *Windsor C-1 Sch. Dist.*, 29 IDELR 170 (SEA MO 1998):

> The Panel rejects the District's position that because Student's ultimate diagnosis of Asperger's Syndrome escaped the experts for a time and was difficult to pinpoint, the District was relieved of its responsibility to identify and evaluate at an early stage. The District is never relieved of its burden to identify, locate, and evaluate children with disabilities within its borders who are in need of special education and related services. Otherwise, the IDEA's goal of providing full educational opportunity could not be met.

However stirring the panel's words, it is not altogether clear when a school district should have reason to suspect that the behaviors of a heretofore unidentified student suggest Asperger's Syndrome. Although a particular state or school district might have general guidelines, it cannot be reduced to a legal issue. Instead, thoughtful observation by the school district personnel who have daily contact with the student, particularly teachers, is the key. These individuals on the frontline must identify the need for further assessment in the absence of parental awareness.

Of course, hindsight is easy, once a student is actually identified. Thus, there is a raft of published administrative decisions involving parental claims that the school district should have identified the student sooner. Sometimes the parents' claims have merit; the student should have been referred for an evaluation months, or perhaps years, earlier. I could go on for pages and pages summarizing now-immortalized school district lapses, but just two examples of administrative decisions finding untimely identification will suffice.

West Des Moines Community Sch. Dist., 36 IDELR 222 (SEA IA 2002) illustrates a school district's need to educate front-line personnel to be alert to behaviors suggestive of Asperger's Syndrome in elementary school-age students.

Although Alex's kindergarten year (1998–1999) was a success academically and socially (Alex's academics continued to be good during his first-grade year of 1999–2000), he exhibited disruptive and violent behavior right from the start. In addition to name-calling and screaming when angry, he was physically aggressive with other students, kicking, pushing, and even jabbing a classmate with a pencil. In

---

[10] *(continued)*   The Act places a burden on school districts which is not merely very difficult to meet but is impossible to meet in all cases. The District has procedures for notifying parents of the availability of special education and related services. Those procedures seem reasonably calculated to locate and make available for evaluation the vast majority of disabled children residing in the District.

one instance, enraged over the loss of a class privilege, he tried to hit another student over the head with a chair. The school district did not conduct an evaluation in response to these actions, all duly documented. To the contrary, it advised Alex's parents that his behavior was not "discrepant enough."

By April 2000 it was; the school district found Alex IDEA-eligible on the basis of an emotional disturbance. He was not diagnosed as having Asperger's Syndrome until shortly before the start of the next school year when his parents, believing the school district's program did not address Alex's educational needs, engaged an evaluation by an independent psychologist, who diagnosed him as having Asperger's Syndrome. Unlike the school district, the hearing officer found Alex's behavior during the first 2 to 3 months of the 1999–2000 school year significantly atypical for a student his age to have triggered an evaluation before the end of the 1999 calendar year.

The independent psychologist in *West Des Moines Community Sch. Dist., sipra.,* also conducted the first testing of Alex's cognitive abilities with the WISC–III. Alex, it turned out, had a Verbal IQ (144) and Performance (nonverbal) IQ of 104, resulting in a Full-Scale IQ of 127.

Startlingly high verbal intelligence is not, of course, a comorbid condition for students with Asperger's Syndrome. On the other hand, the presence of one does not rule out the existence of the other. In that regard, the administrative review panel decision in *Quaker Valley Sch. Dist.,* 31 IDELR 255 (SEA PA 1999) is a good example of why school districts must avoid being so dazzled by the intellectual giftedness of a student with Asperger's Syndrome that they neglect the obligation to investigate significant social deficits.

Christopher, the student at issue, was a 14-year-old ninth grader identified as an exceptional child on the basis of intellectual giftedness under state law. Prior to ninth grade his school career was marked by difficulties with social skills and developing friendships, initiating conversations, maintaining eye contact, accepting constructive criticism, and a markedly restricted repertoire of activities and interests. During ninth grade (the 1996–1997 school year) Christopher added eccentric behavior (talking aloud to himself and neglecting personal hygiene) to his social difficulties. Nevertheless, he was not identified as possibly disabled.

In October of his 10th-grade year (the 1997–1998 school year), however, the school district identified Christopher as requiring supplemental support on the basis of an (unspecified) emotional disturbance. A psychiatric evaluation the following February (1998) resulted in a diagnosis of adjustment and anxiety disorders and a menu of counseling and social skills training intended to address them. It was not until after Christopher threatened to blow up the school in May 1998 that two additional independent evaluations diagnosed Asperger's Syndrome, an assessment the school district refused to accept.

Both the hearing officer and the review panel accepted it, however, holding that Christopher was educationally disabled on account of Asperger's Syndrome. It held that the school district, which should have identified and programmed for his disability long before the final incident, had violated the IDEA by focusing only on Christopher's academic strengths.[11]

Nonetheless, even as a child advocate, I can appreciate the challenge faced by a teacher whose class includes such a student. Because the student has above-average measured intelligence and academic skills, the teacher does not have to be concerned about ability to master the curriculum. If that student's in-school behavior is neither provocative nor disruptive, the issue of whether to refer the student is reduced to whether the social deficits go beyond the more typical social skills problems that children have to work out on their own and is one that might well fly under the radar.

EVALUATION

Before a school district begins providing special education and related services to a student with Asperger's Syndrome (or any student) it must conduct a full and individual evaluation (34 C.F.R. § 300.531). The purpose of the evaluation is twofold: to determine whether the student has a qualifying disabling condition, such as Asperger's Syndrome, and to assess the student's disability-related educational needs (34 C.F.R. § 300.320).

The evaluation must be conduced in accordance with IDEA regulations at 34 C.F.R. §§ 300.532-300.533. Among these regulatory requirements: (a) a variety of assessment tools and strategies must be used to gather relevant functional and developmental information about the student; (b) the assessments must address all areas related to the student's disability, including if appropriate, health, vision, hearing, social and emotional status, general intelligence, academic performance, communicative status, and motor abilities; (c) and any standardized test must be validated for that particular use and administered by trained and knowledgeable personnel.

The requirements are, on the whole, procedural in nature. They are also for the most part generic, with the same rules governing evaluations of students who might be eligible on the basis of, for instance, mental retardation, an emotional disturbance, or blindness. Selection of particular tests, instruments, or protocols for evaluating an student with Asperger's Syndrome (or indeed any disabled student) is left to the states and school districts. See *Letter to Warrington*, 20 IDELR 539 (OSEP 1993). The end result is that, so far as the IDEA is concerned, the evaluation does not have to be conducted by a neurologist, neuropsychologist, or psychologist who could be considered to be an expert in Asperger's Syndrome. Generally speaking, state-licensed school psychologists take the lead role in the team of professionals

---

[11]A foundation principle of the IDEA is that educational needs are not just academic. They encompass social, health, emotional, communicative, physical, and vocational needs, as well. See, for example, H.R. Rep. No. 410, 98th Cong., 1st Sess. 19 (1983), reprinted in 1983 U.S. Code Cong. & Admin. News 2088, 2106.

conducting the evaluations, although a school district might retain consultants with more targeted expertise or experience.

Parents are members of the team empowered with deciding how to conduct the evaluation, including selecting tests and other assessment materials and appropriate testing personnel (34 C.F.R. § 300.533). However, their influence is limited, as it should be in most instances, consistent with their probable lack of professional expertise and certain lack of objectivity.

The IDEA, though, gives parents who disagree with an evaluation the right to obtain an independent evaluation (IEE; 34 C.F.R. § 300.502). In some instances the school district is required to reimburse the parents for their costs, but in all instances it must "consider" its results. A parent deciding to go the route of obtaining an IEE typically selects a professional with more direct experience with students disabled by Asperger's Syndrome than the psychologist the school district has relied on. In addition, the IEE typically consists of more tests. The multiplicity of tests helps to level the playing field with the school, which can claim the advantage of familiarity with the student over time and in a range of nontest situations.[12] For example, it is unlikely a school district evaluation for a student suspected of having Asperger's Syndrome will include all the tests performed by the independently practicing clinical psychologist who conducted the IEE in *Windsor C-1 Sch. Dist., supra*: Woodcock–Johnson Psychoeducational Battery–Revised; Word Definitions Differential Ability Scales; Leiter International Performance Scale–Revised; NEPSY Arrows; Developmental Test of Visual Motor Integration; Gestalt Closure Kaufman Assessment Battery for Children; Gordon Diagnostic System; NEPSY Attention/Executive Domain; Grooved Pegboard; Finger Tapping; and NEPSY Sensorimotor Functions.

Of course, diagnostic testing is not an end in itself. An IEE report will be, more likely than not, far more detailed than the school district's and its recommended interventions more intensive. Ideally, an IEE such as the one the school district was ordered to implement in *West Des Moines Community Sch. Dist., supra*, uses the testing as the basis for very relevant information about program planning in such areas as social skill needs and structural planning in areas such as recess, lunch, and other opportunities for peer interaction. As a real-world issue, if this were not the case, the parent would not be presenting the report to the school.

PROVISION OF INTERVENTIONS

The individualized education program (IEP) is the cornerstone of the IDEA. As stated by the U.S. Supreme Court in *Burlington School Comm. v. Dep't of Educ.*, 471 U.S. 359, 368 (1985), "[t]he IEP is, in brief, a comprehensive statement of the educational needs of a handicapped child and the specially designed instruction and re-

---

[12]The victorious school district in *Tredyffrin/Easttown Sch. Dist.*, 36 IDELR 149 (SEA PA 2002), for example, helped its own case considerably by having the student's social interactions in the school setting observed by credible autism consultants who found them appropriate.

lated services to be employed to meet those needs." An IEP includes, but is by no means limited to, special education and related services (i.e., interventions) that a school district must offer to a student with a disability to meet its obligation under the IDEA to provide a free appropriate public education (FAPE).

The IDEA does not contain a list of approved services, based on the identified disability category. In fact, such a mix-and-match approach to programming is a blatant violation of the law. As the Department of Education stated in its often-quoted *Letter to New*, EHLR 211:464 (OSEP 1988), when a school district operates on the assumption that children with similar disabilities have identical educational needs and will benefit from uniform programming, it "fails to reflect the critical requirement of 'individuality' imposed by Federal law."

Nor does the statute impose substantive standards of program design or professional qualifications of service providers for any such services. As the Supreme Court opined in *Board of Education of the Hendrick Hudson Central School District v. Rowley*, 459 U.S. 176 (1982), the first of only the handful of cases interpreting the IDEA that have come before it, school districts have discretion to determine issues of methodology, so long as the selected approach meets the needs of the student and is reasonably calculated to provide an educational benefit.

Thus, in response to questions concerning specific services for children with Asperger's Syndrome, OSEP responded in *Letter to Williams, supra*, as follows:

> Part B [of the IDEA] does not dictate the services to be provided to individual children based solely on the disability category in which the child has been classified. Whether speech pathology or any other related service is required for a particular child with a disability is a determination that must be made on an individual basis by the child's IEP team. The same is true with respect to social skills training, even though Part B does not identify social skills training as a related service. The related services listed in Part B are examples of related services that could be provided if required to assist a child with a disability to benefit from special education, and this list is not intended to be exhaustive.

Social skills training is arguably the most critical intervention a school district can provide to a student with Asperger's Syndrome. Although issues about how that intervention should be delivered are critical, they are largely pedagogical rather than legal in nature. See, for example, *Desert Sands Unified Sch. Dist.*, 35 IDELR 114 (SEA CA 2001), in which the hearing officer had no jurisdiction to resolve a dispute about the manner in which the student's social skills program should be implemented.

Notwithstanding this, uniform IDEA requirements still govern a school district's provision of social skills training to students with Asperger's Syndrome. These include most notably the requirement that the IEP team develop measurable annual goals, related to, among other things, meeting each of the student's disability-related needs (34 C.F.R. § 300.347(a)(3)).

However, as illustrated by the hearing officer's decision in *Lewisville Indep. Sch. Dist.*, 35 IDELR 236 (SEA TX 2001), this can be easier said than done. The primary areas of concern for the high school student at issue in *Lewisville Indep. Sch. Dist* were poor social skills with peers and difficulty following directions in class. With regard to the latter, the IEP team developed goals for increasing appropriate responses to questions in class and reducing inappropriate, off-topic interruptions. These goals, being quantifiable and observable, were capable of measurement. As to peer interaction, the initial goal for the social skills training was "making [the student] tolerable to others" by "decreasing those behaviors that are most likely to elicit an intense negative response from others." The district proposed to measure the student's progress toward achieving this goal with quizzes and tests.

The hearing officer agreed with the parents that the district's social skills training program did not comply with the IDEA because the curriculum emphasized quizzes or tests, "which is inconsistent with the way to measure progress in social skills." No alternatives—let alone alternatives that are both legally compliant and feasible—were proposed. In my opinion, coming up with some is a challenge educators and psychologist must be prepared to meet.

In addition to social skills training, the IEP for a student with Asperger's Syndrome must also include programming to address all other disability-related educational needs. As discussed earlier, what those needs are and how to address them are questions better approached from a pedagogical perspective. However, on the legal end of things, published decisions reflect support for provision of the following interventions:

- Speech and language therapy to address deficits in semantic language or prosody. See, for example, *Lewisville Indep. Sch. Dist.*, *supra.*
- Occupational therapy (sensory integration) to address sensory processing problems, such as those involving oral textures, visual attending, auditory processing, olfactory function, or tactile defensiveness. See, for example, *Groton Bd. of Educ.*, 37 IDELR 85 (SEA CT 2002).
- Occupational therapy for fine motor deficits, such as poor handwriting. See, for example, *Dublin Unified Sch. Dist.*, *supra.*
- Psychotherapy, psychological counseling, or family therapy to address emotional or behavioral issues such as rigidity, anger, self-esteem, fear, ritualistic behaviors, or family conflict. See, for example, *Quaker Valley Sch. Dist.*, *supra.*
- Parent counseling and training when needed to assist parents in understanding the special needs of their disabled child.

Although the law requires that an IEP address all disability-related needs, there is nothing in the IDEA that requires a school district to address a disabled student's strengths. The hearing officer in *West Des Moines Community Sch. Dist.*, *supra.*, for instance, observed that it "would seem important to take into account [the student's] 'giftedness' in planning for his educational program." The student at issue, if you recall, was a second-grade boy with a gifted-level verbal IQ given to fits of anger and inclined to respond with physical aggression when he did not get his way. Providing academically challenging work would both provide enrichment and defuse his anger, the hearing officer opined, also noting that the IEP team was under no obligation to program for enrichment.[13]

Unlike the identification of the particular interventions required to address the educational needs of a student with Asperger's Syndrome, identification of the quantum, or level, of the instruction or service is a matter of law. Parents understandably want the best for their children, but that is not the applicable legal standard. In *Rowley, supra*, the Supreme Court held that the IDEA does not require that a disabled student be provided with the best available special education instruction or services, or that those services maximize a student's potential. Instead, what is required is a "basic floor of opportunity," the provision of special education and related services individually reasonably likely to provide a meaningful educational benefit.

In 1993 the Circuit Court for the Sixth Circuit Court of Appeals came up with an effective way to explain the *Rowley* standard that still has legs, or maybe, wheels:

> The [IDEA] requires that the [school district] provide the educational equivalent of a serviceable Chevrolet to every handicapped student. [The parent], however, demands ... a Cadillac solely for [the student's] use.... [W]e hold that the school board is not required to provide a Cadillac, and that the proposed IEP is reasonably calculated to provide educational benefits to [the student], and therefore is in compliance with the requirements of the IDEA. *Doe v. Bd. of Educ. of Tullahoma City Schools*, 9 F.3d 455, 459-460 (6th Cir. 1993).

All the other federal circuit courts of appeals have also relied on *Rowley* to endorse the proposition that the IDEA does not require states to provide children with disabilities with the best education possible. See, for example, *Walczak v. Florida Union Free Sch. Dist.*,142 F.3d 119 (2d Cir. 1998); *Fort Zumwalt School Dist. v. Clynes*, 119 F.3d 607, 615 (8th Cir.1997); *Cypress-Fairbanks Indep. Sch. Dist. v. Michael F.*,118 F.3d 245, 247-48 (5th Cir. 1997); *Board of Educ. of Community Consol. Sch. Dist. 21 v. Illinois State Bd. of Educ.*, 938 F.2d at 715 (7th Cir. 1994); and *Johnson v. Independent Sch. Dist. No. 4*, 921 F.2d 1022 (10th Cir. 1990).

---

[13]The administrative decision in *Wells Oqunqit CSD*, 36 IDELR 204 (SEA ME 2002) illustrates what can happen in the absence of a state classification of exceptionality on the basis of intellectual giftedness. That dispute involved an IDEA-eligible student with Asperger's Syndrome so extraordinarily academically gifted that he entered high school well in advance of his chronological-age peers. The roster for the student's first year in high school was supposed to include a computer course that for unspecified reasons was not offered. The school district, again for reasons that were not specified, did not substitute another course, leaving the student without any educational services for one academic period a day 3 days per week. The parents claimed a denial of the student's rights under the IDEA, but the hearing officer ruled that the student had no entitlement to the computer course under the IDEA that could be enforced because the computer course itself fell within the ambit of regular, and not special education.

Before an IDEA dispute gets to the circuit court level, though, a school district is charged with making the initial quantification of a disabled student's "need" for a particular intervention. In that regard, the decision of the administrative review panel in *Tredyffrin/Easttown Sch. Dist.*, 36 IDELR 149 (SEA 2002) serves as a caveat to parents who show too clearly their desire for the best education possible. When Emily, the student at issue, was privately diagnosed as having Asperger's Syndrome prior to starting kindergarten, the school district accepted the diagnosis, developed an IEP, and provided varying amounts of social skills training, sensory integration therapy (occupational therapy), speech therapy, and a part-time one-to-one aide, as well as enrichment under the state's gifted education program, during her kindergarten, first-grade and second-grade years.

The IEP for Emily's third-grade year added group social skills training and increased the amount of aide support time. As the school district would later claim, these changes were not really needed, but were provided to, in effect, humor the parents. However, that was still not enough for Emily's parents, who requested another increase in aide support about a month before school was to begin, along with "a list of the ... school officials who have had experience with children who have Asperger's Syndrome, the type and quantity of experience they have had, their level of training, and their current position in the school district." Again, the school district complied, but it also requested permission to reevaluate.

The resulting reevaluation concluded that Emily no longer exhibited social or sensory integration problems and did not need an aide. In fact, she no longer needed any special education. The parents responded by demanding the district also fund the additional social skills training and occupational therapy they had been paying for privately.

Perhaps this would have been a good time for the parties to try to compromise, but instead both took it to the mat. The end result was that according to the review panel, by the time Emily started third grade, she no longer "needed"—for purposes of establishing IDEA eligibility—social skills training. Even if she had, the "considerable social skills training that the District had provided" met the requisite *Rowley* standard of "reasonably calculated benefit."

EDUCATIONAL SETTING OR PLACEMENT

It is hard to argue with a parent who believes a student with Asperger's Syndrome should be educated in a private school for students with atypical learning styles related to their disabling conditions. However, the *Rowley* standard shields school districts from parental demands for the best program, so long as what is offered is good enough.

Over and above that consideration, the IDEA's least restrictive environment (LRE) requirement embodies the law's strong preference for educating disabled children with their nondisabled peers in the school they would attend if not disabled, whenever reasonably possible (34 CFR §§ 300.550-300.554). The LRE mandate itself, set out at 20 U.S.C. § 1415(a)(5)(A), states:

> To the maximum extent appropriate, children with disabilities, including children in public or private institutions or other care facilities, are educated with children who are not disabled, and special classes, separate schooling, or other removal of children with disabilities from the regular educational environment occurs only when the nature or severity of the disability of a child is such that education in regular classes with the use of supplementary aids and services cannot be achieved satisfactorily.

The LRE mandate was a key provision of the IDEA legislation first enacted in 1975, reflecting the revulsion of Congress to its finding that over half of the nation's disabled students were not permitted to attend public school, with 1 million children with disabilities being denied any public education. To the extent callousness, ignorance, or prejudice might have been the reasons disabled children were so poorly served prior to 1975, the barrier to full compliance with the LRE mandate is now largely economic. Hoewever, the Department of Education has made it clear that placement decisions "may not be made based solely on factors such as category of disability, significance of disability, availability of special education and related services, availability of space, configuration of the service delivery system, or administrative convenience" (*Letter to Williams, supra*). Similarly, lack of adequate personnel or resources do not relieve school districts of their obligations to make FAPE available to each disabled student in the least restrictive educational setting in which the appropriate IEP can be implemented (*Id.*).

Without a doubt, then, it will not always be either convenient or economically sensible to educate a student with Asperger's Syndrome in regular classrooms with no disabled peers. However, when the parents of a student with Asperger's Syndrome object to a proposal by a school district's business-types to fund a private school, they will almost always win the support of administrative and judicial decision makers. Simply put, the law is overwhelmingly on their side.

Thus the appeals panel in *Quaker Valley Sch. Dist., supra,* let loose the following condemnation of a school district looking to take the easy way out:

> [The school district] argues that, "in a high school of over 600 students, it is impossible to control the educational environment so as to be able to appropriately address [the student's] social and emotional inadequacies, as circumstances present themselves … [The student] would continue to experience great difficulty in the normal high school environment because of the many uncontrollable stressors that were present." The District may not abrogate its responsibilities so glibly…. [The student] may be inconvenient, but the District shall provide an appropriate environment.

The key to complying with the LRE mandate is providing needed "supplementary aids and services," as explicitly required under 34 C.F.R. § 300.552. "Supplementary aids and services" is a legal term, or term of art, defined unhelpfully in the IDEA regulations at 4 C.F.R. § 300.28 as "aids, services, and other supports that are provided in regular education classes or other education-related settings to enable children with disabilities to be educated with no disabled children to the maximum extent appropriate." Federal law does not further define the aids, services, and so on, making it a matter of professional judgment and state law in the first instance. As a matter of law, though, provision of a one-to-one aide falls with the ambit of supplementary aids and services. As a result, whenever provision is needed to prevent the removal of a student with Asperger's Syndrome from the regular education classroom, the school district must provide that costly service.

The particular service a one-to-one aide provides to a student with Asperger's Syndrome is, generally speaking, a pedagogical concern. Typically, the aide's responsibilities include facilitating generalization of learned social skills, but the totality of a student's individual needs drive the determination. The disabled high school student in *Dublin Unified Sch. Dist., supra.*, for example, had difficulties initiating or sustaining interactions with peers, reading nonverbal cues, and appreciating the needs of others. He talked aloud to himself and made self-stimulatory hand gestures. On top of that, he was often forgetful and poorly organized; he required frequent redirection to finish tasks or transition to new tasks. The duties of the student's one-to-one aide included facilitating class-to-class transitions, assisting the student to come prepared to class, and redirecting him when off-task.

One exception, though, relates to the IDEA requirement discussed earlier with respect to establishing measurable annual goals for all areas of need, including social skills deficits. Almost invariably, a one-to-one aide must become a data collector, charting the student's progress in specifically identified discrete items of social interaction.[14]

The decision to provide a one-to-one aide is not unilateral, but instead made by the student's IEP team (34 C.F.R. § 300.347(a)(3)). Typically parents welcome the provision of a one-to-one aide for younger children. When students get older, however, the parents—and the student at issue—might start to feel uncomfortable with the situation.[15] Generally, however, a school district is not obligated to fund a private school placement where the student would not require an aide if the student can be "satisfactorily educated" in the public school with an aide.

---

[14]Among the lacerating criticisms of the school district delivered by the administrative review panel in *Quaker Valley Sch. Dist.*, 31 IDELR 255 (SEA PA 1999) was the following: "[T]he methods of evaluation [for interactions with peers and teachers] are so ethereal they would be humorous if this were not such a serious matter."

[15]The parent in *Dublin Unified Sch. Dist.*, 37 IDELR 22 (SEA CA 2002), for instance, unsuccessfully challenged the school district's provision of a female one-to- one for her teenage son. In denying the parent's request for a male aide, the hearing officer identified the problematic nature of one-to-one assistance for older students with Asperger's Syndrome: "The Hearing Officer considers that, by definition, any adult aide may potentially hinder the student's socialization with peers. While the student may claim that having Ms. N. as his aide is like having his mother around all day, it is not clear that STUDENT would feel much less constrained having a father-like individual with him at school all day."

Training and education of teachers, aides and other school district personnel so they can understand the nature of the educational needs of a student with Asperger's Syndrome is also essential to successful inclusion in the regular education environment. Generally, staff selection and training is under the sole control of the states (34 C.F.R. §§ 300.380-300.382). However, a 1997 change to the IDEA put determinations about required supports for school personnel that will be provided for or on behalf of the child within the control of the IEP team (34 C.F.R. § 300.347(a)(3)). According to the Department of Education, supports for school personnel can include training and professional development. As a result, the IEP team is charged with deciding, as a threshold matter, if such training should be included in the IEP, as well as what that training should be, who should provide it, and who should receive it. See *Letter to Williams, supra.*

Administrative decision makers have recognized that school districts must respond to the unique challenges of including students with Asperger's Syndrome by placing a teacher with the training, education, and experience necessary to effectively deal with the particular student's learning needs and behaviors in the classroom.[16] See, for example, *West Des Moines Community Sch. Dist.; supra; Lewisville Indep. Sch. Dist., supra.* In that regard, if the student has behavior problems that impede his or her learning or that of classmates, the IEP team must consider whether there are strategies, including positive behavioral interventions, strategies, and supports that will address the behavior sufficiently to allow the student to remain in the classroom (34 C.F.R. § 300.346(a)(2)(i)). Any resulting strategies must be included in a written behavior management plan.

TRANSITION SERVICES

In my opinion, the transition services obligation of the IDEA, which applies to all identified students, has the potential to be particularly beneficial to students with Asperger's Syndrome. Regrettably, the entitlement is little understood, typically treated more as a paperwork exercise than an opportunity to enable students with disabilities to move with greater ease from the school environment to a postschool environment.

Enacted in 1990 and reinforced in 1997, the transition services mandate of the IDEA, codified at 20 U.S.C. § 1414(d)(1)(A)(vii)(II),(viii)(1), obligates school districts to "assist disabled students in making the transition from high school to adult life" (Individuals with Disabilities Education Act, P.L. 101-477 [Oct. 30, 1990]; H.Rep.101-544, H.C. Rep. 101-787). That assistance, defined in the law as "transition services," concerns how the student will navigate in all areas of postschool life

---

[16]A school might also have to provide training to help prevent taunting, teasing, name-calling, ridicule, and every other form of children's cruelty to other children who are different. All such behavior, when it is based on exploiting the student's disability, is considered disability harassment under Section 504 and the Americans with Disabilities Act. School districts have an obligation educate students about the types of disability-related behaviors they might observe in a classmate with Asperger's Syndrome and remain alert for problems.

that are impacted by the disability, including "post-secondary education, vocational training, integrated employment, continuing and adult education, adult services, independent living or community participation" (20 U.S.C. § 1414 (d)(1)(A)(vii)). Under the law, the school district must provide "transition services" in the form of special education, related services, and identification of "linkages" starting at age 16 (or earlier if needed).

Linkages is an important concept. Once a disabled student receives a high school diploma, the school district's obligation under the IDEA ends and the days of one-stop shopping for all the services the school district provided are over. In some cases other public agencies are obligated to continue providing them or to provide other forms of assistance.

In the postsecondary education arena, transition services for a college-bound student with Asperger's Syndrome should include, in my opinion, counseling about the rights of, and protections for, college students with disabilities. In this regard, here is the briefest possible summary of those rights:

Whereas the IDEA establishes a disabled student's positive right to a "free appropriate public education," the disability laws concerning college students—Section 504 of the Rehabilitation Act of 1973 (Section 504) and Title III of the Americans with Disabilities Act—bar colleges from discriminating on the basis of disability. Unlawful discrimination includes the refusal to make "reasonable accommodations" required for an "otherwise qualified student with a disability" to participate in a college's program when provision does not impose an undue financial or administrative burden on the college or work a fundamental alteration to the nature of the program (34 C.F.R. § 104.4(a)); *Southeastern Community College v. Davis,* 442 U.S. 397 [1979].

The issue of what is a reasonable accommodation in the postsecondary education context typically comes up in the context of students with learning disabilities such as dyslexia or attention deficit disorder and relates to test taking (extended time, untimed), provision of classroom notes, or elimination of the foreign language requirement. The published legal literature does not disclose, to my knowledge, disputes about requests for reasonable accommodations by students with Asperger's Syndrome. This is likely because students with Asperger's Syndrome are not as likely to need the types of academic accommodations available under Section 504 as they are to need continued interventions, such as social skills training, sensory integration, or speech therapy. However, Section 504 does not extend that far.

That said, in my opinion, helping prepare a student with Asperger's Syndrome for college is only a small piece of what school districts need to do to fulfill their legal obligation to provide transition services to students with Asperger's Syndrome. They should also address how the student will continue to improve his or her social skills and ability to interact successfully with others, not only at college, but also later in life in the workplace, and with family and peers. They should identify all possible resources the student will be able to turn to.

CONCLUSION

When educational psychologist Nancy Wasson testified for the parents of a bright 14-year-old student she suspected might have Asperger's Syndrome in *Autauga County Bd. of Educ*, 28 IDELR 539 (SEA Al 1998), she was asked on cross-examination why her IEE did not reference his academics. According to the hearing officer, "Dr. Wasson [responded] that this Child has many areas that need to be addressed. In this Child's case, she would rather see him make all 'D's' and advance socially and be able to interact and hold down a job one day." I understand Dr. Wasson's concern about how a student with an impaired ability to interact socially will fare, but I close this chapter by emphasizing to all readers who think they would make the same choice between academics and social skills training for a student with Asperger's Syndrome that you do not have to choose. Under the IDEA, the student is entitled to both.

Author Index

Subject Index